NAUVOO TEMPLE

A STORY OF FAITH

NAUVOO TEMPLE

A STORY OF FAITH

DON F. COLVIN

Published by Covenant Communications, Inc.
American Fork, Utah

Printed in Canada
First Printing: April 2002

08 07 06 05 04 03 02 01   10 9 8 7 6 5 4 3 2 1

ISBN 1-59156-014-4

Library of Congress Cataloging-in-Publication Data

Colvin, Don F., 1927-
      Nauvoo Temple : a story of faith / Don F. Colvin.
            p.   cm.
      Includes bibliographical references.
      ISBN 1-59156-014-4
      1. Nauvoo Temple (Nauvoo, Ill.) I. Title

BX8685.N3 C65 2002
246'.95'0977343--dc21   2002019411

To

My wife, Delsa, for her love, constant support, and encouragement.

It is she, together with our sons, Scott and Roger, our daughters-in-law,

Marilyn and Sonya, and our ten grandchildren—Sara, Amy, April, Stacey,

Shane, Jamie, Christopher, Jana, Laura, and Nicholas—who make my life

happy and full of joy.

ACKNOWLEDGMENTS

I am indebted to many who have researched and written on the Nauvoo Temple. The diaries and writings of Brigham Young, William Clayton, and Heber C. Kimball, as well as the *History of the Church*, compiled by B. H. Roberts, have been particularly valuable sources. Special recognition must also be given to the voluminous research and unpublished writings of James Earl Arrington. His contributions on this area of Church history are very significant.

The most valuable collections of materials and original sources on this subject have been found in the Church History Library of The Church of Jesus Christ of Latter-day Saints, and the Special Collections Section of the Brigham Young University Library. Other helpful sources have been the Bancroft Library at the University of California and the University of Utah Library in Salt Lake City. I am indebted to the staffs and personnel at each of these libraries for their courteous and helpful assistance. Several individuals from the Church History Library and Archives deserve special recognition: Scott Christensen for his encouragement, interest, and very helpful assistance; Ronald G. Watt for his close collaboration and assistance in finding resources; Bill Slaughter for his help in acquiring illustrations; and Ron Barney for his encouragement and assistance with resources. Special thanks also to Randall Dixon, Linda Haslam, Veneese Nelson, and April Williamson for their cheerful and helpful service. Thanks also to Donald L. Enders, a senior curator of historic sites for The Church of Jesus Christ of Latter-day Saints, for his encouragement, consultation, and helpful contribution of information.

I would also like to extend appreciation to those who provided resources and assistance in refining the manuscript. To Dr. Kenneth Godfrey, who read the entire manuscript and provided valuable insights, criticism, and resources, his assistance is most appreciated. To James Kimball Jr., who read some chapters and provided helpful critique and direction to other valuable sources of information, his interest, encouragement, and assistance was very helpful. Also, to my wife, Delsa, who read and evaluated all of the chapters, along with typing some portions of the manuscript. In addition, to our granddaughters Sara and Amy, who each read several chapters, offering their helpful suggestions and criticisms.

I am particularly grateful to Roger Jackson, Steve Goodwin, and Gerald Tim Maxwell, architects of the FFKR architectural firm (architects assigned to the Nauvoo Temple reconstruction project) for their helpful assistance and collaboration on this project. Steve and Tim also read and critiqued those chapters concerning the external and internal features of the temple. They provided helpful insights and suggestions, and Steve unselfishly prepared several illustrations for publication. Special recognition is also given to F. Keith Stepan, managing director of the Temple Construction Department, and to Robert T. Dewey, Church architect assigned to oversee the Nauvoo Temple reconstruction project. Their consultation and helpful cooperation in obtaining approval for the use of illustrations are most appreciated.

Special thanks and appreciation is also extended to Dr. Kent P. Jackson and Dr. Richard D. Draper, directors, and to their staff at the Brigham Young University Religious Studies Center for their assistance in preparing the manuscript for publication, especially the work of Charlotte Pollard, Peter Christopherson, Peter Jasinski, Mary Frances Nielson, Rex Nielson, H. L. Rogers, Rob Schwartz, and Devan Jensen.

PREFACE

While researching this history I have developed great respect and appreciation for those pioneer builders who sacrificed so much and worked so hard to construct the magnificent Nauvoo Temple. I have been constantly amazed by the skill of their work and the excellence of their efforts. The quality of their labor did not diminish even when they were faced with leaving it all behind. Theirs was a sacrifice of devotion and a gift to God. They gave their very best in spite of difficult circumstances. My deepest gratitude goes to those who left behind firsthand descriptions, experiences, and observations in writing. Their journals, letters, and articles have been invaluable sources of information.

This book reveals the dedicated struggle of pioneers, who, in the face of great obstacles, sacrificed for the fulfillment of their religious ideals and convictions. It reviews the early setting in which the Nauvoo Temple was constructed, the theology that led to its erection, and the struggle of construction from when the building was first contemplated until its dedication. The text brings together in more complete form than previously published the pertinent information relating to the temple's construction, varied uses, and eventual fate. It also brings into focus the faith and dedication of its builders, who steadily pushed the project to completion in spite of intense persecution. Insights are also provided into the sacrifices involved in supplying the manpower, skills, means, and materials essential to the temple's construction, showing that some even gave all their earthly possessions toward the building's erection.

In a more complete form than ever before published, this book brings together the most detailed and pertinent information and descriptions regarding the external and internal physical features of the Nauvoo Temple. Helpful illustrations are also included, enabling readers to visualize the intricate designs, features, and architecture of this majestic building.

The problems and issues surrounding the temple's completion are treated in detail in relation to each section of the building. From the point of view of architectural design, the temple was not totally finished, and had the builders been permitted to remain in the city, they would have further embellished the building, giving a finer finish to several areas of the structure. Clear evidence, however, shows that from a functional point of view the building was completed and contained all of its designed sections, of which each was accessible. Though only roughed in, some portions of the building were still put to effective use while the building stood. This book also concludes that the temple was graced by a golden statue of an angel placed at or near the apex of the tower, lying in a horizontal position, which served as a weather vane. The destruction of the temple by fire, the eventual demolition of the walls, and the disposition of the temple site are all traced to the present time.

To the greatest degree possible, this study has concerned itself with material from original sources such as private journals, newspaper accounts, historic writings, letters, and other written materials originating in the period when the temple was built. I have endeavored to honestly quote and give proper credit to all these valuable sources of information. This text is limited only to those parts of that history that have direct bearing on the story of the temple. It does not attempt to address problems between the Mormons and their neighbors, nor does it deal with other areas of interest that developed over the period of construction.

This book also addresses the nature and early practice of temple ordinances along with the great desire of church members to obtain these sacred blessings. This study furnishes valuable insights into the historical development of these temple ordinances as practiced by The Church of Jesus Christ of Latter-day Saints. Additional ordinances such as baptisms for healing, plural marriages, and other higher temple ordinances were also performed in the Nauvoo Temple, but these are not emphasized in this book for two reasons: first, they were not the primary purposes of temple ordinances, and second, the information dealing with higher ordinances approaches an area of sacredness that I feel would be improper to write upon.

The impact of the Nauvoo Temple on Church doctrine and practice has been significant and long-lasting, and the nature of this influence is traced within the book. The construction of this temple not only proved to be a spiritual blessing to the Mormon people, but it physically unified them in a common goal. The economic impact of this construction project was also important as the temple provided jobs for numerous individuals and fostered numerous support industries and businesses that contributed significantly to the economic growth of the city.

From a personal frame of reference I must pay special tribute to my own great-great-grandparents Richard and Louisa Sprague. Richard Demont Sprague worked as a stonemason, assisting in building the walls of the Nauvoo Temple. He was selected by the city council to serve as a police officer, and he stood guard over the temple and other buildings in the city. On 22 January 1846 they received their endowments in the Nauvoo Temple, and one week later, on 29 January 1846, they were sealed in the temple as husband and wife for time and for all eternity. To these noble pioneers, my great-great-grandparents, I will be forever indebted. Their faith, sacrifice, devotion, integrity, and character are a rich legacy for me and my family.

Though I write from a position of faith, it has been my endeavor to be honest and accurate. I do possess strong convictions and a firm testimony that the hand of God attended the construction of this great temple. It is my observation that God's Spirit guided this work and was clearly manifested in meetings and ordinances conducted within this sacred building. I come away from this experience with my faith deeply enriched.

TABLE OF CONTENTS

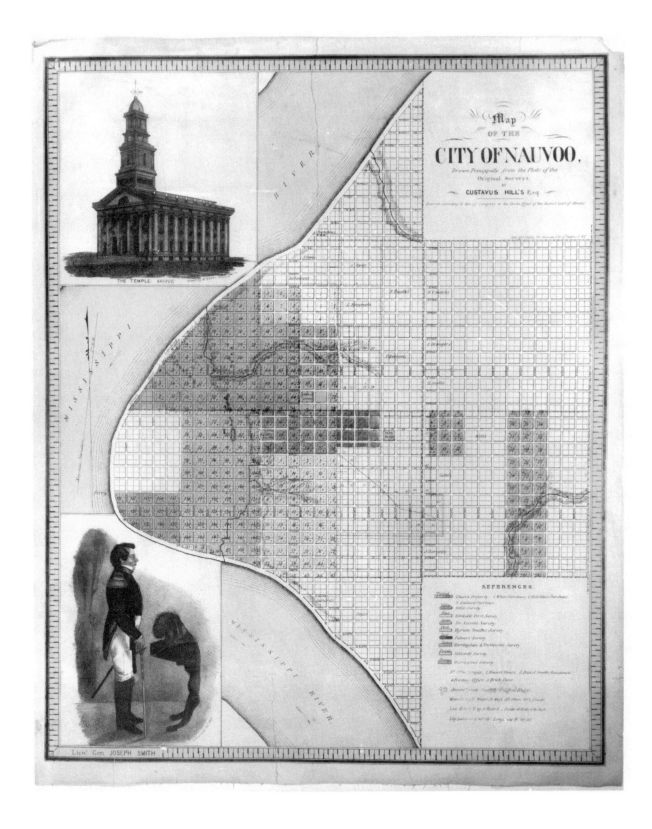

Figure 1.1 Map of the City of Nauvoo, drawing, 1842, Gustavus Hill, © by Intellectual Reserve, Inc., courtesy of LDS Church Archives, used by permission. Gustavus Hill drew this map principally from the plat of the original surveys. In the upper left corner is the first known drawing of the Nauvoo Temple as proposed by architect William Weeks.

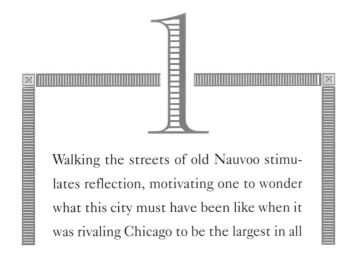

Walking the streets of old Nauvoo stimulates reflection, motivating one to wonder what this city must have been like when it was rivaling Chicago to be the largest in all

CHAPTER ONE

NAUVOO ☙ A PLACE WHERE

WE CAN BUILD A TEMPLE

of Illinois. Just prior to the forced exodus of its citizens to the West, when the city was at its height, Nauvoo boasted a population of twelve to fifteen thousand citizens.[1] One observer reported that Nauvoo's inhabitants were housed in

"at least two thousand houses in the city proper, and in the suburbs five hundred more." Twelve hundred of these were described as "tolerably fit residences," with probably five hundred being good brick houses, some of which were "elegantly and handsomely finished residences."[2] By January 1846 the population of Nauvoo had swelled to its greatest numbers as persecution and mobbings drove Church members from their homes in surrounding communities to seek refuge in the city. Many of these new citizens

"larger than any building west of Cincinnati and north of St. Louis," and he described it as "the finest building in the west."[3] Another visitor praised it in somewhat exaggerated terms as "the most splendid and imposing architectural monument in the new world . . . unique and wonderful as the faith of its builders."[4] The Nauvoo Temple was unquestionably one of the finest structures of nineteenth-century America. Built at great cost and sacrifice, its erection was a dominant concern of the entire Church during the Nauvoo period of

were housed in wagons or temporary shanties as they made preparations to leave the city and cross the plains to the West.

As impressive and substantial as are some of the restored homes now standing in Nauvoo, they are insignificant when compared to the city's most prominent structure, the Nauvoo Temple. Visible from a long distance, it stood on a bluff overlooking the city and the mighty Mississippi River. One non-Mormon visitor noted that the temple was

Latter-day Saint history. The building has forever left its imprint on the history of Mormonism and the state of Illinois.

Who Were the Latter-day Saints?

Who were these people who built so much and so well in just a few short years? What was it that motivated them to sacrifice so much of their time, means, and energy—even under intense persecution—to build such a building

and such a city, only to walk away and leave it all to the elements and to their persecutors? Commonly called Mormons, they were members of The Church of Jesus Christ of Latter-day Saints. The bulk of them had formerly been residents of New England, the eastern states, and southern Canada. Later, as the city grew, these were joined by converts from the southern states and the British Isles. Organized in Fayette, New York, 6 April 1830, the Church claimed to be the original Church of Jesus

apostasy and persecution, Church members left Ohio in 1837 and 1838 to the other main center of the Church in western Missouri. Their arrival in large numbers was perceived as an economic, social, and religious threat to earlier settlers, resulting in opposition and persecution. Motivated by political and religious reasons, armed mobs plundered Mormon homes and settlements. As the Saints marshaled their members for defense, a near state of war existed in western Missouri. Siding with the mob element,

s are some of the restored homes

e insignificant when compared to the city's

e Nauvoo Temple.

Christ, restored to earth in the latter days. A basic belief was acceptance of their Church president, Joseph Smith (as well as each of his successors), as a true prophet of God.

From New York the movement spread west as early as 1831, establishing settlements in northeastern Ohio and western Missouri. Kirtland, Ohio, was the main center of activity in the early 1830s, and it was here that the Latter-day Saints constructed their first temple. Due to

Missouri governor Lilburn W. Boggs issued an order of extermination in October 1838. In part it read: "The Mormons must be treated as enemies, and must be exterminated or driven from the state if necessary for the public peace."[5]

As the extermination order was put into effect, Church leaders were imprisoned and held under threat of the penalty of death. Church members were forced to leave their homes and lands and flee the state. Many spent

the winter of 1838–39 as guests of the city of Quincy, Illinois, whose citizens were moved to sympathy for the refugee Latter-day Saints. Some wintered in wagons, in barns, or in dugouts along the riverbank, while others found similar refuge in Iowa.

After six long months of incarceration, Joseph Smith and those with him were allowed to escape from prison. They joined the main body of Church members on 16 April 1839 at Quincy, Illinois. The question of where to go to build anew now occupied the attention of all. After investigating possible sites, Church members purchased large farms at Commerce, Illinois, and in Iowa. The terms of purchase were generous, allowing for long-term payment. Sparsely inhabited and undeveloped, Commerce became the new home of the exiles.

THE CITY OF NAUVOO

Commerce, with but few residents, was largely a "paper town," ushered into existence by eastern speculators who in 1837 established on paper what was to be the city.[6] Due in part to the financial panic of 1837, the intentions of these early founders were never realized, and the land awaited development under its new owners, the Latter-day Saints. Joseph Smith described the appearance of the settlement as he arrived to take up residence.

> When I made the purchase . . . there were one stone house, three frame houses, and two block houses, which constituted the whole city of Commerce. Between Commerce and Mr. Davidson Hibbard's, there was one stone house and three log houses, including the one that I live in, and these were all the houses in this vicinity, and the place was literally a wilderness. The land was mostly covered with trees and bushes, and much of it so wet that it was with the utmost difficulty a footman could get through, and totally impossible for teams. Commerce was so unhealthful, very few could live there; but believing that it might become a healthful place by the blessing of heaven to the Saints, and no more eligible place presenting itself, I considered it wisdom to make an attempt to build up a city.[7]

Throughout the summer of 1839 the Saints continued to gather on lands purchased by Church authorities. Presenting a general appearance of great destitution, the Saints occupied the lower ground along the bank of the river. Extending a considerable distance above the camps was a succession of ponds filled with stagnant water and decaying vegetation. Men were put to work cutting ditches to the river for the purpose of draining the swampy land. This project was completed during the summer of 1840. During this time many fell prey to sickness, mostly in the form of malaria fever carried by mosquitoes bred in the swampy land upon which they were settling. After the land had been drained, conditions were improved greatly, and the land was claimed for habitation and cultivation.

In September 1839 streets and lots were laid out in what was to be a new city called Nauvoo, meaning a beautiful situation or place.

Figure 1.2 *Nauvoo Temple Rendering, painting, 1960s, Visual Resources Department, The Church of Jesus Christ of Latter-day Saints; hereafter cited as Church Visual Resources Department. Steven T. Baird and architectural staff of Nauvoo Restoration produced this drawing in the 1960s.*

The city was given official status on 21 April 1840, when the United States Postal Department changed the name of the local post office at Commerce to Nauvoo. On 16 December 1840 the Illinois governor signed into law an act officially chartering the city.[8]

Nauvoo was a well-planned city laid out with broad streets; it evidenced many features now common in zoning and farsighted city planning. It grew in both population and improvements at a phenomenal rate. By August 1840 the population was estimated at more than three thousand inhabitants.[9] By the summer of 1841, it had grown to some eight or nine thousand citizens, and from then on it vied with Chicago for claim as the largest city in the state.[10]

The first large group of Saints left their homes on 4 February 1846.

Previous page: Figure 1.3 Saints Crossing the Mississippi River in the Dead-Cold of Winter, detail of mural, 1959, Lynn Fausett, LDS Church Archives. This mural, painted by Lynn Fausett, depicts the Saints leaving Nauvoo and crossing the Mississippi River in February 1846. It is located in the tourist center adjacent to This Is the Place Monument in Salt Lake City, Utah.

The Saints from far and near were urged to gather and build up the city. This call resulted in a swelling of the population by a steady flow of new citizens. Converts came from all parts of the United States as well as from Canada and England. The influx of Church members from England began as early as June 1840. By 1846 a total of five thousand Saints had immigrated to America, the greater part of whom settled in Nauvoo.[11] The effect of these new citizens upon the culture, beauty, and industry of the city was considerable. They brought skills that contributed to the growth of industry and building. In addition, they contributed their talents in the cultural and intellectual activities of the city.

EXODUS FROM ILLINOIS

In the short space of six years, Nauvoo rose to attract the interest and attention of people from far and near. It was visited by a number of notable travelers of the time, with favorable comment. It fast became an industrial and shipping center and gave promise of becoming a cultural center as well. Due to its rapidly growing population, Nauvoo had significant political impact in Hancock County and the state of Illinois. As the city grew in power and influence, attitudes of many of its neighbors changed. Some developed bitter opposition to the cause of Mormonism. Most of these feelings grew out of political motivation. Added to this was continued harassment and agitation against Church leaders by old enemies from Missouri. Another source of the growing difficulty came from apostates and dissenters who showed their bitterness by striking out in acts of aggression against the Church and its leaders. Still another influence was that of envy and jealousy on the part of some citizens in neighboring towns who looked upon the rising wealth and industry of Nauvoo as diminishing the economy and growth of its neighbors. The unity and hard work of the Mormons were producing material growth while the rest of the state languished in a financial depression. To others the liberal Nauvoo Charter and the presence of the Nauvoo Legion excited fears and suspicions of religious oppression by zealous Mormons.[12]

A combination of these factors, along with rumors and other influences, united in an ever-growing storm of opposition and persecution. The situation gradually worsened, culminating in mob violence on 27 June 1844, when Church president Joseph Smith and his brother Hyrum were murdered by an armed mob.[13] A mournful silence settled over Nauvoo and the Latter-day Saints. Stunned by the tragic events, Church members waited for direction. The void of leadership was filled when the Twelve Apostles returned from their missions in the eastern states and were sustained as the new presiding authorities.[14] Under this new leadership, every effort was exacted toward completion of the temple and continued expansion of the Church. Contrary to the hopes of its enemies, it soon became apparent that the movement had taken on a new vitality.

Mob action resumed and increased, forcing members of outlying Mormon settlements to flee to Nauvoo for refuge. The Nauvoo Charter was repealed by the state legislature, leaving the city without protection of city law. Mob forces, checked only in part by the state militia, threatened the destruction of the city unless the Mormons would leave. Agreements were made in the fall of 1845 between the Church and its enemies that allowed the Saints to leave the following spring.[15] Aggressive acts and harassment continued however, forcing a premature departure in the cold and snows of winter.

The first large group of Saints left their homes on 4 February 1846. Having ferried across the Mississippi River to Iowa, they gathered at Sugar Creek.[16] At this point of assembly, they organized for their journey across the plains. As weather conditions dictated, groups continued to cross the river on the ice and by ferry. Most left during the winter and spring and others during the summer. As fall approached, the only Latter-day Saints remaining in the city were the poor, the sick, the aged, and widows, along with their children. These, numbering nearly five hundred souls, had remained behind, awaiting the time when they could be picked up and assisted by their fellow Saints. Exodus of Church leaders along with the vast majority of members still failed to appease the mob. In September 1846, after overcoming a brief defense, the mobs drove the last of the Saints from their homes—away from their city and into the exposure of the open prairie.

Once again the people were exiles. This time their journey would eventually lead to the Great Basin of the Rocky Mountains near the Great Salt

Lake. Here the industry that made Nauvoo would be put to work making the desert blossom. They would contribute a vital part in taming and colonizing the wilderness of the West. Nauvoo and its central structure, the temple, were to remain a silent symbol of the industry, faith, sacrifice, ideals, and dreams of its builders. As stated by historian B. H. Roberts, Nauvoo had enjoyed an adventurous career, "the most prosperous, but the briefest, and the saddest career of all American cities in modern times."[17]

NOTES

1. Thomas Ford, *A History of Illinois* (Chicago: Lakeside, 1946), 2:290. Ford lists the population at fifteen thousand. This figure may have been correct in February 1846 due to an influx of people from surrounding communities as refugees from persecution. During the summer and fall of 1845, as well as in early 1846, mobs drove families of Church members from their homes, burning houses, barns, and crops. These people fled to Nauvoo for safety. The most accurate figures on population are those compiled by Susan Easton Black, who concluded that the Ford figure was too high and that the population was probably eleven to twelve thousand. She compiled data "from over one thousand sources. . . . It acknowledges, highlights, and reconstructs the contribution and commitment of a total of 23,200 known people who were members of the Church at any time during the years from 1830 to 1848. A synthesis of all these noncensus data indicates that the population of Nauvoo grew from 100 in 1839 to about 4,000 in 1842, rose to about 12,000 in 1844, and stood at around 11,000 in 1845." "How Large Was the Population of Nauvoo?" *BYU Studies* 35, no. 2 (1995): 93.

2. Thomas Gregg, *Missouri Republican,* as quoted in David R. Crockett, *Saints in the Wilderness* (Tucson: LDS Gems, 1997), 186.

3. J. R. Smith, a traveling artist and lecturer, as quoted by Glen M. Leonard and T. Edgar Lyon, "The Nauvoo Years," *Ensign,* September 1979, 11.

4. John Greenleaf Whittier, a famous poet and traveler, as quoted by William Mulder and A. Russell Mortensen, ed., *Among the Mormons* (Lincoln: University of Nebraska Press, 1973), 159.

5. B. H. Roberts, *A Comprehensive History of the Church of Jesus Christ of Latter-day Saints* (Salt Lake City: Deseret News, 1930), 1:479.

6. Gregg, *History of Hancock County,* Illinois (Chicago: C. C. Chapman, 1880), 2:245.

7. Joseph Smith, *History of the Church of Jesus Christ of Latter-day Saints,* ed. B. H. Roberts, 2d ed., rev. (Salt Lake City: Deseret Book, 1957), 3:375.

8. Ibid., 4:239–49.

9. Ibid., 4:178.

10. Roberts, *Comprehensive History,* 2:84–85.

11. Gustive O. Larson, *Prelude to the Kingdom* (Francestown, N. H.: M. Jones, 1947), 50; also, Richard L. Jensen, "Transplanted to Zion: The Impact of British Latter-day Saint Immigration upon Nauvoo," *BYU Studies* 31, no. 1 (winter 1991): 78. He records that from 1840 to 1845 some 4,666 individuals came to Nauvoo from the British Isles.

12. Kenneth Godfrey, "Causes of Mormon Non-Mormon Conflict in Hancock County, Illinois, 1839–1846" (Ph.D. diss., Brigham Young University, 1967). This dissertation presents a detailed survey of these conflicts; pages 112–44 are particularly insightful.

13. Smith, *History of the Church,* 6:612–22.

14. Roberts, *Comprehensive History,* 2:416–20.

15. Ibid., 2:504–6.

16. William E. Berrett and Alma P. Burton, *Readings in LDS Church History from Original Manuscripts* (Salt Lake City: Deseret Book, 1955), 2:122–23.

17. Roberts, *Comprehensive History,* 2:60.

Architectural Drawing No. 2 of Nauvoo Temple, drawing, 1842 or 1843, William Weeks, LDS Church Archives. This is a second preliminary or proposed architectural drawing of the Nauvoo Temple by architect William Weeks. This drawing has some significant changes from the earlier proposal: star stones, star windows, and a boxlike front attic section along with an octagonal tower capped by an angelic weather vane.

In less than ten years from its founding, The Church of Jesus Christ of Latter-day Saints had built a temple in Kirtland, Ohio, and, if not deterred by persecution,

CHAPTER TWO

A SIX-YEAR

BUILDING PROGRAM

would have built on two sites dedicated in Missouri. It is therefore not unusual that the Saints would direct their thoughts toward constructing such a building as they began to settle in Illinois. The first printed mention of a temple to be erected

in Nauvoo dates to 1 August 1840. A communication from the First Presidency of the Church declared that "the time has now come, when it is necessary to erect a house of prayer, a house of order, a house for the worship of our God, where the ordinances can be attended to agreeably to His divine will, in this region of the country—to accomplish which, considerable exertion must be made, and means will be required."[1]

A site was selected on the east bench, the highest elevation in the city. It was a striking loca-

Several plans for the building were submitted by various individuals, only one of which was satisfactory to the Prophet—the drawing of William Weeks. Weeks, a recent convert to the Church, had been an architect and builder in New England prior to coming to Nauvoo. When he came and showed his proposed plans, "Joseph Smith grabbed him, hugged him and said, 'You are the man I want.'"[3] He was appointed as official architect and supervised the work during most of the construction period.

The time has now come, whe a house of order, a house fo which, considerable exertio

tion. Plans and decisions were carried into formal action at the October 1840 general conference in Nauvoo as the Prophet Joseph Smith spoke of the necessity of building a "House of the Lord" in Nauvoo and presented the matter to Church membership for approval. "Whereupon it was Resolved: That the Saints build a house for the worship of God, and that Reynolds Cahoon, Elias Higbee, and Alpheus Cutler be appointed a committee to build the same."[2]

William Clayton, who served as a secretary to Joseph Smith and whose journal became known as the "History of the Nauvoo Temple," reports that less than ten days following the October conference approval of the project, the "brethren commenced to open a quarry to dig the stone for the building. Brother Elisha Everett was the man who struck the first blow."[4] On 15 January 1841 the First Presidency declared that "the Temple of the Lord is in

progress of erection here," explaining that the building would be constructed so that all functions of the priesthood could be exercised. It was to be a place where instructions from the "Most High" would be received and from Nauvoo go forth to distant lands.[5]

Construction of the building was given divine confirmation, and the steps taken thus far were approved in a revelation issued by the Prophet on 19 January 1841. A more detailed account of the design and functions of the

commandment from God to build the temple and hasten its completion (D&C 124:26–44).

1841: Organizing and Moving Forward

From the beginning Albert P. Rockwood and Charles Drury, both skilled stoneworkers, were in charge of crews working in the quarries.[6] Work was slow at first, with only one day in ten being spent on the project. As spring arrived in 1841, work picked up momentum. Employment of regular hired hands to labor on

t is necessary to erect a house of prayer,

e worship of our God . . . to accomplish

ust be made and means will be required.

proposed structure was now made clear. The temple was to contain a baptismal font for performing baptisms in behalf of the dead. It was to be a place where God could restore that which was lost, where sacred ordinances could be revealed unto his people—"even the fulness of the priesthood." The Prophet was to be shown all things pertaining to the building, and it was to be erected on the spot that had been selected previously. From that date on, the Church was under

the project gave a new consistency to the effort. This consistency was later aided by division of the city into ten wards, with each ward crew working once every ten days.[7]

The foundation was laid out by the temple committee in February 1841. The work began with the digging of the basement.[8] During the first week in March, workers began laying stones for the basement walls.[9] William Clayton reported that "by the 6th day of April walls

were sufficiently high at the corners [at ground level] to lay the cornerstones, and notwithstanding the extreme poverty of the church everything moved on rapidly and prospects looked very cheering and pleasing."[10] It should be noted that most likely only the four corners had been trenched out at that time; indications are that the center of the basement and the sides had not yet been excavated. This is borne out by the report of Norton Jacob, a carpenter who helped build the Nauvoo Temple. He explained that "not much had been excavated then except about the corners where trenches had been sunk to the depth of the intended basement and filed with rough walls so as to receive the corner stones."[11]

Church members eagerly awaited the annual conference of 6 April 1841. The Saints had been gathering to Nauvoo for several days in anticipation of this event. A very special conference, it was to begin with the ceremony of laying the cornerstones of the temple. As the day arrived, an estimated ten thousand people were present to witness the

Figure 2.1 Nauvoo Temple from Hill's Map of Nauvoo, drawing, 1842, William Weeks, LDS Church Archives. This is the earliest known sketch of the Nauvoo Temple by its architect, William Weeks. It was printed on Gustavus Hill's map of Nauvoo (see Figure 1.1).

festivities. Commencing at 7:30 A.M., sixteen companies of the Nauvoo Legion paraded in general review. Following the review, a procession was organized and moved forward to the temple block, arriving there at noon. At the temple site, generals of the Nauvoo Legion, their staffs, and distinguished visitors took up positions inside the center of the foundation. Ladies were seated next, just inside the foundation walls. Immediately behind and outside the walls stood the gentlemen, behind them the infantry, and in the rear the cavalry. Superior officers, speakers, architects, and other dignitaries were conducted to the stand located at the southeast or principal cornerstone. With the site fully enclosed, the services were ready to begin.[12]

The chorus, led by B. S. Wilber, began the meeting by singing a hymn from the new hymnbook. Next came an address to the assembly by President Sidney Rigdon. His oration, lasting more than one hour, was followed by another hymn by the choir. Then came the laying of the principal or southeast cornerstone. By order of the First Presidency, the architects lowered the stone to its place, and Joseph Smith pronounced the benediction: "This principal corner stone in representation of the First Presidency, is now duly laid in honor of the Great God; and may it there remain until the whole fabric is completed; and may the same be accomplished speedily; that the Saints may have a place to worship God, and the Son of Man have where to lay His head."[13]

President Rigdon then stated: "May the persons employed in the erection of this house be preserved from all harm while engaged in its construction, till the whole is completed. . . . Even so, Amen."[14] Following this, services were adjourned for one hour. Upon reassembling, they proceeded to lay the remaining cornerstones, each with appropriate ceremony. The second cornerstone, the southwest corner, was laid under the direction of the President of the high priesthood and his council. President William Marks pronounced the benediction. Third to be laid was the northwest corner. This was superintended by the High Council with a benediction by Elias Higbee. The fourth or northeast cornerstone was laid under direction of the bishops; Bishop Newell K. Whitney pronounced the prayer.[15] Services were then declared to be closed, and the crowd dispersed to their homes and lodgings. Music in addition to the choir had been provided by a military band directed by Captain Duzette of the Nauvoo Legion.[16]

Work on the temple picked up momentum during the remainder of the year. By July plans had been made by the committee to erect a baptismal font in the basement of the building.[17] William Clayton reported that the font was to be located at the east end of the building and was to be made of wood. William Weeks, the architect, drew a sketch of the proposed font, and the plan was accepted by Joseph Smith. On 8 August Weeks commenced laboring on the project with his own hands. On 11 August he began carving the twelve oxen which were to support the font. After a few days he turned the work over to the carpenters. Elijah Fordham, who had earlier been miraculously healed through the ministering of Joseph Smith, took over as principal carver. Work on the font was finished in a little over two months, and on 8 November 1841 it was dedicated and put to use.[18]

William Clayton cites another interesting event as taking place on 25 September 1841, when "a deposit was made in the southeast corner stone of the Temple."[19] Samuel Miles, a convert from England who helped construct the temple, was present on the occasion and indicated that perhaps two hundred persons had assembled to witness the event.[20] Nancy Naomi Alexander Tracy, who lived just one lot beyond the street on the north side of the temple, describes clearly what took place: "One day I looked over toward the temple and saw a large crowd gathered with some two or three women present; so I thought I would go over. I put on my bonnet and shawl and made my way over. Brother Joseph was there and seemed busily engaged over something. Finally, he looked up and saw us women. He said for the brothers to stand back and let the sisters come up. So they gave way, and we went up. In the huge chief corner stone was cut out a square about a foot around and about as deep lined with zinc, and in it Brother Joseph had placed a Bible, a Book of Mormon, hymn book, and other church works along with silver money that had been coined in that year. Then a lid was cemented down, and the temple was reared on the top of this."[21]

This event is often confused with a nearly identical deposit in the Nauvoo House cornerstone which took place just a few days later, on 2 October 1841. Some have felt that there was no such deposit in the temple but only in the Nauvoo House. There is no available evidence to further clarify the matter, and therefore it is possible that very similar deposits were made in each building just one week apart. The walls of the temple were not very high at the time, and the southeast corner could have remained accessible for such a deposit. Further information may in time surface to either corroborate or disprove observations of the above witnesses.

Suitable low-cost timber was not available in Illinois, so in September the temple committee participated in the purchase of lumber mills in Wisconsin to provide lumber for the building (see more about this in chapter 3). This action became a great boon to construction of the temple as well as to the construction of other buildings in Nauvoo.[22]

As winter 1841 began the foundation was laid, and the walls of the basement story were nearly completed. The greater portion of work in the basement had now been accomplished. The wall on the south side was up to the water table (about 5½ feet high), and part of it had been laid. This water table course of stone marked the separation of the foundation and the main wall above it. The structure remained in this condition until the spring of 1842.[23]

To facilitate the project, most stakes of the Church were dissolved except those in the vicinity of Nauvoo and a few others in Illinois. Church members were asked to gather to Nauvoo and areas nearby to assist in building the temple. Further stimulus was given when it was announced that no general conferences of the Church would be held until they could be held in the temple.[24] In December 1841 some two or three hundred elders of the

Figure 2.2 Architectural Drawing No. 1 of the Nauvoo Temple, drawing, 1842, William Weeks, LDS Church Archives. This is the earliest known preliminary or proposed architectural drawing of the Nauvoo Temple by architect William Weeks. There is good evidence to conclude that the gabled roof design and the large, elliptical arched window as shown in the attic section of this drawing were utilized in the completed east or back end of the building.

Church who had offered to go on missions were called instead to accept work missions, providing labor on the temple. These were the first of many labor missionaries who served without pay and assisted in erecting the building.[25]

1842: Steady Progress

During the winter of 1841–42, as many as one hundred men were engaged in quarrying rock for the temple walls.[26] They were assisted by numerous other workmen who hauled stone to the building site. On 21 February the Prophet dictated a letter to the "brethren in Nauvoo," observing that they needed a more equal distribution of labor on the part of the tithing hands: "A super abundance of hands one week, and none the next, tends to retard the progress of the work; therefore every brother is requested to be particular to labor on the day set apart for the same, in his ward. . . . The captains of the respective wards are particularly requested to be at the place of labor on their respective days, and keep an accurate account of each man's work, and be ready to exhibit a list of the same when called for."[27] A report published in the *Wasp* on 23 April 1842 cites the progress being made: "We passed by the Temple, and was delighted at the prospect that here presented itself. A scene of lively industry and animation was there. The sound of the polisher's chisel—converting the rude stone of the quarry into an artful shape—sent forth its busy hum: all were busily employed—the work was fast progressing."[28]

An optimistic article in the *Times and Seasons* of early May declared that work was progressing rapidly and that all workers were strenuously exerting themselves. The report went so far as to predict that the building would either be enclosed or the top stone raised upon it by the next fall.[29] Work on the walls did not get under way until late spring, and what was done was meager until the arrival of William W. Player in June. Coming from England with the intent of working on the temple, Player commenced his labors on 8 June 1842. An expert in his trade, he served as principal stone setter from this time until the last stone was laid on the temple. William Clayton records that Player spent some time regulating the stonework that had already been done. Then on 11 June he set the first plinth on the southwest corner.[30] "During the summer he lost two weeks work having to wait for plinths, which they were cutting. The work progressed but slowly during this season, having but one crane, but the delay arose through the stone not being cut fast enough. By the fall, however, he got all the stone laid round as high as the window sills, and all the window sills, as well as the large sill on the East Venetian window. He had also 2 courses of pilaster stones on the plinths all around."[31] On 4 August the first raft of lumber arrived from the pineries in Wisconsin.[32] As other rafts arrived during October and November, an article in the *Times and Seasons* described what became a common practice as men and teams responded to requests for hauling lumber. "A cheering assemblage of waggons, horses, oxen and men . . . began with zeal and gladness to pull the raft to pieces and haul it up to the Temple," where "a large assemblage of carpenters, joiners &c. . . . succeeded in preparing the lumber and laying the joists."[33]

The work of framing the floor joists for the main floor was completed in October.[34] Also, in late October the temple committee, under instructions from Joseph Smith, proposed that a temporary floor be laid so the Saints could meet in the temple for worship instead of at the grove. Work on the temporary floor began the following day. By Friday, 28 October 1842, the floor was laid and seats fixed ready for meeting. The first meeting in the incomplete building, a worship service, was held on Sunday, 30 October 1842, with the building filled to capacity.[35]

Work on the temple, which had been steady all year, slowed only in late summer due to a temporary lack of funds. By the time winter arrived, the walls were four feet high above the basement story. Here they remained until spring, as stonecutters continued work in the quarries, preparing stones for use during the next year.[36]

1843: Delays and Problems

Information on the work done in 1843 is fragmentary and incomplete. An annual conference of the Church was convened on the temporary floor of the first story on 6 April. It was attended by a large assembly with many coming from Iowa, crossing on ice over the frozen Mississippi. On this occasion the temple walls are described as being from four to twelve feet above the first floor.[37] Construction during the spring was considerably delayed by the illness of Brother Player and the necessity of fixing run-

ways for the crane. This crane and others added later were used for lifting and moving large wooden beams and heavy stones as they were put in place in the building. Work on the walls was again begun by Player on 21 April and continued steadily until the start of an early winter.

Additional problems delayed the project as misunderstandings developed between the temple committee and the architect. The problem was resolved by the Prophet, who stated, "I gave a certificate to William Weeks to carry out my designs and the architecture of the Temple in Nauvoo, and that no person or persons shall interfere with him or his plans in the building of the Temple."[38]

On 8 June 1843 Elias Higbee, a member of the temple committee, died in Nauvoo after a short illness.[39] This vacancy was not filled until October, when Hyrum Smith, a brother of the Prophet, was appointed to the position. He served in this capacity until his death in 1844.[40]

As work slowed in the fall due to a lack of teams and provisions, a call was issued for greater exertions, declaring that if these embarrassments were removed, walls could be completed the next year.[41] As work ended for winter, walls were up as high as the arches of the first tier of windows all around the building.[42]

1844: Renewed Determination

On New Year's Day 1844 a progress report on the building was published in the *Times and Seasons:* "Considering the many improvements that have been made, and the difficulties in many instances under which the committee have had to labor, the Temple has made great progress; and strenuous efforts are now being made in quarrying, hauling, and hewing stone, to place it in a situation that the walls can go up and the building be enclosed by next fall."[43] In early spring, construction of a second crane commenced. It was rigged during the month of March, and on 11 April Brother Player again started work on the walls.[44] Payment of tithes slacked off considerably in the spring, and some workmen went for weeks without pay. Charles Lambert, who began work at this time, reported that "many of the most skillful workmen had left to find employment elsewhere, that it looked for a time as if the work would have to cease unless more funds could be collected."[45] Response to a call by the Prophet for more funds enabled the work to go forward. In June seventy-five to one hundred stonecutters were laboring in the workshop beside the structure, either hewing or laying stones for the temple.[46]

June and July were months of grave crisis for the Church. Persecution had been increasing in Illinois, causing the Church and its leaders considerable difficulty. In June mob action and violence struck what was considered by some to be a fatal blow. On 27 June 1844 Joseph Smith and his brother Hyrum were murdered by a mob at Carthage, Illinois. They were being held in protective custody pending a hearing on charges of treason against the state of Illinois.[47] Following their martyrdom, all work on the temple was suspended as workmen ceased their labor, standing guard over the building to protect it from threatened violence.[48] Not only did work on the temple cease, so did donations toward its erection. Disturbed by the death of their leaders, members were uncertain as to what their future course might be. On Sunday, 7 July, a decision was made to resume work on the building and to finish it as speedily as possible.[49] The following day work began. No food was available to supply needs of workers and their families, yet in spite of this condition workers pitched in, putting their trust in God.

Figure 2.3 Architectural Drawing No. 2 of Nauvoo Temple, drawing, 1842 or 1843, William Weeks, LDS Church Archives. This is a second preliminary or proposed architectural drawing of the Nauvoo Temple by architect William Weeks. This drawing has some significant changes from the earlier proposal: star stones, star windows, and a boxlike front attic section along with an octagonal tower capped by an angelic weather vane.

As the Twelve Apostles assumed the role of Church leadership, Brigham Young as President of the Twelve became the leader and chief force in pushing the temple to completion. Calls for provisions went out; members opened their hearts, and means poured in to sustain the project. A renewed spirit of dedication took hold of workers and Church members as work went forward. Two large rafts of lumber had recently arrived in Nauvoo from the pineries, and men were liberal with their teams, hauling timber to the temple, where it was secured in a few days.

About the middle of July the female members of the LeHarpe and Macedonia branches of the Church offered to collect funds for building an additional crane. Anxious to see the building progress more rapidly, they raised 194 dollars before the end of the month, which was more than enough to do the job. The committee put the carpenters to work, and on 3 August the new crane was put into operation on the north side of the structure.[50] Work now moved ahead with great speed, and on 23 September the first capital stone, or sun stone, weighing about two tons, was placed in position on the walls of the temple.[51] Due to threats of arson, President Young appointed four watchmen to keep watch over the temple at night. This practice continued from 26 September until the Saints left the city.[52]

While attempting to raise one of the sunstone capitals on 25 September, a near fatal mishap occurred. Clayton reports that they had started to raise the stone when the crane fell over in a tremendous crash. Someone had failed to fasten the guy wires. The crane was damaged considerably and barely missed some of the workmen as it fell. However, it was repaired and back in use in a few days.[53]

Crews continued to set the capitals, hoping to complete the task before winter set in. The last of the thirty capital stones was set in place on 6 December 1844. It had been raised halfway when the blocking of the tackle broke, making it impossible either to raise or lower the stone. After some difficulty, workmen were able to make repairs, and the stone was placed on the wall at 12:40 P.M. Clayton reported that it seemed as if the Lord had held up the winter until this important work could be accomplished. Two hours after the stone had been set, a brisk snowstorm commenced, and by nightfall four inches of snow covered the ground.[54]

Early in December, it was decided to employ carpenters during the winter. On 16 December 1844 the carpenters commenced their activities. They were to prepare timbers so they would be available for immediate use upon completion of the stonework. Fifteen persons were selected by the architect for this type of steady employment. The south side of the lower story was weather boarded around, and a shop was made ready.[55] A letter from W. W. Phelps written on Christmas Day was printed in the *Times and Seasons*. It stated that the temple was up as high as the caps of the pilasters and that the inside work was going forward as fast as possible.[56]

1845: SIGNIFICANT ACCOMPLISHMENTS

The Twelve Apostles published an epistle in the *Times and Seasons* of 15 January reporting

progress on the temple. They stated that the temporary wooden font had now been removed and would be replaced by one made of stone. Work on the new font would begin as soon as the stonecutters had finished cutting the last stone for the walls of the building. It was further reported that they anticipated that all the stones would be cut by the start of spring and that great numbers of carpenters, masons, and other workmen were daily engaged in the building's erection. The plan was to rush the work forward, enclosing the building and preparing to commence endowment ordinances in the fall (these are explained in chapters 4 and 5).[57] The desire to complete the temple as early as possible occupied the attention of all in Nauvoo.

On 24 May 1845 the Saints assembled for the laying of the capstone.

On Wednesday, 12 March, Brother Player again renewed work on the walls. Under his supervision, by the close of the month they had put up the last trumpet stone.[58] Church authorities decided to put all their help on the temple to build a drain for the font, to build a wall on the south side of the temple block, and to keep the cranes going.[59]

On 16 March President Young expressed some displeasure at the project's slow progress and issued a renewed call for greater effort. He reported that the stonecutters and joiners were at work and that the joiners had far exceeded their expectations during the winter. The lumber was reported to be holding out, and there was no lack of provisions. Men were asked to rededicate themselves to the task at hand, and a call for four hundred men was issued.[60] On the following day, "one hundred and five extra laborers and about thirty teams commenced work" in response to the request of their leader.[61]

On 1 April the *Times and Seasons* reported that a trench about 6 feet wide and 6 feet deep was being excavated around the temple block to enclose an area of 6 to 8 acres. The trench would be filled with stone and an iron fence built on it for the security of the temple and tabernacle. This work was performed by the public hands, or tithing workers.[62] The same issue of the *Times and Seasons* reported: "The work on the Temple goes on as fast as possible, and, in fact, the anxiety is so great to labor upon this great house of the Lord, that the committee frequently have to set men at other work. . . . There never was so great union in the city before."[63]

Figure 2.4 The Mormon Temple, drawing, early 1846, Edward Everett, LDS Church Archives. For two days Edward Everett studied the building, taking measurements and doing preliminary sketches of the temple. Note the angelic weather vane at the top of the steeple.

A regular guard was still in service at the temple to protect it from enemies of the Church. On the night of 2 April the police caught a man entering the structure and severely beat him in the process of capture. The temple committee and others were quite upset by the guard's actions and protested to Hosea Stout, who was in charge of security. Feelings on the issue were calmed after explanation of the circumstances and the orders under which the guard was operating. Following this investigation, President Young approved the police action and requested that the guard be continued.[64] The Church continued efforts to complete the building, while at the same time enemies were massing in an effort to drive all Latter-day Saints from the state. Continued threats of violence and mobbing of outlying Mormon settlements were to result in less than a year's time in a mass exodus to the wilderness of the West. Use of guards for protection of Church property had become a necessity.

Figure 2.5 *The Nauvoo Temple, engraving, date unknown, Vizetelly, LDS Church Archives. This engraving is believed to have been produced by an individual surnamed Vizetelly in the late 1840s or in the 1850s.*

A conference of the Church convened at Nauvoo on 6 April 1845 and lasted four days. It was reportedly attended by about twenty-five thousand people,[65] which seems to be a somewhat exaggerated figure.

On Monday, 21 April, Brother Player put up the first star stone on the southeast corner of the temple.[66] The top of this stone was fifty-five feet from the ground. As the rest of the star stones were placed, they added significantly to the beauty of the building.[67] Walls were then complete in readiness for laying the final stone.

On 24 May 1845 a large number of Saints assembled at the temple to witness the laying of the capstone on the southeast corner of the building. The hour was purposely early so Church leaders could attend unmolested by marshals. The time appointed for gathering was 5:45 A.M. Church leaders in attendance were Brigham Young, Heber C. Kimball, John Taylor, Willard Richards, Amasa M. Lyman, George A. Smith, John E. Page, Orson Hyde, and Orson Pratt (all members of the Twelve); Newel K. Whitney and George Miller (the presiding bishops and trustees in trust); Alpheus Cutler and Reynolds Cahoon (temple committee); William Clayton (temple recorder); John Smith (patriarch); and several members of the Nauvoo Stake high council.[68]

A brass band under the direction of William Pitt was arranged in a circle a short distance from the corner. The band began the program by playing "The Nightingale."[69] At eight minutes past six, William Player spread the mortar, and the stone was lowered into place. President Young stepped onto the stone and by beating on it with a large mallet fitted it precisely into position. The stone was pronounced set at 6:22 A.M. The band then played the "Capstone March," composed especially for the occasion by Brother Pitt.[70] Heber C. Kimball described the scene: "The singers sang their sweetest notes, and their voices thrilled the hearts of the assemblage; the music of the band, which played on the occasion, never sounded so charming."[71] President Young then remarked, "The last stone is now laid upon the temple and I pray the Almighty in the name of Jesus to defend us in this place and sustain us until the temple is finished and we have all got our endowments."[72] This was followed by the entire congregation shouting three times in unison, "Hosanna, Hosanna, Hosanna, to God and the Lamb, Amen, Amen, and Amen." President Young concluded by saying: "So let it be, Lord Almighty." He then dismissed the workmen for the day, admonishing the people to hallow the day and spend it giving thanks to God.[73]

The congregation was now dismissed, and the Saints returned to their homes. As they began to leave, the band continued to play, and John Kay stood on the stone singing "The Capstone Song," composed by W. W. Phelps. Though the morning had been very cold, members had been warmed by the services and the realization that the walls were now complete.[74]

On 28 May the carpenters began raising the timbers for the attic story of the building.[75] By the middle of June, the roof was nearly on, and on 26 June workers laid the first stones for the new baptismal font.[76] On 27 June President Young wrote a letter to the editor of the *Millennial Star* in England. In it he reported progress on the structure as it then stood:

> The frame-work of the roof is on the building, and the next week the brethren expect to put on the shingles; the frame work around the foundation of the tower is all up, and the first timbers for the tower itself were raised this day. The new stone font is mostly cut, and the first stone was laid to-day at about four o'clock. We expect in about five or six weeks the attic story of the Temple and the font will be all finished and ready for dedication, and just as soon as they are ready we shall dedicate them. We have all the timbers for the temple on the ground, and above one hundred thousand shingles for the roof. The lead for the eaves and tin for the dome of the tower are also bought. . . .
>
> We are building a stone wall round the Temple-block, eight feet high and about five feet thick at the base, the wall on the north side is nearly built, the most of the woodwork for the tem-

ple is finished, all the window-frames and sashes are made, and the glaziers are ready to set the glass, which we expect here in a few days, the frame and ornamental-work of the tower is all ready to be put up, and the whole is far on the way of completion.[77]

As July closed, the *Nauvoo Neighbor* reported that when completed, the building would measure 158½ feet from the ground to the top of the steeple and that of this 130 feet were already raised.[78] On 13 August the paper reported: "The

On Sunday, 5 October 1845, the Church held its first general conference in three years. It became the only general conference ever held within the temple after its enclosure. The structure was now fully enclosed, windows were in, and temporary floors had been laid. With temporary seats and pulpits erected, the building was ready to receive the thousands of members who attended this first session of the conference. Services were opened by President Young, who offered a prayer of dedication, "pre-

While the temple was bei[ng]

of the Saints, their zeal wa[s]

seeking their removal fro[m]

Neighbor has been delayed a few hours, in order to say that *the last shingle* has been laid upon the roof of the Temple. The roof is now completed, and, the sash and window frames having been made ready, the house of the Lord may be considered 'enclosed.'"[79] The dome and cap of the temple tower were raised on 23 August.[80] A letter from Brigham Young to Samuel Brannan written 15 September declared that as of that date the attic story and steeple were nearly complete.[81]

senting the Temple, thus far completed, as a monument of the Saints' liberality, fidelity, and faith—concluding, 'Lord we dedicate this house and ourselves to thee.'"[82]

While the temple was being rushed to completion by the united energies of the Saints, their zeal was matched in part by the bitterness of enemies seeking their removal from the state. Due to threats and repeated mob violence, the fall of 1845 became not only a time of great

activity in an effort to complete the temple but also a time to stock provisions, prepare wagons, sell property, and make preparations to leave. The decision had been made to leave in the spring for the wilderness of the West.[83]

Following general conference, worship meetings were held in the temple each Sunday. This procedure lasted but a short time, being interrupted on 9 November as workmen started removing the floor of the first story to put in new timbers. The original sleepers put in at the large main room of the east attic story for heating, and on the twenty-ninth workers laid carpets on the main floor of the attic story and in several rooms on the side.[86] This portion of the building was pushed to completion preparatory to administering endowment ordinances to Church members.

On 30 November 1845 the attic story was ready for use. In services held that morning by several Church authorities, President Young dedicated this portion of the building.[87] The

...shed to completion by the united energies

...atched in part by the bitterness of enemies

...e state.

commencement of the structure had rotted.[84] This had probably resulted from three years of exposure to the elements prior to enclosing and roofing the building. Until other rooms could be prepared and the new floor put in, all large meetings were held outside the temple.

By 22 November plasterers finished their work in the attic story.[85] They were followed by the painters, who put on the last coat of paint by 26 November. Two stoves were put in the next few days were spent in arranging rooms for endowment ordinances, which began on 10 December 1845.[88] This completed portion of the structure remained in almost constant use as long as the Church remained in Nauvoo.

Without question, 1845 was the most productive period of temple construction. It was a period of great accomplishment, and the year closed with work continuing at a rapid pace. The floor of the main hall on the lower story

was nearly finished, and the pulpits were arranged for installation.[89] The temple was now in constant use for sacred ordinances, fulfilling the primary purpose for which it had been erected. By 29 December one thousand persons had received endowment ordinances in the temple.[90]

1846: COMPLETION, DEDICATION, AND EXODUS

New Year's Day of 1846 proved to be no holiday for temple workmen; it was instead a day of continued activity. Brigham Young announced, "The plasterers have commenced to plaster the arched ceiling of the lower hall, the floor is laid, the framework of the pulpits and seats for the choir and band are put up; and the work of finishing the room for dedication progresses rapidly."[91]

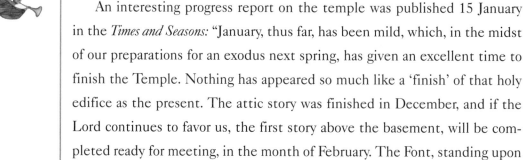

By 29 December 1845 one thousand persons had received endowment ordinances in the temple.

On 7 January 1846 a new altar was put to use for the first time in performance of sacred temple ordinances such as eternal marriages and sealings. This altar, about 2½ feet high, was covered on the sides by white linen, with scarlet damask cushions on its top. It was located in Room 1 of the attic story.[92]

An interesting progress report on the temple was published 15 January in the *Times and Seasons:* "January, thus far, has been mild, which, in the midst of our preparations for an exodus next spring, has given an excellent time to finish the Temple. Nothing has appeared so much like a 'finish' of that holy edifice as the present. The attic story was finished in December, and if the Lord continues to favor us, the first story above the basement, will be completed ready for meeting, in the month of February. The Font, standing upon twelve stone oxen, is about ready, and the floor of the second story is laid, so that all speculation about the Temple of God at Nauvoo, must cease."[93]

On 24 January "a general meeting of the official members of the Church" met on the newly laid floor of the second story to consider plans and preparations for an early exodus. At that meeting a committee was selected to dispose of property of both the Church and its members.[94] A crew of workers was asked to remain behind to finish the first story and prepare the building for dedication. Other members were busily engaged in packing and preparing for the journey ahead. As the month closed, another interesting feature was added to the temple. A weather vane (the angel) was put into place on the tower of the

City of Joseph February 13. 1846

I, William Weeks, by the authority vested in me by Joseph Smith and his Councillors & the Twelve, do appoint Truman O Angel to be my successor as Superintendant over the finishing of the Temple & Nauvoo House in the City of Joseph according to the plans and designs given by me to him. and, no person or persons shall interfere with him in the carrying out of these plans and designs

William Weeks Architect

I wish Br T. O Angel to carry out the doing of the Temple & Nauvoo House

Nauvoo feby 13 1846

Brigham Young

Figure 2.6 (Above) Letter Appointing Truman Angell, letter, 1846, William Weeks, LDS Church Archives. As the Saints began to leave Nauvoo in February 1846, William Weeks was asked by Church leaders to accompany them in the exodus to the West. Truman Angell was asked to remain behind in charge of completing the temple and preparing it for dedication. This letter is an official letter of appointment from William Weeks, the temple architect, and is cosigned by President Brigham Young.

Figure 2.7 (Next page) Crossing the Mississippi on the Ice, tempura on muslin, c. 1865, C. C. A. Christensen. Courtesy Brigham Young University Museum of Art. All rights reserved. In the late 1870s, Christensen painted his panoramic murals. This section depicts Church members leaving Nauvoo in February 1846 as they crossed the frozen Mississippi on the ice.

temple at 9:00 A.M. on 30 January.[95] The topmost point of the temple was now finally in place.

On 4 February 1846 the Latter-day Saints began driving their heavily laden wagons toward the Mississippi. One of the routes taken was down Parley Street, which came to be known as the "street of tears." Coming to the river, the Saints crossed by skiffs and flat-bottom ferryboats to the plains of Iowa. The exodus from Nauvoo had begun. A second interesting development was taking place early that morning at the temple. Here could be seen a number of persons busily removing articles of furniture, stoves, carpets, pictures, and other furnishings. These items were to be taken west with the exiles or sold to finance the journey.[96]

Five days after beginning the exodus, exiles looking back across the river witnessed an alarming scene as smoke and fire issued forth from the roof of the temple. The fire started at 3:30 P.M. and burned nearly half an hour. The cause of the blaze was an overheated stovepipe, which ignited clothing drying in the attic story. It was put out by a bucket brigade. Damage was to the roof and was not extensive, but it necessitated repair. The area covered by the fire was in the west end of the main attic section. "It burned from the west stovepipe from the ridge to the railing, about sixteen feet north and south, and about ten feet east and west on the north side. The shingles on the north were broken in several places."[97] Thomas Bullock reported on 17 February: "The burnt part of the roof of the Temple was this day relaid and covered over with lead."[98]

Considerable excitement took place on 22 February 1846, when some Saints crossed back over the river from Iowa to join those still in Nauvoo in meeting for the first time on the new floor of the first story. A large crowd gathered for these services, and the great weight of this group caused the new truss floor to settle nearly to its proper position. President Young reported the incident as follows: "While settling, an inch-board or some light timber underneath was caught and cracked, the sound of which created great alarm in the congregation and some jumped out of the windows, smashing the glass and all before them; . . . others ran out of the doors and many of those who remained jumped up and down with all their might crying Oh! Oh!! Oh!!! as though they could not settle the floor fast enough, but at the same time so agitated that they knew not what they did. I attempted to call the assembly in order to explain the cause of the settling of the floor, but failing to get their attention I adjourned the meeting to the grove. I went below, examined the floor and found it had hardly settled to its designated position."[99]

As reported in the *Warsaw Signal*, damage to the building was between five hundred to a thousand dollars.[100] Since no structural damage was reported, injury to the building probably came in the form of broken windows, etc., caused by the frightened congregation.

Though many Church members were leaving the city daily, the crew at the temple continued its work of completing the first story of the building. The first story was plastered, and

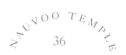

joiner work was completed on 22 April 1846. On the following day the building was swept out so the work of painting the lower story could begin in preparation for the temple dedication.[101] Workmen continued at their jobs day and night, and the painting was completed on Thursday, 29 April. The next day workers were busy sweeping out rooms and making final preparations for the dedication, which was to take place privately that night and publicly on 1 May, the day following.[102] With the temple now dedicated and construction ended, workmen settled for their final wages. They then either traveled west to join the main body of Church members on the prairies of Iowa or departed on missions to spread the message of the restored gospel.

The major portion of the construction had been under the direction of the temple committee and the architect, William Weeks. Brother Weeks departed Nauvoo early in 1846. Following his departure, Truman O. Angell, who later served as architect for the St. George and Salt Lake Temples, was placed in charge. He supervised final completion of the lower story according to the design of Weeks and remained to see the building dedicated.[103] The struggle of building a house to God had now drawn to a close. Undertaken by a people in destitute circumstances, the Nauvoo Temple had with considerable sacrifice and toil risen stone upon stone, a symbol of the faith and devotion of its builders.

Notes

1. Joseph Smith, *History of the Church of Jesus Christ of Latter-day Saints*, ed. B. H. Roberts, 2d ed., rev. (Salt Lake City: Deseret Book, 1957), 4:186.

2. Ibid., 4:205.

3. J. Earl Arrington, "William Weeks, Architect of the Nauvoo Temple," *BYU Studies* 19, no. 3 (spring 1979): 340, 359, as told to Arrington on 7 March 1932 by F. M. Weeks, who was well acquainted with his uncle William Weeks and was the family member who wrote his uncle's obituary. He claimed that William Weeks had personally told him of this experience.

4. Journal of William Clayton, "History of the Nauvoo Temple," 4, LDS Church Archives. William Clayton was appointed as official temple recorder for the Nauvoo Temple on 7 October 1842. As part of his journal he wrote or included a history of the Nauvoo Temple. He summarized events prior to his appointment and recorded events as they transpired following his call to office. This portion of his journal has been placed in one unpublished handwritten document of one hundred plus pages and is also on microfilm in the LDS Church Archives; also, Smith, *History of the Church*, 4:229; also, Diary of William Huntington, 12, typescript, 1952–53, Harold B. Lee Library, Brigham Young University.

5. *Times and Seasons* 2 (15 January 1841): 274.

6. Journal History, 31 December 1844, LDS Church Archives.

7. Diary of William Huntington, 12; and Andrew Jenson, *Church Chronology*, 2d ed., rev. (Salt Lake City: Deseret News, 1914), 22.

8. Andrew Jenson, *Historical Record* 8 (June 1889): 857–58.

9. Diary of William Huntington, 12. He explains: "I was one who assisted in laying the first stone that was laid

in the bottom of the foundation of the temple." This was on 8 March 1841.

10. Journal of William Clayton, 6.

11. Norton Jacob, "The Life of Norton Jacob," 5, typescript, 1937, Harold B. Lee Library, Brigham Young University.

12. *Times and Seasons* 2 (15 April 1841): 375.

13. Smith, *History of the Church*, 4:329.

14. Ibid.

15. Ibid., 4:329–31.

16. *Times and Seasons* 2 (15 April 1841): 377.

17. Ibid., 1 July 1841, 455.

18. Journal History, 8 November 1841.

19. Jenson, *Historical Record* 8 (June 1889): 857, quoting the writings of William Clayton.

20. Samuel Miles, "Recollections of the Prophet Joseph Smith," *Juvenile Instructor* 27 (15 March 1892): 174.

21. Nancy Naomi Alexander Tracy, as quoted by Carol Cornwall Madsen, *In Their Own Words* (Salt Lake City: Deseret Book, 1994), 252. Madsen explains that Nancy Tracy may have confused this with a nearly identical occurrence at the cornerstone of the Nauvoo House just one week later (2 October 1841) when similar deposits were made there. The additional observations of William Clayton and Samuel Miles, combined with the fact that Nancy Tracy lived very near the temple, lends credence to the accuracy of her report. It is very likely that nearly identical deposits were made in cornerstones of both the temple and the Nauvoo House. The walls of the temple were not high at the time, and it is entirely possible that this corner was left at this level in anticipation of such a deposit. No further documentation has been found yet on this issue.

22. *Times and Seasons* 2 (15 September 1841): 543.

23. Jenson, *Historical Record* 8 (June 1889): 860.

24. Smith, *History of the Church*, 4:443–44.

25. *Times and Seasons* 3 (15 December 1841): 626.

26. Ibid., 2 May 1842, 775.

27. Journal History, 21 February 1842; also, Times and Seasons 3 (1 March 1842): 715.

28. *The Wasp*, 23 April 1842.

29. *Times and Seasons* 3 (2 May 1842): 775.

30. Journal History, 11 October 1842.

31. Ibid.; also, Journal of William Clayton, 22–23.

32. *The Wasp*, 30 July 1842.

33. *Times and Seasons* 4 (15 November 1842): 10; also, John C. Bennett, *History of the Saints* (Boston: Leland and Whiting, 1842), 191. Here Bennett explains that the portion of lumber needing additional finishing was prepared in two steam saw mills which were in operation in the city. *Times and Seasons* 3 (1 October 1842): 937, explains that two extensive steam mills had been put into operation that season. These may have been used to saw wood as well as in other manufacturing.

34. "Time Book C. for the Temple, Account Book 16," 10, LDS Church Archives, Work by Carpenters and Joiners recorded by William F. Cahoon and Curtis E. Bolton. The Nauvoo Temple Committee, appointed at the October Conference of 1840, kept meticulous detailed records on all phases of construction relating to the Nauvoo Temple. These records, consisting of daybooks, ledgers, account books, time books, and other financial volumes, were kept by Elias Higbee (of the temple committee), William Clayton (temple recorder), James Whitehead, John McEwan, and Curtis E. Bolton (clerks); as well as the Carpenters Time Book kept by William F. Cahoon. These volumes include accounts by Nauvoo Trustees, Bishops Newell K. Whitney and George Miller, as well as by Joseph L. Heywood, Almon W. Babbitt, and John S. Fullmer. The records also contain

detailed measurements of stones used in walls of the building as well as numerous pieces of wood used for pulpits, moldings, door and window frames, columns, and so on. They were a treasure trove of information to the architects who designed the reconstruction plans for rebuilding the Nauvoo Temple.

Never published, these records have been preserved for many years in vaults of the Church Office Building. During 1999 the records were all placed on microfilm (consisting of five complete reels of microfilm), making them available for detailed study. Years ago the author was able to access the original documents and has more recently accessed the microfilm copies.

35. Journal History, 23 October 1842.

36. Ibid., 30 October 1842.

37. Ibid., 6 April 1843.

38. Ibid., 12 April 1843.

39. Smith, *History of the Church*, 5:420.

40. Journal History, 10 October 1843.

41. Smith, *History of the Church*, 6:49.

42. Jenson, *Historical Record* 8 (June 1889): 864.

43. *Times and Seasons* 5 (1 January 1844): 392.

44. Jenson, *Historical Record* 8 (June 1889): 866.

45. Charles C. Lambert, "Reminiscences and Diaries, 1844–1881," 12, LDS Church Archives.

46. Journal History, 12 June 1844.

47. Smith, *History of the Church*, 6:561–62, 602–22.

48. Jenson, *Historical Record* 8 (June 1889): 866.

49. Ibid.; also, Autobiography of William Adams, 1822–1894, 14, Harold B. Lee Library, Brigham Young University.

50. Jenson, *Historical Record* 8 (June 1889): 866.

51. Journal History, 23 September 1844.

52. Ibid., 26 September 1844.

53. Jenson, *Historical Record* 8 (June 1889): 867.

54. B. H. Roberts, ed., *History of the Church of Jesus Christ of Latter-day Saints, Period 2: Apostolic Interregnum* (Salt Lake City: Deseret Book, 1957), 7:323–24; also, Journal History, 5 December 1844.

55. Journal History, 16 December 1844.

56. *Times and Seasons* 5 (1 January 1845): 759.

57. Ibid. 6 (15 January 1845): 779.

58. Jenson, *Historical Record* 8 (June 1889): 868–69.

59. Journal History, 15 March 1845.

60. Ibid., 16 March 1845.

61. Ibid., 17 March 1845.

62. *Times and Seasons* 6 (1 April 1845): 856; also, Roberts, *History of the Church*, 7:399, 407.

63. *Times and Seasons* 6 (1 April 1845): 846.

64. Hosea Stout, *On the Mormon Frontier, the Diary of Hosea Stout*, 1844–1861, ed. Juanita Brooks (Salt Lake City: University of Utah Press, 1964), 1:32.

65. Jenson, *Church Chronology*, 27.

66. Journal History, 21 April 1845; also, Jenson, *Historical Record* 8 (June 1889): 869.

67. Jenson, *Historical Record* 8 (June 1889): 869–70.

68. Journal History, 24 May 1845.

69. Roberts, *History of the Church*, 7:417.

70. Ibid.

71. Helen Mar Whitney, "Scenes in Nauvoo after the Martyrdom of the Prophet and the Patriarch," *Woman's Exponent* 11 (15 April 1883): 169.

72. Roberts, *History of the Church*, 7:417–18.

73. Ibid.

74. Ibid.

75. Journal History, 28 May 1845.

76. Ibid., 26 June 1845.

77. *Millennial Star* 6 (1 September 1845): 91.

78. *Nauvoo Neighbor*, 30 July 1845.

79. Ibid., 13 August 1845.

80. Jenson, *Church Chronology*, 27; also, "Time Book C.," 33.

81. *New-York Messenger*, 11 October 1845.

82. Journal History, 5 October 1845; also, Roberts, *History of the Church*, 7:456–57.

83. Roberts, *History of the Church*, 7:439–40.

84. Ibid., 519; also, Jacob, "The Life of Norton Jacob," 16, 18. Jacob describes that he "replaced the lower girders, they having lain four years in the weather and being exposed were so decayed as not to be safe." He went on to explain: "Bro. Wm. Weeks the architect of the temple requested me this morning to go ahead and put in the truss timbers for the lower floor of the temple."

85. Roberts, *History of the Church*, 7:531.

86. Whitney, "Scenes in Nauvoo and Incidents from H. C. Kimball's Journal," *Woman's Exponent* 12 (15 June 1883): 10.

87. Roberts, *History of the Church*, 7:534.

88. Journal History, 10 December 1845.

89. Roberts, *History of the Church*, 7:546.

90. Ibid., 556, 566; also, Journal History, 1 January 1846; also, Brigham Young, *The Journal of Brigham*, comp. Leland R. Nelson (Provo, Utah: Council, 1980), 118–19.

91. Roberts, *History of the Church*, 7:560.

92. Journal History, 7 January 1846. The location of Room 1 can be seen in Figure 8.18.

93. *Times and Seasons* 6 (15 January 1846): 1096.

94. Roberts, *History of the Church*, 7:573.

95. Journal History, 30 January 1846.

96. Ibid., 4 February 1846; and Whitney, "The Last Chapter of Scenes in Nauvoo," *Woman's Exponent* 12 (1 November 1883): 81.

97. Roberts, *History of the Church*, 7:581.

98. Thomas Bullock, as quoted in Gregory R. Knight, "Journal of Thomas Bullock, 1816–1885," *BYU Studies* 31, no. 1 (winter 1991): 52.

99. Roberts, *History of the Church*, 7:594.

100. *Warsaw Signal*, 25 February 1846.

101. Diary of Samuel Whitney Richards, 1:16–18, Harold B. Lee Library, Brigham Young University.

102. Ibid., 18–20.

103. Kate B. Carter, comp., *Heart Throbs of the West* (Salt Lake City: Daughters of Utah Pioneers, 1939), 3:67, quoting the journal of Truman O. Angell Sr., 3.

View of Nauvoo and the Temple from across the River, lithograph (detail of panorama painting), 1848, Henry Lewis, Missouri Historical Society. Henry Lewis was an adventurer traveling through the United States when he painted this view of the Nauvoo Temple as part of his Mississippi panorama. The lithograph was made by Josef Arnz in 1849 and first published in Das Illustrirte Mississippienthal *in 1849.*

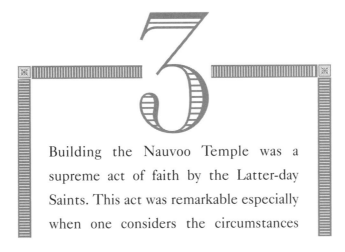

3

Building the Nauvoo Temple was a supreme act of faith by the Latter-day Saints. This act was remarkable especially when one considers the circumstances

CHAPTER THREE

MEANS AND MATERIALS

USED IN CONSTRUCTION

existing when the call to build was given. The decision of Church leaders to build the temple presented a dramatic challenge for Church members and their resources. It would be no easy task to assemble a workforce of sufficient numbers, let alone one possessing the skills required to accomplish such a project. In August 1840 when the temple was first announced, it was estimated that only two thousand eight hundred Saints lived in and about Nauvoo, with another two thousand on the other side of the river in Iowa.[1] Some three thousand others were scattered mainly throughout Ohio, Illinois, and Iowa.

Not only were the Saints lacking in numbers and skills, they also lacked the wealth to

were suffering from disease, sickness, and death, each of which would take a heavy toll during the years of temple construction. Many families battled daily with hunger: "Even the best providers were often short of flour, milk, butter, eggs, and other staples. Almost every letter from this period deals with the great struggle for food."[3] On balance it should be reported that food supplies were much better by the fall of 1845. Fruit trees planted earlier were now in production, and grain and veg-

The construction of this temp nothing short of miraculo devotion, consecration, ar

fund such a building. Most were impoverished, having lost all they owned when just months before they had been driven by mobs from the state of Missouri. They had left behind homes, shops, farms, and possessions. How could they possibly finance such a large structure as the temple, a building which would ultimately (in labor and materials) cost a million dollars or more?[2] In Nauvoo, they struggled to find adequate shelter for themselves. Many families

etable products were plentiful. Distribution of these commodities now became the problem as farmers in outlying areas were driven from their farms by mobs, and crops were destroyed.

Even if the workforce and the financial means could somehow be assembled, there would yet remain formidable challenges. How and where could they obtain the nails, glass, metals, stone, lumber, tools, equipment, and other building materials? The construction of this temple in the

1840s under these conditions was nothing short of miraculous. It was a demonstration of great faith, devotion, consecration, and sacrifice.

METHODS OF FINANCE

The funds required to finance the construction of the Nauvoo Temple came largely from the tithes and offerings of Church members. The law of tithing, instituted in the Church through revelation in July 1838 (D&C 119), was employed in connection with the temple from the very beginning. This was in fact the first full-scale implementation of this principle in the Church. In the revelation of 19 January 1841, Church members were also called upon to contribute gold, silver, and other precious things of the earth for the temple's construction (D&C 124:26–27).

At first, contributions of money and property were turned over to the temple committee, which issued receipts to the contributors.[4] The role of bishops and ward clerks in collecting tithes from Church members was not in place at this early date in Church history. On 13 December 1841 the Prophet appointed Willard Richards to serve as recorder for the temple. He opened his office in the accounting room of Joseph Smith's new brick store, located on Water Street. From this date, a regular record was kept of tithing contributions in what was called the Book of the Law of the Lord. John Sanders, a convert from Scotland, was the first recorded contributor—for a sum of five dollars.[5]

the 1840s under these conditions was

t was a demonstration of great faith,

crifice.

The temple committee was then instructed to receive no further tithing and to leave the entire work to Brother Richards.

As Church leaders, particularly members of the Twelve Apostles, visited various conference gatherings of the Church, they made a plea for members to contribute tithes. At these conferences a vote was usually taken, and Church members pledged themselves to contribute of their time and means. An epistle sent to all

Church members by the Twelve urged participation and furnished an explanation of the tithing expected. Members living even thousands of miles away were told: "You will find your names, tithings and consecrations written in the Book of the Law of the Lord, to be kept in the Temple. . . . The temple is to be built by tithing and consecration, and every one is at liberty to consecrate all they find in their hearts so to do; but the tithings required, is one-tenth of all anyone possessed at the commencement of the building, and one-tenth part of all his increase from that time until the completion of the same, whether it be money, or whatever he may be blessed with."[6]

Two types of tithing were expected: Members contributed their regular tithing on increase or earnings and another tithe on time, when each person was expected to work every tenth day on the temple without pay. This donation of labor was encouraged so the workforce would expand, especially in the case of skilled craftsmen.

As the flow of contributions increased, Brother Richards's time became crowded. To avoid neglect of his other duties, he found it necessary to devote all day Saturday of each week to receive and record the tithing as it came in. As donations continued to increase, he could not keep pace with the work, so William Clayton was called to assist, which he did beginning 14 February 1842.[7]

Figure 3.1 The Mormon Temple, lithograph (panorama painting), 1848, Henry Lewis, Missouri Historical Society. The lithograph was made by Josef Arnz in 1849 and first published in Das Illustrirte Mississippienthal *in 1849.*

The spring of 1842 was a time of great exertion and sacrifice as contributions to the temple increased. Even some members of other faiths gave liberally. An editorial in the *Times and Seasons* declared, "Never since the foundation of this church was laid, have we seen manifested a greater willingness to comply with the requisitions of Jehovah."[8] Gratitude was expressed for the help given as the people responded to the call of their leaders. It was a time of optimism, a time to push ahead and forget the past. A bright new future, full of promise, loomed on the horizon. On 11 June 1842 the record-keeping staff was again increased as James Whitehead was appointed as an assistant recorder. Money continued to come in at a steadily increasing flow.[9] Members of the Church were urged to send in their contributions from "abroad and near by" that the work might progress.[10]

Even some members of other faiths gave liberally.

The press of business in the recorder's office justified the need for better accommodations, and a small brick office was built near the temple to facilitate the handling of donations. In November the recorder moved in with his books and records,[11] and work was conducted at this location for the next two years.

Since Latter-day Saints in outlying areas and missions could not come to Nauvoo to contribute, they donated to local authorities, visiting Church leaders, and others who pledged to take their donations to Nauvoo. Some agents had been sent on special missions to raise funds. These were sent with letters of introduction, and their names were published by mission authorities. A number of regular missionaries were authorized to act in this capacity.[12]

It became apparent that not all money was being properly receipted, and in some cases the money was not reaching its destination, being diverted to other causes. The decision was made to require that each individual authorized to collect funds be placed under a two-thousand-dollar bond. The Twelve Apostles were the first to comply with the new ruling.[13] "The wisdom of this order was soon manifest; for, although it was well understood and universally believed that the Twelve would invariably make correct returns, there were others who might not be so careful or scrupulous. And, inasmuch as members of this first quorum were required to give bonds, no other man could justly complain if he were brought under the same rule."[14]

Figure 3.2 The Nauvoo Temple, detail of panorama painting, 1846, J. R. Smith, LDS Church Archives. J. R. Smith included the Nauvoo Temple in his panorama painting, which was published in Grahams Magazine, *April 1849.*

There were occasional slack periods in the flow of contributions and provisions. One came at the deaths of Joseph and Hyrum Smith, when work on the temple lapsed for about six weeks, as did also the flow of contributions. For many it was a time of uncertainty. As the Twelve Apostles assumed their role of leadership, elders were again sent out to collect funds. An epistle by the Twelve was published in Church periodicals urging a renewed effort and announcing that work on the temple would be pushed to completion.[15] The regular payment of tithes continued, and though slack at times, eventually enough money was donated to allow completion of the building.

Many members had little or no cash and therefore donated as conditions permitted. Daniel Tyler reports that in the early days of Nauvoo the Saints were generally poor. Corn sold for twenty-five cents a bushel and wheat for thirty to fifty cents a bushel. Those who had these provisions not only faced low prices but lacked a ready market. There was also a shortage of jobs.[16] Such conditions explain in large part the types of contributions received. Many Saints donated extra days in labor since they had nothing else to give. Louisa Decker records that her mother sold her best china dishes and a fine bed quilt to contribute her part.[17] Many contributed horses, wagons, cows, grain, beef, pork, and other provisions for use by the temple workmen and their families. Workmens' wages were in large part paid from those resources.

Women unable to donate money or work on the building gave blankets, clothes, and other items, or spent their time knitting socks and mittens and making other clothing for the workmen. Some farmers contributed the use of teams and wagons. Others sold part of their land and donated the money to the temple. On a number of occasions a call was sent forth for bench and moulding planes to be contributed as tithing.[18] These and other tools were donated. So many watches and old guns were received that a request was made that no more be turned in, but rather other items that could be used more easily.[19]

As items came in that had to be exchanged for money or usable materials, the work of temple recorders became more interesting and challenging. On occasion it became necessary to advertise for cows that had strayed from the temple yards and were lost. Anyone who could furnish information regarding their whereabouts was asked to report to the temple committee or the temple recorder. Recorders also had the problem of dealing with the collection of debts. Many had responded to a request of the Twelve Apostles that all old notes, deeds, and obligations members held against each other could be turned over as a donation toward building the temple.[20] This resulted in some members reporting to work as payment for debts they had contracted, because notes against them had been turned over to the temple committee as tithing.[21]

In the April conference of 1844, the women's Relief Society was called upon to participate in a special fund for purchasing nails and glass. The women were given the privilege

of donating one cent per week or fifty cents per year. The call was to raise at least one thousand dollars by this method.[22] By December nearly six hundred dollars had been collected, and by March 1845, just one year from when the challenge was issued, the full amount of one thousand dollars had been received. Women were then invited to continue their fund-raising efforts until the temple was finished.[23]

Many Church members went beyond their expected tithe, giving of their means far above that required. One outstanding illustration of such unselfish sacrifice was the donation of Joseph Toronto. A native of Sicily and a recent convert to the Church, he had come to Nauvoo during the late spring of 1845. Upon arrival he heard strong appeals from Brigham Young and others for additional funds to build the temple. He responded by giving his life's savings, which amounted to twenty-five hundred dollars in gold.[24]

Brigham Young later commented on the occasion of the Toronto contribution:

> A few months after the martyrdom of Joseph the Prophet, in the autumn and winter of 1844 we did much hard labor on the Nauvoo temple, during which time it was difficult to get bread and other provisions for the workmen to eat. I counseled the committee who had charge of the temple funds to deal out all the flour they had, and God would give them more; they did so; and it was but a short time before Brother Toronto came and brought me twenty five hundred dollars in gold. The bishop and the committee met, and I met

> with them; and they said, that the law was to lay the gold at the apostles' feet. Yes, I said and I will lay it at the bishop's feet; so I opened the mouth of the bag and took hold of the bottom end, and gave it a jerk towards the bishop, and strewed the gold across the room and said, now go and buy flour for the workmen on the temple and do not distrust the Lord any more; for we will have what we need.[25]

True, there were times when funds necessary to carry on were hard to come by, and workmen went without pay. But in general, requests were met. Thus funds were furnished by tithes, offerings, and sacrifice, and the Latter-day Saints at Nauvoo built a house to God.

THE LABOR FORCE

Construction of the temple was almost entirely accomplished by a working force from Church membership. Recruiting, organizing, and supervising work crews for such a massive structure was no small task. Not only was there a need for workmen on the building itself, but additional work crews were required to obtain some of the principal building materials and prepare them for use.

A significant factor in providing the needed workers was the principle of gathering. As work on the temple commenced, members from far and near were urged to gather to Nauvoo. They came in increasing numbers from the eastern United States, Canada, and England. Among those members were artisans skilled in carpentry, mechanics, metalwork, stonework, plastering, painting, and so forth, along with a large pool of unskilled laborers. Had this policy of gathering not been implemented, it is very doubtful that the temple could have been built.

At first the workforce consisted almost entirely of workmen donating one day's labor in ten as their payment of a tithe. As the work's tempo picked up, however, the need for an effective organization of this labor became apparent. A workable plan was devised by the temple committee and announced 22 February 1841.[26] At the suggestion of Joseph Smith, the city council divided the city into four geographical divisions or municipal wards.[27] Though this division of political or geographic wards was not totally related to the temple, it nevertheless became a great asset in organizing the workforce.[28] In November 1842 the number was increased to ten wards by action of the high council. Bishops were then appointed to preside over each ward. This designation of ward bishops later became standard Church procedure. Each ward was assigned a specific day on which its workmen were to

Figure 3.3 The Great Mormon Temple, drawing, before 1848, John Jackson, J. Reuben Clark collection, LDS Church Archives. John Jackson sketched this view of the temple some time before 1848.

report for work with their tools, wagons, and teams. If a worker could not make it on the appointed day, he was expected to be there the next or as soon thereafter as possible. Workers were urged to keep their appointments and labor on the date set apart for their ward. The Prophet Joseph issued the following notice respecting the work as it then functioned: "The captains of the respective wards are particularly requested to be at the place of labor on their respective days, and keep an accurate account of each man's work, and be ready to exhibit a list of the same when called for."[29] This effective organization pushed the work along rapidly.

Since donations were now arriving in the form of money and provisions, the committee was able to expand the labor force. It employed several stonecutters on a regular basis. About eighteen were so employed to dress the rock at the time the cornerstones were laid.[30] Prior to this, nearly all work had been done by donated labor. Alpheus Cutler and Reynolds Cahoon, members of the temple committee, hired the workmen as the work progressed.[31] As sufficient means came in, the number of skilled workmen regularly employed increased. Donated labor was also kept at a high level by the influx of new converts arriving from England.

On the occasions when lumber arrived from the pinery in Wisconsin and when special efforts were required, the regular schedule of work was stepped up, and calls were made to assist in the activity needing attention. A comment printed in the *Times and Seasons* is typical of such an effort: "Last Sabbath the committee for the building of the Temple, stated before the congregation that a large raft of pine lumber had lately arrived and was now laying in the river at this place. They requested all the brethren who had teams to turn out with their teams to assist in hauling lumber to the Temple. The first, second, third, fourth and fifth wards of the city were requested to be on the ground on Monday, Tuesday and Wednesday; and the sixth, seventh, eighth, ninth and tenth on Thursday, Friday, and Saturday."[32] A further request was made for carpenters to prepare timbers for the first floor, so all who were able could come on Friday and Saturday to lay a temporary floor and prepare seats so the Saints could meet within the walls of the temple. It is reported that all of these requests were filled as desired.[33]

The size of the workforce fluctuated considerably according to need at the various periods of construction and the availability of workmen. Some glimpses into the size of crews are available, indicating that at one time approximately one thousand men were donating every tenth day in work on the temple.[34] At least 150 men were at one time working in the pineries of Wisconsin harvesting lumber for the temple.[35] It was reported that as many as one hundred men were removing stone from the quarries, while multitudes were engaged in hauling the stone to the temple and performing other kinds of labor.[36] In June 1844 seventy-five to one hundred stonecutters worked at the temple, preparing stones for the walls.[37] Carpenters were hired, and at least twenty-five were regularly working in the joiner shops.[38] In August 1845 it was reported that 350 hired men were zealously at work on the building.[39]

A "time book" kept for the temple hands from 13 June 1842 to 6 June 1846 furnishes interesting information on the employed section of the workforce. It records a total of 1,221 employed and registered in the book over its four-year period. Of this number 885 persons are reported as having completed at least one full month's labor during this time of construction, and some individuals worked through the entire period of the time book. The book records forty-six registered workers in 1842, with some working as many as seven months, with an average of 2.2 months each. In 1843 forty are registered, each averaging 2.2 months, with some working all twelve months. The number increased to 123 registered in 1844, some working as many as ten months, with an average of 2.2. In 1845 there were 602 registered people working an average of 3.3 months each. In 1846 there were 410 registered workers averaging 1.2 months of work.[40] This record is only for the hired labor and probably does not include the entire workforce.

The temple made a significant contribution to the industry and economy of Nauvoo, both as a public works project and in the support industries that it stimulated. It was a major project, providing needed employment for those who were poor or unemployed. Those people were given a small wage or allowance and were mostly paid in food, clothing, housing, and other provisions. They would usually work until their dependent status was relieved or they found other employment. As a result of the building project, new industries and businesses arose, providing employment such as millwork, brickmaking, and other support projects that served temple needs directly or the needs of those working on the project.

The length of the working day is uncertain prior to 9 October 1845. It is recorded that from that date on, time would be calculated at nine hours per day.[41] This was later extended on 13 January 1846 to nine and one-half hours. Wages were paid from the tithing collected, and since a great deal of this was received as in-kind contributions in the form of provisions, most wages were paid in the form of food, clothing, and other supplies. Some workers received lumber as wages, which enabled them to build their own homes; others were given room and board. Anything of value that had been contributed was exchanged where possible for labor. In 1844 the stonecutters met and agreed that one-sixth of their wages should be in cash, one-third in store goods, and the balance in other property or provisions they might need.[42]

There were occasions when sufficient funds were not available to pay the wages of the skilled workers. Men struggling to maintain a living for their families were naturally forced to seek employment elsewhere. Some workers

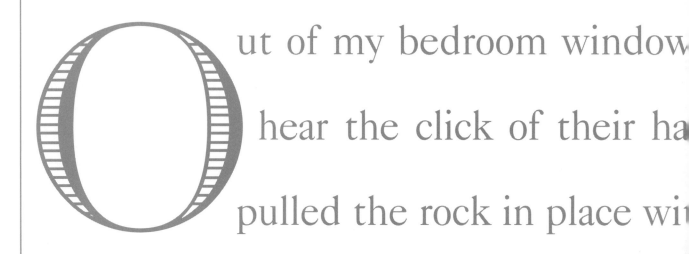

Out of my bedroom window
hear the click of their ha
pulled the rock in place wi

continued with no pay for certain periods, existing as best they could. In the early part of 1844, work was nearly at a standstill due to the lack of funds. Most of the skilled hands had to leave for other employment.[43]

Working conditions were typical of most frontier construction projects of that period. Generally speaking, some phase of the work was in production during each of the winters, though it occasionally ceased entirely because of bitter cold and snow. Most of the work, however, had to

cial events. Workers who belonged to the Nauvoo Legion, which included nearly all men between the ages of eighteen and forty-five, were required to parade on those occasions.[44] The work on other days proceeded generally without interruption. Some special breaks were allowed, however, as evidenced by a report that on the day the capstone was laid the entire working force was given the rest of the day off.[45] Also on 23 July 1845 the entire crew was released to enjoy a watermelon feast for workmen then on the job.[46]

uld see the masons at work and could

ers and hear their sailor songs as they

e pulleys. It was grand to see.

be done in the favorable weather of the spring, summer, or fall. Conditions were aggravated by the lack of available tools as well as by a heterogeneous workforce that was in a constant state of flux. Despite these difficulties, the various building forces were well organized and coordinated by the temple committee and other leaders. This effort brought unity, dedication, and purpose.

Days off from the regular routine of work took place every Sunday and on holidays or spe-

Nancy Naomi Alexander Tracy, an observer watching the stone walls being built, furnished insights regarding the labor and the attitudes of the workmen: "Out of my bedroom window I could see the masons at work and could hear the click of their hammers and hear their sailor songs as they pulled the rock in place with pulleys. It was grand to see."[47] Apparently some workers had been seamen or had learned songs from sailors while traveling across the ocean.

Labor disputes also became part of the scene. From the records available, workers employed on the building organized when it was deemed necessary and protested what they considered unfair practices. Concerns were amicably settled, and no disputes hindered the temple's construction. Workers in the main were dedicated and sacrificed considerably in wages and energy.

Stonecutters met in August 1844 to consider a request for an increase in pay. Even Church authorities encouraged such an increase. The workers, however, decided on a different course of action, resolving instead to reduce wages, and in the future have their pay estimated and priced according to the reduced scale.[48] Such was the spirit and dedication of those engaged in building the temple.

The building was constructed with relatively few accidents. One man was killed in the stone quarry[49] and another in the pineries of Wisconsin.[50] Two young boys also lost their lives at the temple site while playing in the pile of sand used for making mortar. They had tunneled into the sand pile, and it collapsed, causing them to suffocate.[51] One death was miraculously averted when Stephen Goddard was hurt. While working on the temple wall he was struck on the head by a pole from a scaffold he was helping to dismantle. This knocked him off the wall, but his fall was broken by two floor joists that prevented him falling to the basement sixty-two feet below. Cut and bruised, he was back on the job two days later.[52] Another close call was reported by William Clayton: "As the brethren were just beginning to raise one of the capitals, having neglected to fasten the guys, the crane fell over with a tremendous crash, breaking it considerably. As soon as it was perceived that the crane was falling the hands fled to get out of the way. Brother Thomas Jaap unfortunately was directly in the course in which the crane fell. He barely escaped being killed. The crane struck the ground and was within a foot of striking his head. This circumstance hindered the workmen some, but in a few days the crane was mended, reared; and the brethren again went to work on it."[53] Lorenzo Brown cites another serious accident: "January 8, 1846 This day A.M. whilst working on the scaffold in the lower room of the Temple the Scaffold gave way and myself and five others were precipitated from a height of from 12 to 15 feet on to the floor beneath among tools timber plank etc. I was the only one that escaped injury. Jesse Haven fell by my side with a very heavy plank lying across him. I sprang to his relief thinking him dead. He revived shortly after . . . but was badly hurt. Br Josiah Perry struck on his feet and has never recovered their use."[54] Few other accidents are noted.

In the latter stages of construction, when persecution was on the rise, a new type of employee could be found at the temple. Due to threats of defacing the temple and burning it, or the lumber stocked nearby, it became necessary to establish a regular force of watchmen to guard the temple at night.[55] The entire working force had participated in such action for a time just prior to and following the martyrdom of Joseph and Hyrum Smith.[56] In 1845 the practice became common as persecution continued and increased.

Other workmen worthy of special mention were those called to serve on work missions for the Church. Many elders were asked to stay at home and serve their missions by working on the temple instead of going abroad to preach the gospel. Some were called to labor six months, some one year, and others two years. They were to be furnished board and room by Church members in Nauvoo, many of whom had offered to board laborers on the temple.[57]

Stories of great sacrifice on the part of individual workers could fill many pages. Brigham Young commented that there were those who worked on the temple without shoes for their feet or a shirt to cover their arms "even at the risk of their lives and the sacrifice of their labor and earthly goods."[58] A few accounts showing the dedication and observations of those workers have been preserved in private journals, of which the following are typical.

Charles Lambert, a master workman and contractor in England, arrived in Nauvoo in the early part of 1844 as a convert to Mormonism.

Figure 3.4 The Nauvoo Temple, 1846–48, drawing, Amelia Stevens Translot, LDS Church Archives. Amelia Stevens Translot sketched the temple from memory as she traveled on the plains of Iowa after leaving Nauvoo in 1846. Note that she draws a clock face on the temple tower. Some question remains as to whether such a clock ever existed or was fully installed, but this sketch suggests that whether or not the clock was fully installed and functioning, it was certainly intended.

Showing his credentials, he applied for work at the temple. He recounted that Reynolds Cahoon of the building committee said, "'If you can work we can do with your work but we have nothing to give you'. I replied sharply I have not come here to work for pay I have come to help build that house, pointing to the temple."[59] Though many skilled workmen left for other employment because of lack of tithes to pay wages, Charles Lambert did not. Having no working clothes, since he had not worked as a tradesman for some time, he appeared for work in what he had worn while a contractor in England. He reported to the workshop in a good suit and a high silk hat, put on an apron, and commenced work.[60] Generous with his labor, he later cut a capstone, "bought it, and when finished he gave the stone and labor free of all charges."[61]

William W. Player was the principal setter of stones on the temple, laboring on its walls from June 1842 until they were completed. As a new convert to the Church and apparently recruited by Church leaders, he had come from England with the full intention of working on the temple. During the fall and early winter of 1842, he continued at his post in spite of sickness and cold weather. Before work on the walls stopped for the winter season, he nearly lost the use of his hands and feet, and he fell several times on his way home because of fatigue and weakness.[62] Highly skilled at his trade, he was also put in charge of the stoneworkers who built the stone baptismal font.

When William Player started to build the walls of the temple in 1842, he was assisted by Elisha Everett, who served as the "principal backer up" to do the inside stone surfaces of the main inner walls of the temple. Elisha Everett, assisted by a crew of stonemasons that included his brothers Elijah and John Everett, was credited with building most of the inside walls of the temple. He took an active part in placing the last capstone and also assisted in setting the moon stones, the capitals (sun stones), and the star stones in the walls of the temple.[63]

William Weeks and Joseph Smith commissioned Elijah Fordham to do the ornamental carving on the wooden baptistry. Fordham is the same man who was near death and was miraculously healed through the administration of the Prophet Joseph (for full story, see note 64).[64] He spent eight months on this carving project, receiving praise from Joseph Smith and many others for his skillful work. As a result of his skill and workmanship, he was later employed as the principal wood-carver for the temple. He was

also appointed to serve on a committee to look after lumber for the temple.[65]

John Carling, a wood sculptor, is reported to have carved the first pattern of the oxen.[66] The pattern of oxen supporting the baptismal font as used in the Nauvoo Temple became the prototype for all fonts in subsequent temples built by the Church. Carling also was employed in carving other ornaments for the temple.[67]

Wandle Mace, a blacksmith, wheelwright, mechanic, and successful inventor, was called home from a mission to work on the temple. Placed in charge of the sawmill at the temple, he was also assigned as foreman over the timber framing and superintended that work until its completion.[68]

Norton Jacob, who also served as a foreman of timber framing, was foreman of framing the roof, tower structure, and dome of the tower. In November 1845 he was also assigned by William Weeks "to go ahead and put in truss timbers for the lower floor of the temple." These long timber beams 1 foot in diameter and 82 to 83 feet long replaced the earlier timbers, which had rotted out due to exposure.[69]

Philip B. Lewis was the professional tinner employed to cover the steeple dome.[70] He along with other tinners fashioned the angelic weather vane and balls that were placed at the top of the steeple.

Miles Romney, an early convert from England, was a skilled carpenter, wood-carver, and master builder. He labored on the temple from its commencement to its completion. In 1844 he was placed in charge of the ornamental work of the cornices. He also did the ornamental work in the steeple and the spiral staircases in the temple vestibule.[71]

W. P. Vance worked on the temple as a young man in payment of his father's tithing. While boarding at the Smith home, he had the opportunity to become well acquainted with the Prophet Joseph Smith. "My work on the Temple applied as tithing for my father, and my board answered the same purpose for Brother Joseph."[72] His observations, acquired while living in the Smith home, provide interesting insights into qualities possessed by Joseph Smith. "I watched the Prophet closely; I was anxious to know whether he was a Prophet of God, so, of course I watched him, and from all I could discover, he was not only a Prophet of God, but a mighty and great, as well as a good man. . . . He certainly had a very peculiar expression in his face, always pleasant, cheerful and lively. . . . He was sympathetic and kindly perhaps, even to a fault. . . . He was with us enough to enable us to witness much of his peculiar faculties, powers and disposition which was always exercised in nobleness and kindness."[73]

Luman Andrus Shurtliff, who worked faithfully in building the temple, summarizes conditions endured by many workers:

> My cloths was worn out and my family was so destitute I thought best to stay at home and labor to get something before hand that I could leave my family comfortable in the fall. I had helped lay the foundation of our tem-

ple and now wished to do something more towards the building of it. Accordingly I went to the temple committee and hired to them to work on the boat to boat rock, timber, wood and etc. I here got provision to keep my family alive and that was all I expected. The committee did the best they could but they had nothing better in their hands to give us. We labored 10 hours in a day, day after day, on and in the water and at night go to the temple office to get something to take our families for supper and breakfast. Many times we got nothing at other times ½ pound of butter or three pounds of fresh beef and nothing to cook it with. Sometimes a peck of corn meal or a few pounds of flour and before any more provisions came into the office the hands that worked steady would sometimes be entirely out of provisions and have to live on herbs boiled without any seasoning except salt or on parch corn anything we could get to sustain us.

I had some milk from my cows and by putting it half water and then we could get corn or corn meal we could live well for them times that is we could hull or boil corn and put that with milk and water and ate it sweetly and work ten hours on the temple or if we had meal make a cake wet up with water or a mush in a cup for dinner go onto the boat at six and at noon eat my dinner of the above mentioned food and thank God that I and my family was thus blessed. . . . The reader may think the above mentioned scarcity of provision was confined to my family. Not so my family was as well off as the majority of my neighbors. I had seen those that cut stone by the year eat nothing but parched or browned corn for breakfast and take some in their pocket for dinner and go to work singing the songs of Zion. I mention this not to find fault or complain but to let my children know how the temple in Nauvoo was built and how their parents as well as hundreds of others suffered to lay a foundation on which they could build.[74]

Truman O. Angell, an early convert to the Church, was a skilled carpenter and builder. He

ment upon the Temple, having been appointed superintendent of joiner work under Architect William Weeks, and God gave me wisdom to carry out to the architect's designs which gained me the goodwill and esteem of the brethren."[77] When William Weeks left Nauvoo to go west in February 1846, Truman O. Angell was left in charge of the temple project "to bring out the design and finishing of the lower hall which was fully in my charge from then on to its completion, and was dedicated by a few of us."[78] Later

T hey labored faithfully wit

would all be left behind a

West. Their labors becan

did the significant supervision of carpentry work on the Kirtland Temple.[75] Angell was selected as one of the steady carpenters working on the temple in Nauvoo and was appointed as foreman over the joiners. The fine interior joinery work of the temple was considered a monument to his name.[76] He observed: "My privations, the persecutions, sickness of my family and missions have tended to keep me low in purse, but my health is improving. I had steady employ-

in the West, Angell was appointed architect for the Church. In that capacity he was the chief architect in drawing plans and supervising the building of the St. George and Salt Lake Temples.

The labor force was unique in many aspects but succeeded in building a monument that, had it not been destroyed later by fire and wind, may yet have stood to testify to their zeal and sacrifice. They labored faithfully with quality and detail, knowing full well it would all be left behind as they departed into the wilderness of the West. Their labors became an offering given with reverence and devotion.

LUMBER FOR THE TEMPLE: THE PINERY EXPEDITION

The acquisition of lumber in sufficient quantity and quality for the extensive building programs of the Church at Nauvoo prompted the investigation of reasonable and reliable established four sawmills and six logging camps on the Black River. The initial purchase was reported in the *Times and Seasons:* "We are informed that the committees of those two buildings have purchased extensive mills, and water privileges in the pineries of Wisconsin, and a company of several men, in their employ, will leave here in a few days for that country."[79] On 25 September 1841 the assigned company departed Nauvoo to work in the Wisconsin pine country. Their initial task was to establish a

ality and detail, knowing full well it

ey departed into the wilderness of the

offering with reverence and devotion.

sources of wood. Lumber in Illinois was both scarce and expensive. The temple committee along with the Nauvoo House building committee jointly concluded to purchase lumber mills in the pineries of Wisconsin on the Black River, a tributary of the Mississippi. This wise decision resulted in the provision of good quality lumber in the quantity needed and at a fraction of what lumber would have cost on the open market in Illinois. The Church eventually settlement and prepare for the work of the ensuing summer. Alpheus Cutler of the temple committee and Peter Haws of the Nauvoo house committee led the group.[80]

They traveled up the Mississippi River some five or six hundred miles north of Nauvoo, making most of the journey by water.[81] Their camp was located on the Black River about fifteen miles below the Black River Falls at the present site of the village of Melrose.[82]

Here they spent the winter cutting timber and remodeling the mill. The group suffered from the cold winter climate and inadequate provisions but in general fared well.[83] During the following spring a second company journeyed north from Nauvoo. This group was sent to relieve the first group and continue operation of the mills.[84] Additional reinforcements were reported to have left Nauvoo in July 1842. "Two keel boats, sloop-rigged, and laden with provisions and apparatus necessary for the occasion, and manned with fifty of the brethren, started this morning on an expedition to the upper Mississippi, among the pineries, where they can join those already there, and erect mills, saw boards and plank, make shingles, hew timber, and return the next spring with rafts, for the Temple of God."[85] The first tangible results of the pineries expedition reached Nauvoo on 4 August 1842. "Our *big raft* for the Temple and Nauvoo House, is just in; it covers but little less than an acre of surface, and contains 100,000 feet sawed lumber, and 16,000 cubic, or 192,000 square feet hewn timber."[86] In October another raft arrived from Wisconsin with about ninety thousand feet of boards and twenty-four thousand cubic feet of timber.[87] As these and future rafts arrived at the waterfront in Nauvoo, they were met by teams and wagons. The rafts were dismantled and the lumber hauled to the temple for use in the building.

Figure 3.5 View of Nauvoo and the Temple from across the River, lithograph, 1848, Henry Lewis, Missouri Historical Society. The lithograph was made by Josef Arnz in 1849 and first published in Das Illustrirte Mississippienthal *in 1849.*

Haws, Cutler, and twelve men returned to Nauvoo with the raft on 13 October after having remodeled the mill, making it almost new. The committees decided that Bishop George Miller should be sent to the pineries to extricate the establishment from debt and produce greater quantities of lumber.[88] Sometime during October 1842 Miller headed north, taking with him his ailing wife, his children, and a hired girl. At Prairie Du Chein he met Jacob Spaulding, owner of some mills located at Black River Falls, fifteen miles upriver from those then owned by the Church.[89] Spaulding, a millwright by profession, had come from Illinois to Wisconsin in 1838. He had made the first permanent settlement at Black River Falls, which was the outpost on the Black River at this time.[90] Miller reported that he had claims against Spaulding on a suit pending between him and the Church. Arrangements were made to get possession of Spaulding's mills in lieu of turning over the Church mills to him, which, according to Miller, were of little or no value anyway.[91] The new mill site was described by Joseph Holbrook, who traveled to the mills with Miller, as having the best of water privileges, the country being broken and somewhat mountainous. Some land that was suitable for cultivation could be found in the fertile valleys, and the streams were abundant with fish.[92]

The winter of 1842 was one of hardship and near starvation for both the company and their animals. A major part of the provisions had been left down river. Time was spent in preparing the mills for operation and transporting upriver, mainly by backpack, the essential supplies to sustain life.[93]

In the spring of 1843, the mills daily turned out over twelve thousand feet of lumber.[94] Timber was cut that spring and summer on what came to be known in later years as the Mormon Clearings. These clearings are found in what is now Clark County, Wisconsin. An area was also worked some ten miles north of the Black River Falls. At this point two miles of rapids, confined in high canyon walls and known today as the Mormon Riffles, emerge from the southern boundary of the Wisconsin forest tract. Here and above, the timber was cut. After being cut, logs were floated down river to the mills for processing, then later rafted to Nauvoo.[95]

The first raft of the season arrived in Nauvoo at sunrise on Friday, 12 May 1843. Guided down river by Bishop Miller and others, it contained fifty thousand feet of pine lumber.[96] A second raft arriving in early July 1843 brought the total to over two hundred thousand feet of sawed lumber suitable for use on the temple along with a large amount of shingles and barn boards.[97] Two additional large rafts containing over four hundred thousand feet of prime lumber arrived in August.[98] The journey from the Black River Falls to Nauvoo usually took two weeks.[99] The huge rafts were difficult to maneuver in the currents of the river. They were steered by oars or rudders fastened to each end of the raft. Because of rapids, dams, snags, and other hazards, travel on the river was dangerous and generally done in the daytime.

As evening approached, the rafters would tie and snub the raft to trees along the shore. The next morning they would continue their journey down river. Larger rafts were often huge in size, a hundred or more feet in width, usually several hundred feet in length, covering one or more acres. Temporary shanties were built on the rafts for sheltering crews from the weather and to provide facilities for cooking food while on the journey to Nauvoo.[100] Lyman Wight's son described this practice: "On one of these rafts was fixed a shelter with lumber, or you might say a cabin. In front of it some rock was placed on which to build a fire. This was our home as we floated down the river."[101]

Miller reported that two saws were employed in the production of lumber at the pineries, each producing over five thousand feet per day and capable of doing so year-round. These saws were long up-and-down saw blades that cut on the downstroke and were powered by waterwheels. Miller further reported that he had bought out all claims on the mills for twelve thousand dollars payable in lumber at the mills in three years and that one-third of this amount was already paid.[102]

In the spring of 1843, the mills daily turned out over twelve thousand feet of lumber.

Several groups went north in the summer of 1843 to relieve, supply, and increase the numbers working at the mills; the largest of these left 21 July on the *Maid of Iowa*. Consisting of several families, the group was headed by Apostle Lyman Wight, assisted by Bishop George Miller. Cattle and milk cows were driven to the mills, fifty acres of ground was cleared and planted with wheat, and permanent houses were built for the convenience of the families.[103]

The work was now up to schedule. All requests for lumber and shingles were filled in full over the summer. When Miller arrived on the last two rafts in the fall, he became greatly distressed over events in Nauvoo. A great deal of the lumber he and others had labored so hard to provide for the temple and Nauvoo House had been used for other purposes. A large part of it had been used to build houses for the men working on the temple.[104] The temple committee decided that, since the mills had proven to be so productive, some lumber could be used in this manner to pay the wages of the workmen. The Prophet quieted Miller, saying that he would see to it that all would be made right.

During the winter of 1843 one hundred and fifty men, plus a number of women and children, were established in the pineries. A branch of the Church was organized among them, with Lyman Wight presiding.[105] The expedition was now firmly established and well housed. On 15 February 1844 it was reported that by the end of July they should be able to send one million feet of lumber down the river, which would be a great deal more than needed to build the temple and Nauvoo House.[106]

As winter turned to spring, rafts of lumber again floated south to Nauvoo. Bishop Miller and Lyman Wight arrived in Nauvoo on 1 May 1844. Soon after their arrival, Wight was sent to Maryland and Miller to Kentucky. They were called on special missions in connection with Joseph Smith's candidacy for president of the United States.[107]

Two large rafts arrived in July 1844. Sufficient lumber was supplied that year to complete not only the needs of the temple but additional uses as well.[108] These appear to be the last

big rafts to arrive at Nauvoo from the pineries. However, in November 1845 the Church purchased a raft of lumber containing one hundred thousand feet of pine boards for six hundred dollars.[109] These boards were used in the final completion of the temple. The supply source for this lumber is uncertain. It may have come from the pineries, but this is in question since the pinery property was no longer in Church hands.

After the death of Joseph Smith in June 1844, the work in the pineries met with new problems. There was an evident void of leadership created by the extended absence of Wight and Miller. This was further confused by the martyrdom of Church leaders and the subsequent uncertainty that arose among some Church members. Upon return from his mission, Miller found that the expedition had been abandoned and the mills sold. He reported: "The man left in charge of the mills in the pinery, sold out possession of the whole concern [the mills being on Indian land, possession was the best title], for a few hundred thousand feet of

Figure 3.6 The Great Mormon Temple at Nauvoo, Illinois, painting, early 1862, Emille Vallet, LDS Church Archives. Emille Vallet, one of the French Icarians, painted the temple after observing the temple ruins, talking with the local citizens who had seen the building, and examining a drawing of the building made in 1847 by William Murphy, formerly from Nauvoo.

Pine lumber. Those mills and appurtenances, worth at least $20,000, those passed out of our hands for a mere trifle, by the act of an indiscreet man. He brought part of the lumber to Nauvoo and all the company that had been engaged in the pineries."[110] Some Latter-day Saints apparently did not return to Nauvoo with the main body. Mormon settlers were found at Black River Falls and north along the river as late as the early 1850s.[111]

So ends an interesting chapter in the dramatic struggle to furnish lumber for the construction of the Nauvoo Temple. Only one major accident was ever recorded, that being the death of a Brother Cunningham, who drowned in a whirlpool when he fell into the river while rafting logs in the summer of 1843.[112] Yet the Pinery Mission was a great success. Lumber, timbers, and shingles were provided not only for the temple but for many other buildings as well.

STONE FOR BUILDING THE TEMPLE

The main building material used in the construction of the temple was a native grayish-white fine-grained limestone, which underlay the entire area around Nauvoo. Resembling marble in appearance and hardness, the stone was of excellent quality, easily tooled and dressed.[113] Following the decision to build a temple, the brethren opened quarries from which to obtain stone for the building. Work began on 12 October 1840 with Elisha Everett striking the first blow on the project.[114]

William Huntington, a stonecutter and member of the Nauvoo high council, reported that stone was cut and then hauled to the temple site, where on 8 March 1841 workers commenced laying the foundation. By 5 April 1841 enough stone had been cut and hauled that the temple walls in the basement were 5 feet high, bringing them up to ground level and ready for laying the cornerstones.[115]

Workers labored in the quarries without letup during the greater part of the construction period. Work even continued at times in the winter when weather permitted, as stones were prepared for use during the other seasons of the year.[116] The *Times and Seasons* reported that "frequently, during the winter [1841–42], as many as one hundred hands [were engaged in] quarrying rock, while at the same time multitudes of others have been engaged in hauling, and in other kinds of labor."[117] The stoneworkers were so successful that at the general conference held in April 1844 Hyrum Smith informed the Saints, "The quarry is blockaded, it is filled with rock; the stone cutters are wanting work; come on with your teams as soon as conference is over.'[118]

Regularly employed men became part of the scene in the quarries as early as the spring of 1841. Albert P. Rockwood became the overseer, or captain, of the work, assisted by Charles Drury. These men supervised the project from the beginning and continued until all the stone was cut for the temple.[119] Stones taken from the quarries varied in size, depending on their use. Some are reported to have weighed as much as two tons.[120]

As a young boy, the Prophet's son Joseph, who in later years became president of the

Reorganized Church of Jesus Christ of Latter-day Saints, witnessed the hauling of stones from the quarries to the temple. He described them as being hauled on "great carts drawn by oxen, with the stones swinging under the axle of the great high, broad-tired wheels, usually two yoke of cattle drawing them."[121] Only the rough work was done in the quarry. The stones were cut to size, dressed, and polished for their particular use at the stone shop near the temple.[122] Gilbert Belnap, first bishop of the Hooper Utah Ward, described his visit to the stone shop upon exiting the temple: "I then went to the stone cutter's shop, where the sound of many workmen's mallet and the sharpening of the smith's anvil all bore the unmistakable evidence of a determined purpose to complete the mighty structure."[123] Specially constructed two-wheel carts with giant wheels and strong axles were used in moving the large building stones around the temple grounds. The finished stones were hauled by those carts from the stone shop to the large cranes at the temple walls.

Work at the quarry had only one serious accident, when Moses Horn was killed by a stone that fell on his head while rocks were being blasted.[124] Albert P. Rockwood reported the accident as follows: "For three and one half years that I have been in charge of the Temple quarry, with from twenty to one hundred and fifty hands, Brother Moses Horn has been the

Figure 3.7 Contemporary View of the Nauvoo Temple, daguerreotype, 1846 or 1847, Thomas M. Easterly, Missouri Historical Society. Several windows of the temple are open, indicating that this daguerreotype was taken during the summer or warm months of 1846 or 1847.

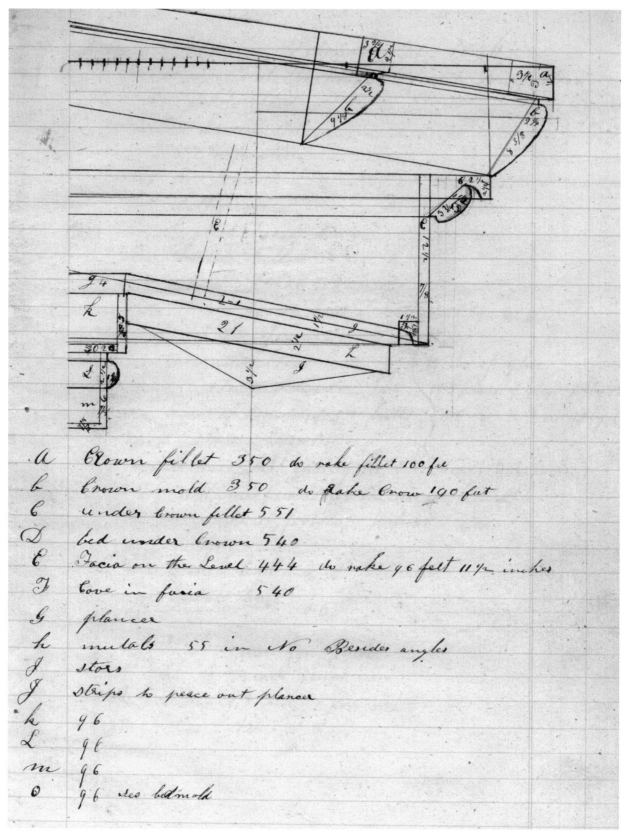

A Crown fillet 350 do rake fillet 100 fee

b Crown mold 350 do rake Crown 190 feet

C under Crown fillet 551

D bed under Crown 540

E Facia on the Level 444 do rake 96 feet 11½ inches

F Cove in facia 540

G plancer

h metals 55 in No Besides angles

J stors

J strips to peace out plancer

k 96

L 96

m 96

O 96 see bedmold

Figure 3.8 Purchase Order from Temple Ledger Account Books, ledger account, 1845–46, Box 8, Folder 1, Carpenters Daybook, LDS Church Archives. Detailed ledger books of expenditures, purchase orders, time records of workers, and so on were kept by temple recorders. This account lists materials needed for a cornice and soffit area that was part of the building.

first man that met accident in blasting. During this time, according to my best judgment, about one hundred casks of powder have been used. Mr. Horn died from a skull fracture."[125] Stone was taken from the quarries for use on the temple until as late as the spring of 1845, when on 24 May the final stone was placed on the structure.[126] Whether stone was quarried for the new font after this date is unknown.

The location of the quarry has been the subject of uncertainty among writers and observers. Two separate locations are discussed in the various sources. Gregg, in referring to the temple, stated: "Its walls were built of beautiful dressed limestone from extensive quarries on the Mississippi Bluff, two miles below the city."[127] This location is upheld by Reta Latimer Halford in her thesis on Nauvoo.[128] At variance with this view is S. A. Burgess, once a historian of the Reorganized Church of Jesus Christ of Latter-day Saints. He referred to the quarry being located on the north side of the city in a river bed.[129] His view is supported by Charles Lanman, who visited Nauvoo in 1846 and described the quarry as being located "within the limits of the city, in the bed of a dry stream."[130] John C. Bennett, who served as mayor of Nauvoo, also declared that stone for the temple was secured from a quarry within the bounds of the city.[131] If one were to visit Nauvoo today and ask where the temple quarry was located, directions would be given to a spot on the north side of the old city, north-west from the intersection of Main and Young Streets. Standing on an overlook one would be able to see the remains of an old quarry, extensive in size. The Prophet's son Joseph cleared up the matter by stating that "the stones came from a quarry in the north side of the city along the river bank, and some of them from down the river."[132] It is evident that quarries were located at both sites mentioned, with the main quarry in all probability being that located on the north side of the city.

Limestone taken from the quarries was mainly used in building the walls of the temple proper. Stone left over was used in building a wall around the temple block. Another use for the stone was that of a permanent baptismal font to replace the original wooden font.

On 24 May 1845 the final stone was placed on the structure.

THE TEMPLE BELL

From the beginning, plans for the temple included a belfry. By November 1845 the exterior of the temple was near completion, and work was rapidly moving forward on the interior. A visitor to the city at that time noted that the Saints "are finishing the Temple, putting in carpets, &c., and intend to hang a bell."[133] Beyond that point, information on the subject is somewhat confusing and limited. From what can be determined, a bell was acquired and installed in the belfry of the temple. Detailed information on the Nauvoo Temple bell and its fate are thoroughly examined in chapter 11.

ADDITIONAL BUILDING MATERIALS

Other materials used in the temple construction were purchased as follows. The sixty-five hundred pounds of lead for the eaves came from Galena, Illinois. Paint, nails, tin, and hardware were purchased in Chicago or St. Louis.[134] Bricks were manufactured in large quantities within the city. The glass for windows was purchased in large quantities at Detroit, Michigan, by George Dykes, who served as president of the Norway Illinois Stake. He bought the glass in behalf of the Church and then had it shipped to Chicago. From there he succeeded in transporting it by land to Nauvoo, where he arrived on the second day of September 1845.[135] The glass used in most of the windows "was typical thin, pale blue-green window glass, similar to that found in other . . . buildings in Nauvoo. The glass was fairly uniform in thickness, ranging from 1.0 to 1.3 mm., which is actually thinner than present-day 'single strength' window glass."[136]

The clock for the steeple was to be purchased by the Saints in England, but if indeed it was ever purchased, this may have taken place in the United States. There is no known record of any purchase, shipment, or installation. A clock may have been shipped with the bell and installed at the same time. Careful examination of the Chaffin daguerreotype (believed to have been taken in the early summer of 1846) shows no clock hands or numbers visible on the area where the clockface would have been. It could still have been installed after this photograph was taken or it may be that a clock was installed on the face of the front or west end of the steeple. A correspondent of the *Palmyra Courier-Journal* reported seeing the octagonal temple steeple in 1847, "having on four sides a clock" below the dome.[137] There is also other evidence of the existence and installation of the clock. Visitors to the ruins of the temple reported seeing parts of a clock among the stone ruins.[138]

Assembling the means, the workforce, and the materials for construction of the Nauvoo Temple was a magnificent accomplishment. The building was a tribute to the faith and dedication of those who sacrificed so much in its construction. Had it not been destroyed, the building would likely be usable today.

NOTES

1. *Niles' Register* 59 (26 September 1840): 57, quoting an article from the *Cincinnati Chronicle*, 26 August 1840.

2. Andrew Jenson, *Historical Record* 8 (June 1889): 872; also, *Deseret News Church Almanac* (Salt Lake City: Deseret News, 1975), F4. These figures would include both cost of materials and paid labor.

3. Kenneth W. Godfrey, "Some Thoughts Regarding an Unwritten History of Nauvoo," *BYU Studies* 15, no. 4 (summer 1975): 420. "During this time, times were very hard. I have known families that had nothing to subsist upon but potatoes and salt, our own family in particular." Unpublished biographical sketch of Eliza Ann Sprague Tracy, in author's possession, 2.

4. Jenson, *Historical Record* 8 (June 1889): 860.

5. Ibid., 861.

6. Joseph Smith, *History of the Church of Jesus Christ of Latter-day Saints*, ed. B. H. Roberts, 2d ed., rev. (Salt Lake City: Deseret Book, 1957), 4:473.

7. Journal History, 14 February 1842, LDS Church Archives.

8. *Times and Seasons* 3 (2 May 1842): 775.

9. Jenson, *Historical Record* 8 (June 1889): 864.

10. *Times and Seasons* 3 (1 September 1842): 909.

11. Journal History, 23 October 1842.

12. Ibid., 9 April 1841.

13. Jenson, *Historical Record* 8 (June 1889): 865.

14. Ibid.

15. B. H. Roberts, ed. *History of the Church of Jesus Christ of Latter-day Saints, Period 2: Apostolic Interregnum* (Salt Lake City: Deseret Book, 1957), 7:250–51.

16. Daniel Tyler, "Temples," *Juvenile Instructor* 15 (1 June 1880): 122.

17. Louisa Decker, "Reminiscences of Nauvoo," *Woman's Exponent* 37 (March 1909): 41.

18. *The Wasp*, 9 July 1842.

19. *Times and Seasons* 5 (1 August 1844): 596.

20. Ibid. 3 (2 May 1842): 768.

21. *The Wasp*, 25 June 1842.

22. *Times and Seasons* 5 (1 August 1844): 596. Invitation issued by Hyrum Smith in April conference of 1844.

23. *Times and Seasons* 6 (15 March 1845): 847.

24. E. Cecil McGavin, *Nauvoo the Beautiful* (Salt Lake City: Stevens and Wallis, 1949), 26–27; and Roberts, History of the Church, 7:433.

25. B. H. Roberts, *A Comprehensive History of the Church of Jesus Christ of Latter-day Saints* (Salt Lake City: Deseret News, 1930), 2:472 n. 17.

26. Jenson, *Historical Record* 8 (June 1889): 858.

27. Joseph Smith, *History of the Church*, 4:305.

28. *Times and Seasons* 4 (15 November 1842): 10.

29. Journal History, 21 February 1842.

30. Jenson, *Historical Record* 8 (June 1889): 860.

31. Ibid.

32. *Times and Seasons* 4 (15 November 1842): 10.

33. Ibid.

34. *Deseret News*, 13 March 1937.

35. George Miller, "Correspondence of Bishop George Miller," 10.

36. *Times and Seasons* 3 (2 May 1842): 775.

37. Journal History, 12 December 1844, quoting an article from the St. Louis Gazette, n.d.

38. Journal History, 16 December 1844; also, Roberts, *History of the Church*, 7:326.

39. Journal History, 6 August 1845.

40. "Time Book C. for the Temple, Account Book 16," 1–56, LDS Church Archives, Work by Carpenters and Joiners recorded by William F. Cahoon and Curtis E. Bolton.

41. Ibid., 44.

42. Ibid., 50.

43. Charles C. Lambert, "Reminiscences and Diaries, 1844–1881," 12, LDS Church Archives.

44. Smith, *History of the Church*, 4:300.

45. Jenson, *Historical Record* 8 (June 1889): 870.

46. "Time Book C.," 33.

47. Nancy Naomi Alexander Tracy, as quoted by Carol Cornwall Madsen, *In Their Own Words* (Salt Lake City: Deseret Book, 1994), 252.

48. Journal History, 15 August 1844.

49. Reta Latimer Halford, "Nauvoo—the City Beautiful" (M.A. thesis, University of Utah, 1945), 189.

50. Joseph Holbrook, "The Life of Joseph Holbrook, 1806–1871," 59, typescript, 1942, Harold B. Lee Library, Brigham Young University.

51. Zina Diantha Huntington Jacobs, "'All Things Move in Order in the City': The Nauvoo Diary of Zina Diantha Huntington Jacobs," ed. Maureen Ursenbach Beecher, *BYU Studies* 19, no. 3 (spring 1979): 312. "Two boys ware smuhered [smothered] in the sand. It caved of yesterday, found to day. They ware at scool, went there at noon, went there to play."

52. Jenson, *Historical Record* 8 (June 1889): 869.

53. Journal of William Clayton, "History of the Nauvoo Temple," 59–60, LDS Church Archives.

54. Journal of Lorenzo Brown, 1823–1900, 1:15, Harold B. Lee Library, Brigham Young University.

55. Journal History, 26 September 1844.

56. Jenson, *Historical Record* 8 (June 1889): 866.

57. Smith, *History of the Church*, 4:474.

58. *Deseret News*, 14 October 1863; also, Manuscript History of the Church, 30 April 1846, 159, LDS Church Archives.

59. Lambert, "Reminiscences and Diaries," 9.

60. Ibid.

61. Journal History, 31 December 1844.

62. Ibid., 11 October 1842.

63. Ibid., 31 December 1844 and 24 May 1845.

64. During July 1839 many Church members were very ill. Weakened by exposure from malnutrition and from the ordeal of being driven by mobs from their homes in Missouri, they had fallen prey to malaria and other diseases. Joseph Smith arose from his own sickbed and with great faith administered to and healed many individuals in Nauvoo and across the river in Montrose, Iowa. Among the places visited was the home of Elijah Fordham, who was near death. "When the company entered the room, the Prophet of God walked up to the dying man and took hold of his right hand and spoke to him; but Brother Fordham was unable to speak, his eyes were set in his head like glass, and he seemed entirely unconscious of all around him. Joseph held his hand and looked into his eyes in silence for a length of time. A change in the countenance of Brother Fordham was soon perceptible to all present. His sight returned, and upon Joseph asking him if he knew him, he, in a low whisper, answered, 'Yes.' Joseph asked him if he had faith to be healed. He answered, 'I fear it is too late; if you had come sooner I think I would have been healed.' The Prophet said, 'Do you believe in Jesus Christ?' He answered in a feeble voice, 'I do.' Joseph then stood erect, still holding his hand in silence several moments, then he spoke in a loud voice, saying, 'Brother Fordham, I command you, in the name of Jesus Christ to arise from this bed and be made whole.' Brother Fordham arose from his bed, and was immediately made whole . . . ; then putting on his clothes, he ate a bowl of bread and milk and followed the Prophet into the street" (Smith, *History of the Church*, 4:4). He then assisted in administering to others.

Elijah Fordham was commissioned to do the ornamental wood-carving on the wooden baptismal font. He was later employed as the principal carver in wood for the entire temple.

65. Ibid., 446; also, Journal History, 31 December 1844; and Roberts, *History of the Church*, 7:183.

66. Kate B. Carter, comp., *Heart Throbs of the West* (Salt Lake City: Daughters of Utah Pioneers, 1939–51), 4:259–60.

67. Mary C. Neeves, as quoted by J. Earl Arrington, "Story of the Nauvoo Temple," 513, LDS Church Archives.

68. Journal History, 31 December 1844; *Deseret Evening News*, 13 December 1890.

69. Norton Jacob, "The Life of Norton Jacob," 16, 18, typescript, 1937, Harold B. Lee Library, Brigham Young University.

70. *Nauvoo Neighbor*, 9 July 1845.

71. Journal History, 31 December 1844; also, Gaskell Romney, as quoted by Arrington, "Story of the Nauvoo Temple," 513.

72. *Deseret News Weekly*, 16 March 1895.

73. Ibid.

74. Autobiography and Personal History of Luman Andros Shurtliff, 1807–64, 250–52, Church History Library.

75. Autobiography of Truman O. Angell, 1884, 3–4, LDS Church Archives.

76. Marvin E. Smith, "The Builder," *Improvement Era*, October 1942, 631.

77. Autobiography of Truman O. Angell, 6–7.

78. Ibid.

79. *Times and Seasons* 2 (15 September 1841): 543.

80. Journal History, 14 February 1842.

81. Ibid., 22 September 1841.

82. F. W. Draper, "Timber for the Nauvoo Temple," *Improvement Era*, February 1943, 76.

83. *Deseret News*, 14 December 1935.

84. *Times and Seasons* 3 (2 May 1842): 775.

85. Smith, *History of the Church*, 5:57–58.

86. *The Wasp*, 30 July 1842.

87. Journal History, 13 October 1842.

88. Miller, "Correspondence of Bishop George Miller," 11.

89. Ibid., 10.

90. Draper, "Timber for the Nauvoo Temple," 76–77.

91. Miller, "Correspondence of Bishop George Miller," 10.

92. Holbrook, "The Life of Joseph Holbrook," 58–59.

93. Miller, "Correspondence of Bishop George Miller," 10.

94. Ibid.

95. Draper, "Timber for the Nauvoo Temple," 77, 125.

96. Journal History, 12 May 1843.

97. *Nauvoo Neighbor*, 12 July 1843.

98. Miller, "Correspondence of Bishop George Miller," 14.

99. Draper, "Timber for the Nauvoo Temple," 127.

100. Dennis Rowley, "The Mormon Experience in the Wisconsin Pineries, 1841–1845," *BYU Studies* 32, nos. 1–2 (winter and spring 1992): 137.

101. *Journal of History 9* (July 1916): 261–62; also, *History of Northern Wisconsin* (Chicago: Western Historical Company, 1881), 460–61.

102. Miller, "Correspondence of Bishop George Miller," 14.

103. Ibid., 15.

104. Rowley, "Wisconsin Pineries," 136.

105. *Deseret News*, 8 April 1978.

106. Draper, "Timber for the Nauvoo Temple," 127.

107. Ibid.

108. *Times and Seasons* 5 (1 January 1844): 392.

109. Helen Mar Whitney, "Scenes from Nauvoo, and Incidents from H. C. Kimball's Journal," *Woman's Exponent* 11 (15 May 1883): 186.

110. Miller, "Correspondence of Bishop George Miller," 23.

111. Draper, "Timber for the Nauvoo Temple," 76.

112. Holbrook, "The Life of Joseph Holbrook," 59.

113. *Valley Tan,* 15 February 1860; Journal History, 7 March 1876; *The Prophet,* 30 November 1844.

114. Jenson, *Historical Record* 8 (June 1889): 858.

115. Diary of William Huntington, 12, typescript, 1952–53, Harold B. Lee Library, Brigham Young University.

116. Jenson, *Historical Record* 8 (June 1889): 864.

117. *Times and Seasons* 3 (2 May 1842): 775.

118. Ibid. 5 (1 August 1844): 597.

119. Journal History, 31 December 1844.

120. Jenson, *Historical Record* 8 (June 1889): 866–67.

121. *Journal of History 3* (April 1910): 142–43, as quoted in the *Saints' Herald,* 26 September 1949.

122. *The Wasp,* 23 April 1842.

123. Autobiography of Gilbert Belnap, 30, typescript, Harold B. Lee Library Special Collections, Brigham Young University.

124. Journal History, 14 March 1845.

125. Albert P. Rockwood, as quoted by Halford, "Nauvoo—the City Beautiful," 189.

126. Roberts, *Comprehensive History,* 2:472–73.

127. Thomas Gregg and Charles J. Scofield, *Historical Encyclopedia of Illinois and History of Hancock County* (Chicago: Munsell Publishing Company, 1921), 2:838.

128. Halford, "Nauvoo—the City Beautiful," 189.

129. S. A. Burgess, *The Early History of Nauvoo* (Independence, Mo.: Reorganized Church of Jesus Christ of Latter-day Saints, 1939), 8.

130. Charles Lanman, *A Summer in the Wilderness* (New York: D. Appleton, 1847), 31.

131. John C. Bennett, *History of the Saints* (Boston: Leland and Whiting, 1842), 190.

132. *Journal of History, 3* (April 1910): 142–43, as quoted in *Saints' Herald,* 26 September 1949.

133. *Burlington Hawkeye,* 20 November 1845.

134. Rowley, "Wisconsin Pineries," 119.

135. Arrington, "Story of the Nauvoo Temple," 1017.

136. Virginia S. Harrington and J. C. Harrington, *Rediscovery of the Nauvoo Temple* (Salt Lake City: Nauvoo Restoration, 1971), 16.

137. *Palmyra Courier-Journal,* 22 September 1847, as quoted by McGavin, *Nauvoo the Beautiful,* 37.

138. Irving B. Richman, *John Brown among the Quakers,* 3d ed. (Des Moines: Historical Department of Iowa, 1904), 142. 4

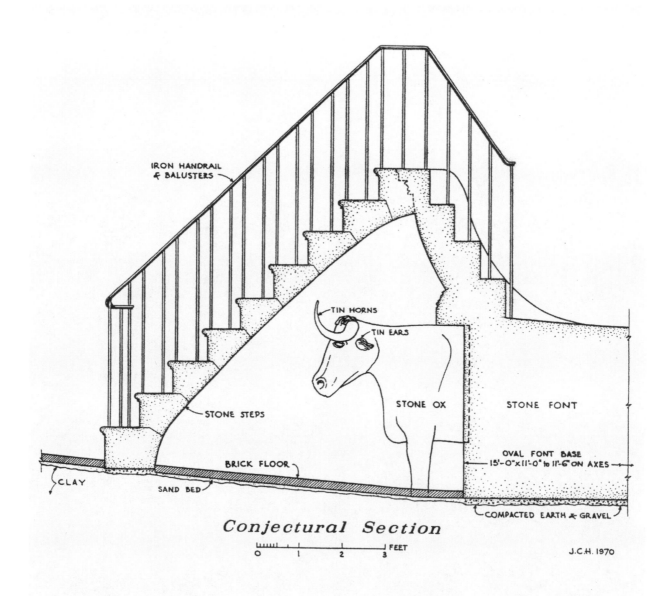

IRON HANDRAIL
& BALUSTERS

TIN HORNS

TIN EARS

STONE STEPS

STONE OX

STONE FONT

OVAL FONT BASE
15'-0"x11'-0" to 11'-6" ON AXES

BRICK FLOOR

CLAY

SAND BED

COMPACTED EARTH & GRAVEL

Conjectural Section

0   1   2   3   FEET

J.C.H. 1970

Conjectural Sketch of Stone Baptismal font, drawing, 1970, LDS Church Archives. This sketch was produced by J. C. Harrington, who worked for Nauvoo Restoration, and was published in 1971 in his book Rediscovery of the Nauvoo Temple, *which was written with his wife, Virginia Harrington.*

The Nauvoo Temple was different from other religious buildings of its day. Some of its functions were singular to the Latter-day Saints. Use of the building,

CHAPTER FOUR

PURPOSES AND FUNCTIONS

OF THE TEMPLE

though varied, was in the main of deep religious import. However, unlike other temples later constructed by the Church, the Nauvoo Temple was truly a multi-purpose building. These uses resulted in large measure from the lack of any

chapels or other large buildings in Nauvoo. The temple filled the role of a Church office building with many offices of Church authorities located in the attic story. It was used as an assembly hall for sacrament meetings, other large meetings, and even general conferences of the Church. The building was even utilized for some recreational purposes. But it was primarily used for the central purpose of its construction, the performance of sacred temple ordinances.

have lived on the earth. He invites all to come unto him and partake of his goodness. It makes no difference what their race, ethnic differences, gender, financial status, or any other conditions may be; all are alike unto God (Acts 10:34–35; 1 Pet. 4:6; 2 Ne. 26:33; Alma 26:37; Moro. 8:17). This implies that if God prescribes any conditions of belief, required patterns of living, or ordinances, all humankind must have equal opportunity to accept and live by these divine requirements.

The theology of temple ordinan[ces]

of his children equally, no matt[er]

He invites all to come unto hi[m]

TEMPLE ORDINANCES IN NAUVOO

Temple ordinance work practiced today by Latter-day Saints in numerous temples throughout the world has most of its development and early practice in connection with the Nauvoo Temple. This is further explained in chapter 5 as it relates to the impact of the temple. The theology of temple ordinance work centers in the belief that God loves all of his children equally, no matter where or when they

Study of the life and teachings of Jesus Christ clearly illustrates that certain beliefs, ordinances, and qualities of life that should be lived by a disciple were plainly enunciated by the Savior. Acceptance of Jesus Christ as our Redeemer, the Son of the Living God, is a fundamental precept. As he himself declared: "I am the way, the truth, and the life: no man cometh unto the Father, but by me" (John 14:6). Salvation as explained in the New

Testament is attained only by acceptance of and faith in the Lord Jesus Christ, by following him and keeping his commandments.

Baptism for the Dead

The Church of Jesus Christ of Latter-day Saints declares that baptism is a basic gospel ordinance essential to salvation. This ordinance required by the Savior and his Apostles is clearly attested by several New Testament scriptures (Matt. 3:13–16; Mark 16:15–16; John

enjoyed adequate opportunity of receiving the gospel when they lived on the earth in mortality (D&C 138). The doctrine and ordinance of vicarious proxy baptism by a living person in behalf of the dead was restored to earth through the Prophet Joseph Smith. He enunciated the doctrine on several occasions during the Nauvoo period:

• "Jesus Christ became a ministering spirit (while His body was lying in the sepulchre) to the spirits in

ork centers in the belief that God loves all

here or when they have lived on the earth.

d partake of his goodness.

3:3–5; 22–26; Acts 2:37–38, 41; 22:16; Rom. 6:3–6; Gal. 3:37; 1 Pet. 3:21). Another fundamental Church doctrine is that between Christs death on the cross and his resurrection, the Lord personally went into the postmortal spirit world and there "preached [his gospel] also to them that are dead" (1 Pet. 4:6; cf. 3:18–20; D&C 138). While there, he organized the faithful and commissioned them to take his gospel message to all the dead who had not

prison, to fulfill an important part of his mission, without which He could not have perfected his work, or entered into His rest. . . . It is no more incredible that God should save the dead, than that he should raise the dead."[1]

• "Aside from knowledge independent of the Bible, I would say that [baptism for the dead] was certainly practiced by the ancient churches. . . . The Saints have the privilege of being baptized for those of their relatives

who are dead, whom they believe would have embraced the Gospel, if they had been privileged with hearing it, and who have received the Gospel in the spirit [world], through the instrumentality of those who have been commissioned to preach to them."[2]

• "If we can, by the authority of the Priesthood of the Son of God, baptize a man in the name of the Father, of the Son, and of the Holy Ghost, for the remission of sins, it is just as much our privilege to act as an agent, and be baptized for the remission of sins for and in behalf of our dead kindred, who have not heard the Gospel, or the fullness of it."[3]

• "Every man that has been baptized and belongs to the kingdom has a right to be baptized for those who have gone before; and as soon as the law of the Gospel is obeyed here by their friends who act as proxy for them, the Lord has administrators there [in the spirit world] to set them free."[4]

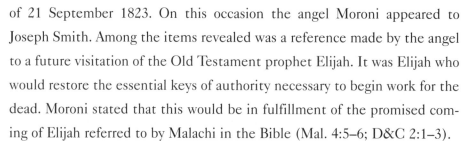

This Latter-day Saint concept of vicarious baptism by a living person in behalf of a dead ancestor is based not alone on latter-day revelation but also on biblical scriptures and clear evidence that such an ordinance was practiced by early Christians (1 Cor. 15:29).[5] The first intimation of vicarious work for the dead in the latter days was given on the night of 21 September 1823. On this occasion the angel Moroni appeared to Joseph Smith. Among the items revealed was a reference made by the angel to a future visitation of the Old Testament prophet Elijah. It was Elijah who would restore the essential keys of authority necessary to begin work for the dead. Moroni stated that this would be in fulfillment of the promised coming of Elijah referred to by Malachi in the Bible (Mal. 4:5–6; D&C 2:1–3).

Though work for the dead was referred to in 1823, the doctrine was not understood nor practiced until some years later. Joseph Smith reported that on 3 April 1836 the prophet Elijah appeared to him at Kirtland, Ohio, and conferred on him the sealing power and keys of authority for this essential work (D&C 110:13–16). The concept was not taught publicly to the Church as doctrine until 10 August 1840 at Nauvoo, Illinois. It is quite likely that though Joseph Smith may have earlier understood the doctrine, its implementation became impossible before this time because of persecution. In a letter to members of the Twelve Apostles in England dated 15 December 1840, Joseph Smith explained: "I presume the doctrine of 'Baptism for the dead' has ere this

It was Elijah who would restore the essential keys of authority necessary to begin work for the dead.

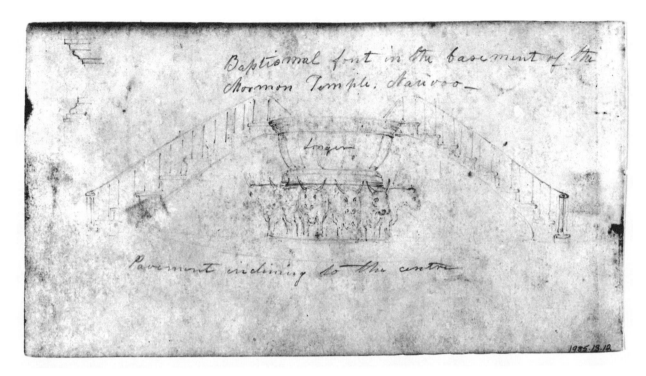

Baptismal font in the basement of the Mormon Temple. Nauvoo—

Imeyer

Pavement inclining to the centre

Figure 4.1 Baptismal Font in the Basement of the Mormon Temple, drawing, 1848, Henry Lewis, Missouri Historical Society, St. Louis, Missouri.

reached your ears, and may have raised some inquiries in your minds respecting the same. I cannot in this letter give you all the information you may desire on the subject. . . . I first mentioned the doctrine in public when preaching the funeral sermon of Bro Brunson [10 August 1840], and have since then given general instructions to the Church on the subject."[6]

During a Church conference in October 1840, the Prophet delivered a discourse on the newly restored doctrine.[7] In the fall of that year vicarious ordinances in behalf of the dead were performed temporarily in the Mississippi River at Nauvoo, Illinois.[8] Other baptisms for the dead were performed in 1840 and 1841, but due to the fact that uniform procedures had not yet been outlined, some irregularities took place that later had to be corrected.[9]

President John Taylor, commenting on the development of the practice, said of Joseph Smith: "At first these things were only partially made known to him, and as they were partially developed he called upon the twelve that were then living . . . to commence and be baptized for the dead, and they were baptized in the Mississippi River. Immediately after these baptisms, the Prophet had a revelation which more clearly developed the order in relation to such baptisms."[10]

The foundation of all ordinance work for the dead was clearly set forth on 19 January 1841 in a revelation to Joseph Smith at Nauvoo. In addition to the enumeration of the vicarious ordinances for the dead, the Lord commanded the building of a temple. This structure was to be the place wherein the sacred ordinances

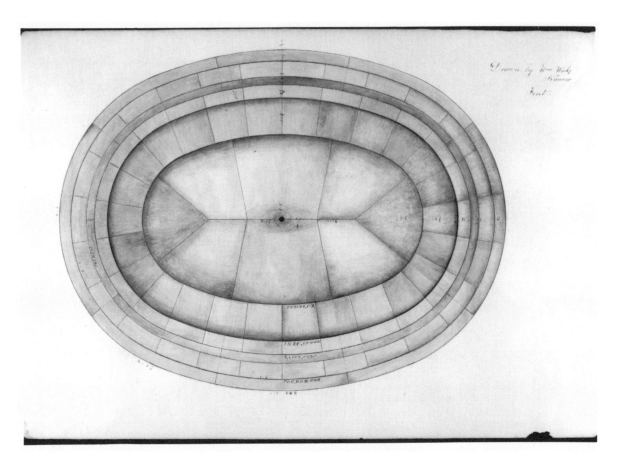

Figure 4.2 *Baptismal Font, drawing, 1845, William Weeks, LDS Church Archives. This is an original architectural drawing by architect William Weeks showing an overhead view looking down into the stone baptismal font.*

could be revealed in their fullness and performed (D&C 124:25–45). During September 1841, additional information was given regarding the subject (D&C 127:4–9; 128:1–19). These two inspired letters, written by Joseph Smith, provided clarification regarding the doctrine of work for the dead. They also outlined the necessity of keeping accurate records and the need for witnesses.

Baptisms in the river were discontinued by revelation on Sunday, 3 October 1841, when the Prophet announced: "There shall be no more baptisms for the dead, until the ordinance can be attended to in the Lord's House; and

the Church shall not hold another General Conference, until they can meet in said house. *For thus saith the Lord!*"[11]

During the summer and fall of 1841, measures had been taken by Church leaders to build a baptismal font in the cellar floor of the temple. This temporary font was dedicated by Brigham Young at 5:00 P.M. on Monday, 8 November. A thorough description of this temporary font and its purposes was recorded by Joseph Smith in his journal.[12] Ordinance work in the font began on Sunday, 21 November, when forty baptisms in behalf of the dead were performed.[13] This temporary font was later replaced by a permanent one made of stone. Elder Erastus Snow reported that the Prophet gave instructions to the effect that none should be allowed to participate in the privileges of the temple unless they could produce a certificate from the general Church recorder certifying that they were full tithe payers.[14] It is reported that a total of 15,626 recorded baptisms for the dead were performed in and about the vicinity of the Nauvoo Temple while the Saints were in Nauvoo.[15]

The Endowment

The revelation calling for the building of the Nauvoo Temple clearly stated: "And verily I say unto you, let this house be built unto my name, that I may reveal mine ordinances therein unto my people." Among the ordinances mentioned were anointings, washings, baptisms for the dead, and the endowment. The Prophet Joseph Smith was to be shown all things pertaining to the building and the priesthood thereof (D&C 124:39–42).

To *endow* means to enrich in some way. How the temple endowment enriches the participant is partially explained by John K. Edmunds, who served as a president of the Salt Lake Temple:

> *"What is the endowment?"* Because of its sacredness and the prohibitions of the Lord established to protect its sanctity, many of the beautiful ordinances of the holy endowment and much of the detailed instruction involved cannot be disclosed or presented except to those who are worthy to receive the ordinances and instruction in the place where God has decreed they shall be administered and revealed—in his holy house. . . .
>
> The endowment comprehends an enrichment not measured nor measurable in terms of money or other material treasures, which are subject to theft and the corrosion of moth and rust. To receive the endowment is to receive the riches of eternity—the knowledge, the power, the keys that unlock the door to the indescribable treasures of heaven and open the way to exaltation in the celestial world. To receive the endowment is to receive a course of instruction in eternal truth, together with all the keys, powers, and ordinances revealed and ordained of God to prepare his children for his greatest gift—the gift of eternal life.
>
> The temple is an institution not only of higher learning but of the highest learning. In the temple, students are taught basic, changeless, everlasting truths applicable to time and eternity.[16]

Elder John A. Widtsoe offered this description of the temple ceremony: "The Temple endowment relates the story of mans eternal journey; sets forth the conditions upon which progress in the eternal journey depends; requires covenants or agreements of those participating, to accept and use the laws of progress; gives tests by which our willingness and fitness for righteousness may be known, and finally points out the ultimate destiny of those who love truth and live by it."[17]

Elder James E. Talmage provided further explanation of the endowment ceremony:

The Temple Endowment, as administered in modern temples, comprises instruction relating to the significance and sequence of past dispensations, and the importance of the present as the greatest and grandest era in human history. This course of instruction includes a recital of the most prominent events of the creative period, the condition of our first parents in the Garden of Eden, their disobedience and consequent expulsion from that blissful abode, their condition in the lone and dreary world when doomed to live by labor and sweat, the plan of redemption by which the great transgression may be atoned, the period of the great apostasy, the restoration of the Gospel with all its ancient powers and privileges, the absolute and indispensable condition of personal purity and devotion to the right in present life, and a strict compliance with Gospel requirements. . . .

The ordinances of the endowment embody certain obligations on the part of the individual, such as covenant and promise to observe the law of strict virtue and chastity, to be charitable, benevolent, tolerant and pure; to devote both talent and material means to the spread of truth and the uplifting of the race; to maintain devotion to the cause of truth; and to seek in every way to contribute to the great preparation that the earth may be made ready to receive her King,— the Lord Jesus Christ. With the taking of each covenant and the assuming of each obligation a promised blessing is pronounced, contingent upon the faithful observance of the conditions.

No jot, iota, or tittle of the temple rites is otherwise than uplifting and sanctifying. In every detail the endowment ceremony contributes to covenants of morality of life, consecration of person to high ideals, devotion to truth, patriotism to nation, and allegiance to God.[18]

The concept of an endowment ceremony originated in the Church as early as 22 June 1834 at Kirtland, Ohio. In a revelation to Joseph Smith on that date, the endowment was significantly related to a temple, one that the Saints had been commanded to build in Kirtland. The revelation declared, "Verily I say unto you, it is expedient in me that the first elders of my church should receive their endowment from on high in my house, which I have commanded to be built unto my name in the land of Kirtland" (D&C 105:33).

The ceremony was first practiced in an incomplete form on 20 January 1836 at a council meeting held in the Kirtland Temple.[19] President Brigham Young, commenting on the endowment as introduced in Kirtland, stated that those who assisted with the building of the temple "received a portion of their endowments, or we might say more clearly, some of the first, or introductory, or initiatory ordinances, preparatory to an endowment."[20]

On 3 April 1836 the Old Testament prophet Elijah appeared to Joseph Smith, restoring to him certain sealing powers of the priesthood. It is mentioned in the revelation given on the occasion of Elijah's visitation that thousands would rejoice in consequence of the blessings that would come through the temple (D&C 110:9, 13–16). Joseph Smith and other

Church leaders connected the visitation of Elijah directly to the authority and nature of temple ordinances. Endowments conducted in Kirtland were limited both in scope and in number. Further development of these ordinances waited until the Church was established at Nauvoo.

The basic temple endowment ceremony, later common to Mormon temple ritual, was first performed by Joseph Smith on 4 May 1842 in the upper room of his brick store in Nauvoo.

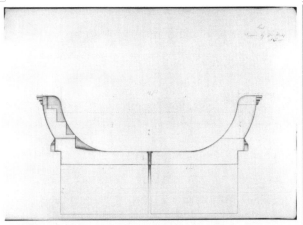

Figure 4.3 Cross-Sectional View of Baptismal Font, drawing, 1845, William Weeks, L.D.S. Church Archives. This is an original architectural drawing by architect William Weeks showing a cross-sectional side view of the stone baptismal font.

> I spent the day in the upper part of the store, that is in my private office . . . in council with General James Adams, of Springfield, Patriarch Hyrum Smith, Bishops Newel K. Whitney and George Miller, and President Brigham Young and Elders Heber C. Kimball and Willard Richards, instructing them in the principles and order of the Priesthood, attending to washings, anointings, endowments and the communication of keys pertaining to the Aaronic Priesthood, and so on to the highest order of the Melchisedek Priesthood, setting forth the order pertaining to the Ancient of Days, and all those plans and principles by which any one is enabled to secure the fullness of those blessings which have been prepared for the Church of the First Born, and come up and abide in the presence of Eloheim in the eternal worlds. In this council was instituted the ancient order of things for the first time in these last days.[21]

John C. Bennett, former mayor of Nauvoo and apostate from the Church, published his

History of the Saints in 1842, furnishing evidence of the endowment ceremony being practiced at this early date. Referring to the practice as a "Holy Order," he provided a description of the room where ordinances were performed along with its symbolic decoration, and he unfolded a garbled account of the ceremony as then practiced. Bennett declared that the ceremonies were being conducted in consequence of a pretended special revelation to Joseph Smith respecting the practice.[22]

Ebenezer Robinson, one-time editor of the *Times and Seasons* who left the Church at the close of the Nauvoo period, wrote that Joseph Smith established a secret order as early as 1843. They held their meetings and performed ordinances in the large room of the second story in Joseph's brick store. Robinson described being a personal witness to the ceremony's existence in June 1844.[23]

Prior to his death, the Prophet Joseph was very concerned with the progress of the temple. As a stimulus to greater effort, he stated that all members who were worthy would receive their endowments and that those recorded as assisting with completion of the temple would have first claim on the ordinances.[24] The following month at the conference of Church members, he commented that as soon as the temple was sufficiently complete, ordinance work would be started and the endowment given. He further declared the ordinances to be essential to exaltation in the celestial degree of glory.[25] Elder Orson Hyde

can confer them upon others, and the hosts of Satan will not be able to tear down the kingdom as fast as you will be able to build it up."[26]

These actions were further explained by Elder Parley P. Pratt:

This great and good man was led, before his death, to call the Twelve together, from time to time, and to instruct them in all things pertaining to the kingdom, ordinances, and government of God. He often observed that

As a stimulus to greater effort, h would receive their endowmer completion of the temple v

recorded that in April 1844 he and other apostles were given their endowments, had conferred upon them the sealing power as well as all the keys of the priesthood, and were then instructed in the ordinances by Joseph Smith: "He conducted us through every ordinance of the holy priesthood, and when he had gone through with all the ordinances he rejoiced very much, and says, now if they kill me you have got all the keys, and all the ordinances, and you

he was laying the foundation, but it would remain for the Twelve to complete the building. Said he, "I know not why; but for some reason I am constrained to hasten my preparations, and to confer upon the Twelve all the ordinances, keys, covenants, endowments, and sealing ordinances of the priesthood, and so set before them a pattern in all things pertaining to the sanctuary and the endowment therein."

Having done this, he rejoiced exceedingly; for, said he, the Lord is

about to lay the burden on your shoulders and let me rest awhile; and if they kill me, continued he, the kingdom of God will roll on, as I have now finished the work which was laid upon me, by committing to you all things for the building up of the kingdom according to the heavenly vision, and the pattern shown me from heaven. With many conversations like this, he comforted the minds of the Twelve, and prepared them for what was soon to follow.

He proceeded to confer on elder Young, the President of the Twelve,

blessing shall be administered pertaining to things of the resurrection and the life to come.

After giving them a very short charge to do all things according to the pattern, he quietly surrendered his liberty and his life into the hands of his blood-thirsty enemies, and all this to save the people for whom he had so long laboured from threatened vengeance.[27]

Following the death of their Prophet, Church members rallied behind new leaders.

ated that all members who were worthy

d that those recorded as assisting with

d have first claim on the ordinances.

the keys of the sealing power, as conferred in the last days by the spirit and power of Elijah, in order to seal the hearts of the fathers to the children, and the hearts of the children to the fathers, lest the whole earth should be smitten with a curse.

This last key of the priesthood is the most sacred of all, and pertains exclusively to the first presidency of the church, without whose sanction and approval or authority, no sealing

Renewing their efforts, they were unified in pushing the temple toward its completion. A letter of the Twelve Apostles on 17 April 1845 reported progress on the temple and declared a stated intention of having the building far enough along by the coming fall so as to "commence administering the ordinances of endowment according to the commandment." Elder Lyman Wight, to whom the letter was addressed, was strongly urged not to depart for

the West before receiving his own endowment.[28]

As the month of November 1845 drew to a close, the temple had been enclosed and outside work completed. Strenuous exertions were now being made to finish the interior, with priority given to the attic story. It was plastered, painted, and ready for use as the month closed. On 30 November at 12:00 P.M., the attic story was dedicated by Brigham Young in the company of the apostles and other Church leaders.[29] Finishing touches were then added; carpets were laid in the large central room as well as in the side rooms of the east attic. The large main room of the east attic was then divided into ordinance rooms by hanging canvas partitions. These partitioned rooms were then furnished and made ready for conducting the endowment ordinances. On 10 December at 4:25 P.M., President Young, Elder Heber C. Kimball, and others commenced administering the ordinances of the endowment. They continued officiating in the ordinances until 3:30 the following morning. After a brief rest, they had breakfast and returned to the temple.[30] Significant among those receiving ordinances the next day (11 December) were the temple committee, their wives, and the Prophet's mother, Lucy Mack Smith.[31] As ordinance work continued over the next several weeks, members of the Twelve Apostles and other specially set-apart brethren officiated in administering the ordinances to others. Women were ministered to by Eliza R. Snow, Vilate Kimball, and Elizabeth Ann Whitney as well as by several other women who were set apart and given authority to officiate in administering the ordinances to female patrons.[32]

John D. Lee reported that as soon as circumstances allowed, Brigham Young organized the work, established rules for the preservation of order, and placed help in the different departments to accommodate large numbers who would come for their ordinances. Lee himself was set apart as a clerk to keep record of work as it was done.[33] He furnished interesting insights on what was expected of those coming to receive their endowments. "A list is made out the day previous. . . . Every person is required to wash himself clean, from head to foot. Also to prepare and bring a good supply of food, of the best quality, for themselves and those who labor in the house of the Lord. In the latter about twenty-five persons are required in the different departments to attend to the [ordinances]."[34]

Typical of those called to assist was Erastus Snow, who recorded that he and his wife received their endowments on 12 December, following which they were assigned to assist others in the work. He continued to assist both day and night for about six weeks, and his wife continued in the female department for about a month.[35] Endowment work continued from its commencement with little interruption, and as time went on, experienced workers were able to work more rapidly, thereby accommodating increasingly larger numbers. William Huntington reported that by 21 December some 560 had received their endowments.[36] By

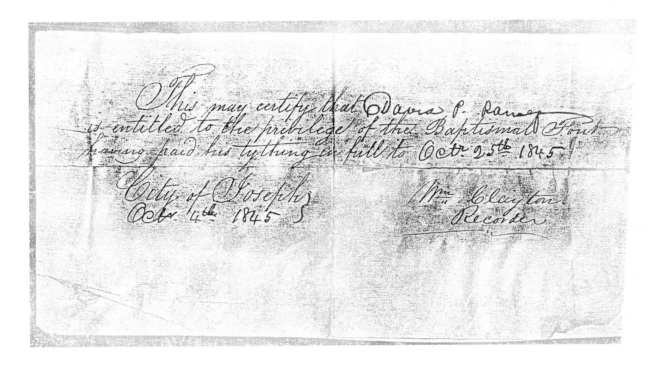

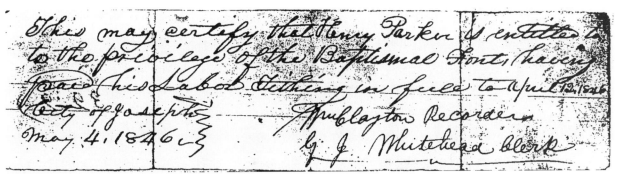

Figure 4.4 (Top) Recommend—Privilege to Use Baptismal Font, photocopy of handwritten document, 25 October 1845, William Clayton, LDS Church Archives. Those who paid their tithing in full were provided with a note such as this, indicating their worthiness to use the baptismal font. Dated 25 October 1845, this certifies that David P. Rainey was entitled to use the temple font. This is a photocopy; the original could not be located.

Figure 4.5 (Bottom) Recommend—Privilege to Use Baptismal Font, photocopy of handwritten document, 4 May 1846, James Whitehead, LDS Church Archives. Acting in behalf of temple recorder William Clayton, James Whitehead, a temple clerk, issued this recommend to Henry Parker, certifying he was entitled to use the temple baptismal font. Note that this recommend was issued only three days after the temple dedication. This is a photocopy; the original could not be located.

the end of the month over one thousand had participated in the ceremony.[37]

Heber C. Kimball gradually assumed the role of supervising all ordinance work.[38] As the pace of temple work accelerated, members assembled in increasing numbers. The work was going early in the mornings and very late into the evenings. Assigning and coordinating the efforts of ordinance workers, laundering temple clothing, and providing food for officiators were not simple tasks. The urgency to provide endowments and sealing ordinances for those who had not yet received them was encumbered by members who wished to linger in the temple enjoying the spiritual blessings found there. It became necessary that steps be taken to maintain proper order. At Elder Kimball's insistence, no one was allowed into the building without an official invitation.[39] Furthermore, strict order and decorum were to be maintained within its holy precincts. Ordinance work continued in the temple until 7 February 1846, when it was closed due to the migration of the Saints out of Nauvoo into the western wilderness. Brigham Young reported that by this time 5,634 had received their endowment ordinances.[40]

In spite of threats and violence from enemies, Church members exhibited great faith and determination to have as many partake of temple ordinances as possible. The Church historian recorded on 20 January 1846: "Public prejudice being so strong against the Saints, and the excitement becoming alarming, the brethren determined to continue the administrations of the ordinances of endowment night and day."[41] Church leaders were under great strain in preparing Church members and their own families for a premature departure. Their energies were also considerably taxed in taking care of the many requests for ordinance work. Brigham Young observed: "Such has been the anxiety manifested by the saints to receive the ordinances (of the Temple), and such the anxiety on our part to administer to them, that I have given myself up entirely to the work of the Lord in the Temple night and day, not taking more than four hours sleep, upon an average, per day, and going home but once a week. Elder Kimball and other apostles were in constant attendance but in consequence of close application some of them had to leave the Temple to rest and recruit their health."[42] The orderly evacuation planned for April was hastened by events during the winter. An indictment issued against Brigham Young and eight other apostles (accusing them of counterfeiting) prompted a decision in late January to have several companies of pioneers ready and prepared to leave the city at a moment's notice. Following this, a warning came from Governor Thomas Ford and others that federal troops planned to intercept the Mormons as they left the city. This resulted in a decision on 2 February to begin the exodus. In spite of announcements that temple ordinance work would cease, members could not be dissuaded from seeking their temple blessings before they left Nauvoo. This was explained by Brigham Young, when on Tuesday, 3 February 1846, he reported:

Ordinance work continued in the temple until 7 February 1846.

Notwithstanding that I had announced that we would not attend to the administration of the ordinances, the House of the Lord was thronged all day, the anxiety being so great to receive, as if the brethren would have us stay here and continue the endowments until our way would be hedged up, and our enemies would intercept us. But I informed the brethren that this was not wise, and that we should build more Temples, and have further opportunities to receive the blessings of the Lord, as soon as the saints were prepared to receive them. In this Temple we have been abundantly rewarded, if we receive no more. I also informed the brethren that I was going to get my wagons started and be off. I walked some distance from the Temple supposing the crowd would disperse, but on returning I found the house filled to overflowing.

Looking upon the multitude and knowing their anxiety, as they were thirsting and hungering for the word, we continued at work diligently in the House of the Lord.

Two hundred and ninety-five persons received ordinances.[43]

On 4 February 1846 the exodus from Nauvoo began. Early on that same morning, as "the sun shone brightly into the east windows of the Temple, . . . a new scene was being enacted. A number of persons were busily engaged removing articles of furniture, stoves, carpets and pictures etc., etc."[44] These articles were removed from the celestial room of the temple as families packed belongings to depart from the city. In spite of these events, ordinance work in the temple continued at a feverish pace. It appears that the large numbers of members desiring temple blessings along with the time factor may have made it impractical to give them the full endowment ordinances. Evidence indicates that members obtaining ordinances after the exodus began may have received only their washings and anointings, or the initiatory part of the endowment. This observation is sustained by the report of Joseph Holbrook, who received his ordinances on 6 February. "I went into the temple at Nauvoo and received my washing and anointing in the House of the Lord. There was a crowd. It being at the closing of giving endowments, so that near 500 passed through their ordinance in the last twenty-four hours, but I felt knowledge for me to improve upon until I could get more."[45] Brigham Young reported that on this day "five hundred and twelve persons received the first ordinances [initiatory portion] of endowment in the Temple." This procedure was likely followed on 7 February, the last day on which ordinances were given, when "upwards of six hundred received the ordinances."[46] Church members felt that the main purpose of erecting the building had now been achieved, and thousands had been blessed by the performance of the promised endowment ordinances.

Celestial or Eternal Marriage

Another ordinance practiced in the Nauvoo Temple was that of celestial marriage. To Latter-day Saints, marriage and the resulting

family units are eternal unions, not dissolved by death but existing beyond the grave. Such a union or covenant, entered into righteously, sealed by proper authority, and confirmed by continued faithfulness is recognized as binding in the heavens as well as on earth in an eternal marriage and family relationship.[47] The eternity of the marriage covenant, as practiced in Nauvoo, had its application in the marriage of a man to one wife, and also to plural marriage, wherein a man was sealed in marriage to more than one wife.

The revelation authorizing such marriages was given to Joseph Smith, who is reported to have received the principle by revelation as early as 1831.[48] He introduced the doctrine to the Twelve Apostles in the summer of 1841.[49] The revelation was committed to writing on 12 July 1843, when the Prophet dictated it to William Clayton.[50] On or about 12 August 1843 it was read by Hyrum Smith to members of the high council.[51]

Celestial marriages—marriages for eternity—were performed in the Nauvoo Temple for the first time on 7 January 1846. Heber C. Kimball records that on that date four individuals and their wives were sealed to each other in a covenant of eternal marriage.[52] An altar had been constructed for this purpose and installed in room 1 of the attic story. These and other eternal marriages were solemnized as couples knelt at the altar, as Samuel

Figure 4.6 View of Nauvoo from the West Bank of the Mississippi River, painting, date unknown (between 1848 and 1854), LDS Church Archives. This painting was painted by an unknown artist and was first printed by Herman J. Meyer in 1854 or 1855.

Whitney Richards records in his Journal: "Friday 23rd. By my interposition Father John Parkers family received their endowments his daughter Mary being my intended wife, after which I obtained permission of Pres Joseph [Joseph Young] for her to have the privelege of spending her time in the temple also, where she commenced her labours on the morn. of the 27th and in the evening of the 29th we were sealed upon the altar, Husband and Wife, for time and all Eternity, by Amasa Lyman, at 25

MEETINGS AND ADMINISTRATIVE FUNCTIONS

Among the multipurpose functions of the temple was the use of the structure as a place of worship for numerous and varied Church meetings. In addition, the building was designed to serve as the administrative office building for the Church.

Meetings

During the time the Saints resided in Nauvoo, there were few suitable locations for

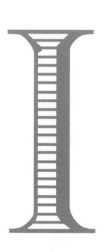

It is reported that there were 2,4 369 sealings of dead spouses and performed in the Nauvoo Temp.

minutes to nine Witnessed by Phinehas Richards and C. W. Wandall and recorded by F. D. Richards."[53]

It is reported that there were 2,420 eternal marriages of living couples plus 369 sealings of dead spouses and 71 sealings of living children to their parents performed in the Nauvoo Temple.[54] The majority of these marriages were monogamous in nature, while others involved a plurality of wives.

conducting religious meetings, and none of those were of sufficient size to accommodate large groups. No chapels or stake centers were ever constructed in Nauvoo during this period. As a result, most Church gatherings of any size were held in the open air, subject to the capricious nature of the elements. The temple was designed to accommodate large audiences, and the Saints were pleased that they could meet indoors.

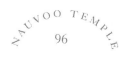

Meetings were held in the temple as early as October 1842, when congregations assembled on the temporary floor of the first story.[55] Since the building was not yet enclosed, those in attendance were exposed to the elements.[56] They met in the temple with some regularity on Sundays when weather permitted, and general conference sessions were convened there on 6 April 1843.[57] The ordinance of the sacrament was administered to the Saints for the first time in the temple during the afternoon of

eral conference of the Church in two and a half years. It was estimated that about five thousand people attended the services.[59] This must have been a solemn occasion with special announcements and votes taken, as reported by George Whitaker:

> At the October Conference a great many people gathered together. We did not know until then what the authorities of the Church had done. We knew that some important busi-

ernal marriages of living couples plus

alings of living children to their parents

Sunday, 21 May 1843.[58] Church gatherings continued in the building until construction needs caused them again to be held outside. Meetings were then often held in the grove near the west end of the temple.

On Sunday morning, 5 October 1845, the temple was opened for the first assembly ever convened in the enclosed structure. This event, an important milestone in temple construction, marked the opening of the first gen-

ness would be transacted. We were told that the spirit of the mob was so bitter against us that we would have to leave the confines of civilization and go beyond the Rocky Mountains into Mexican territory. It was better to leave our houses, our lands, our temple, and our beautiful city than to stay there and fight the mob, and many of us perhaps would lose our lives. . . . This was put to a vote, and we all voted to leave; if they gave us anything for our property to help us out it was

all right, but if they did not we would go anyway. Counsel was given to go to work and finish the temple according to the revelation given to Joseph Smith, so that we might receive our washings and anointings and the keys and powers of the Holy Priesthood, and also the Holy Anointings and Sealings that the power of God might rest upon His servants. It was also prophesied that in less than five years we would be a great deal better off than we were at that time, and many more things were told us that came to pass according to the words that had been spoken. The name of the city of Nauvoo was changed and called the city of Joseph, being called after the Prophet Joseph Smith. A great many things were done at that conference that I cannot write. Suffice it to say, the Spirit of God was with the people and the blessings of the Almighty were upon them.[60]

Meetings in the now enclosed temple continued each Sunday as Church members assembled for worship. This regular use of the structure for public meetings was interrupted during the first week in November 1845, when the first floor of the temple was taken up for the purpose of laying down permanent flooring.[61] Gatherings were also held in other parts of the structure for the purpose of conducting Church business and worship services. Some of these were conducted in the attic story. Illustrative of this practice is the report of a sacrament meeting being conducted there at 10:30 A.M., 28 November 1845, with about two hundred in attendance.[62] The temple was again opened for

public worship on Sunday, 1 February 1846, when those gathered met in the second story.[63] A new permanent floor was ready on the first story by 22 February 1846, and it accommodated a large congregation.[64] The main hall of this story was described in 1847 as having sufficient seating in it to accommodate thirty-five hundred people.[65] This figure, however, seems to be high for a space of 8,000 square feet, especially when considerable space would have been taken up by seats, aisles, and pulpits.

Besides general worship meetings, daily prayer meetings became a practice in 1846, as various-sized groups of priesthood members regularly met in the temple for this purpose. This practice continued even after the dedication of the building.[66]

Administrative Functions

The temple was designed to furnish office space for the various officials and offices of Church government. Leaders of the seventies and high priests were allowed offices in the attic story, as were members of the high council.[67] This was also true of the Twelve Apostles, stake presidency, Presiding Bishops, and others. Numerous meetings and matters of Church business were conducted by those officials in the temple, including plans and organization for the exodus from Nauvoo.

OTHER USES OF THE STRUCTURE

The building was put to additional uses besides those already named. It is doubtful that some of these uses were intended in the begin-

ning, but circumstances relating to the forced exodus made some seem practical and others a necessity.

Residence

The temple became a temporary residence for some Church leaders in January and February 1846. There was great anxiety on the part of both members and leaders to allow as many as possible to receive their temple ordinances. This resulted in an almost round-the-clock activity at the temple. Members of the Twelve and other temple workers gave themselves entirely to the work, taking no more than four hours of sleep per day and going home only once per week.[68] They slept in the side rooms of the attic story, and later in late January and February they may have slept in the second mezzanine half-story or the second story. To accommodate those who stayed day and night in the building, a dining room was set up in the north end of the west front section of the attic story.[69]

> The Twelve and other temple workers gave themselves entirely to the work.

Recreational Functions

The need for a suitable building for recreational purposes was met in part by the temple. The practice was commenced on 30 December 1845. The labors of the day had been brought to a close at 8:30 P.M., and it was decided to enjoy a "season of recreation." Brother Hansen played the violin, joined by Elisha Averett on the flute. Following a few lively musical numbers, the group danced for about an hour. This was followed by several of the group joining together in some songs. The activities were closed with prayer, and the group departed.[70] It was in the attic story where this initial dancing took place. The second floor was still under construction and not available for use until mid-January. The first floor, also under construction, was not usable until late February.

The practice of dancing and musical entertainment was repeated during the following month on various occasions by select groups of members. On one such occasion Brigham Young made a short address to the group. He talked about the privilege the Saints then had of meeting in the temple and stated that they could worship God in dance as well as in other ways. "The way for us to grow and thrive is for us to serve the Lord in all we do. . . . No man is to be filled with lightness. . . . We will praise the Lord as we please. Now, as to dancing in this house—there are thousands of brethren and sisters that have labored to build these walls and put on this roof, and they are shut out from any opportunity of enjoying any amusement among the wicked—or in this world, and shall they have any recreation? Yes! and this is the very place where they can have liberty."[71] The practice evidently came into some question, and on 9 January 1846 Brigham Young issued the following instructions: "I observed to the brethren that it was my wish that all dancing and merriment should cease, lest the brethren and sisters be carried away by vanity; and that the name of the Deity should be held in reverence, with all the due deference that belongeth to an infinite being of his character."[72]

Following the closing of temple ordinance work and the start of the exodus from Nauvoo, the practice of using the temple for recreational functions was renewed. Samuel W. Richards reported that on 9 February 1846, a select company, including several of the Twelve, met in the temple for a dance. Music was provided by the brass band. The social was opened with a prayer offered by Orson Hyde.[73] The building was used for additional social functions in the ensuing weeks by the workmen who were laboring to complete it. Richards furnished interesting accounts of those activities. On 28 April "[at] about noon they ceased and all

hands with their wives repaired to the temple for the feast, a large company were gathered, a plenty of cakes with cheese, and Raisens was furnished by the bretheren and Sisters for the occasion." On 29 April "in the afternoon [I] met in the attic story of the temple with the members who formed the prayer circle in No. 1 and a part of No. 2 with our wives and had a feast of cakes, pies, wine, &c. where we enjoyed ourselves with prayer preaching, administering for healing, blessing children, and music and Dancing untill near Midnight. The other hands completed the painting of the lower room."[74]

A similar social was held the next two days when the temple was dedicated. After the temple had been deserted by the journey of the Saints into the West, the building is reported to have been used for public balls, public meetings, etc., by the local citizens.[75] It is also reported that a fee of twenty-five cents was being collected in 1847 from those desiring a tour of the building.[76]

Astronomical Observatory

An indictment was issued in December 1845 against Brigham Young and eight other apostles by the U.S. District Court in Springfield. "They were accused of instigating and harboring a Nauvoo counterfeiting operation actually conducted by transient river traffickers."[77] Government officials attempted to serve warrants on those Church leaders but were unsuccessful. During this time, Elder Orson Pratt used some spot in the temple both to hide and as a place for an observatory. He spent several nights alone in the temple "quietly camped inside the building taking astronomical measurements by night to prepare for the immense job of navigating the pioneers upon departure. He ascertained the latitude of Nauvoo at 40 degrees, 35 minutes, 48 seconds north on 27 December. From this established base he could later calculate the position of the pioneer wagons on the prairies. All this time the temple was under careful watch by officers.[78]

With the exception of the baptismal font, the building was put into effective use by its builders for the short period of only six to nine months. Though used such a short time, it was considered by the Church as worthy of the sacrifice. Most Church members felt as did their leader, Brigham Young: "This church has obtained already all they have labored for in building this Temple."[79]

NOTES

1. Joseph Smith, *Teachings of the Prophet Joseph Smith*, comp. Joseph Fielding Smith (Salt Lake City: Deseret Book, 1938), 191; Andrew F. Ehat and Lyndon W. Cook, eds., *The Words of Joseph Smith* (Provo, Utah: Religious Studies Center, Brigham Young University, 1980), 77.

2. *Teachings of the Prophet Joseph Smith*, 179.

3. Ibid., 201; *Words of Joseph Smith*, 109–10.

4. Ibid., 367; *Words of Joseph Smith*, 368.

5. James E. Talmage, *The Articles of Faith* (Salt Lake City: Deseret Book, 1987), 145–56; Hugh Nibley, "Baptism for the Dead in Ancient Times," in *Mormonism and Early Christianity*, ed. Todd M. Compton and Stephen

D. Ricks (Salt Lake City: Deseret Book, 1987), 100–67; Richard Lloyd Anderson, "Baptism for the Dead," appendix C in *Understanding Paul* (Salt Lake City: Deseret Book, 1983), 403–15; Robert L. Millet, *The Mormon Faith, a New Look at Christianity* (Salt Lake City: Shadow Mountain, 1998), 197–200; also, Millet, "Was Baptism for the Dead a non-Christian Practice in New Testament Times (see 1 Cor. 15:29), or Was It a Practice of the Church of Jesus Christ as It Is Today?" *Ensign*, August 1987, 19–21; Daniel H. Ludlow, ed., *Encyclopedia of Mormonism* (New York: Macmillan, 1992), 1:95–97.

6. Dean C. Jessee, ed., *The Personal Writings of Joseph Smith* (Salt Lake City: Deseret Book, 1984), 486.

7. Joseph Smith, *History of the Church of Jesus Christ of Latter-day Saints*, B. H. Roberts, 2d ed., rev. (Salt Lake City: Deseret Book, 1957), 4:206.

8. Albert M. Zobell Jr., "If the Dead Rise Not," *Improvement Era*, August 1940, 531.

9. Genealogical Society, "Introduction of Baptism for the Dead," *Improvement Era*, April 1939, 251.

10. *Journal of Discourses* (London: Latter-day Saints' Book Depot, 1854–86), 25:183.

11. Smith, *History of the Church*, 4:426; *Words of Joseph Smith*, 78.

12. Ibid., 4:446–47.

13. Ibid., 4:454.

14. *Journal of Discourses*, 19:337.

15. *Deseret News*, 26 November 1932.

16. John K. Edmunds, Through Temple Doors (Salt Lake City: Bookcraft, 1978), 74–75.

17. John A. Widtsoe, comp., *Priesthood and Church Government in the Church of Jesus Christ of Latter-day Saints* (Salt Lake City: Deseret Book, 1939), 351.

18. James E. Talmage, *The House of the Lord* (Salt Lake City: Deseret Book, 1969), 83–84.

19. Joseph Fielding Smith, *Church History and Modern Revelation* (Salt Lake City: Deseret Book, 1953), 2:304; and Joseph Smith, *History of the Church*, 2:379; see also, 2:308–10.

20. *Journal of Discourses*, 2:31.

21. Smith, *History of the Church*, 5:1–2; see also Dean C. Jessee, ed., *The Papers of Joseph Smith*, vol. 2 (Salt Lake City: Deseret Book, 1992), 380.

22. John C. Bennett, *History of the Saints* (Boston: Leland and Whiting, 1842), 272–77.

23. *The Return 2*, no. 4 (April 1890): 252.

24. Smith, *Teachings of the Prophet Joseph Smith*, 333.

25. Smith, *History of the Church*, 6:319.

26. *Times and Seasons* 5 (15 September 1844): 651; also, *Millennial Star* 5 (December 1844): 104.

27. *Millennial Star* 5 (March 1845): 151.

28. B. H. Roberts, ed., *History of the Church of Jesus Christ of Latter-day Saints, Period 2: Apostolic Interregnum* (Salt Lake City: Deseret Book, 1957), 7:400.

29. *Journal History*, 30 November 1845, LDS Church Archives.

30. Ibid., 10 December 1845.

31. Roberts, *History of the Church*, 7:543–44.

32. Elizabeth Ann Whitney, "A Leaf from an Autobiography," *Woman's Exponent* 7 (15 February 1879): 191; also, "Pen Sketch of an Illustrious Woman," *Woman's Exponent* 9 (15 October 1880): 74.

33. John D. Lee, "Diaries and Official Records," 59–60, Harold B. Lee Library, Brigham Young University.

34. John D. Lee, *Mormonism Unveiled* (St. Louis: Vandawalker, 1892), 169.

35. Erastus Snow Sketch Book, 1818–47, 95, Harold B. Lee Library, Brigham Young University.

36. Diary of William Huntington, 43, typescript, 1952–53, Harold B. Lee Library, Brigham Young University.

37. Journal History, 29 December 1845.

38. Stanley B. Kimball, *Heber C. Kimball, Mormon Patriarch and Pioneer* (Urbana, Ill.: University of Illinois Press, 1981), 117.

39. Ibid., 118.

40. Roberts, *History of the Church*, 7:541–80. These pages list the number of endowments performed on each respective day. Added together, the figures total 5,634.

41. Journal History, 20 January 1846.

42. Roberts, *History of the Church*, 7:567.

43. Ibid., 579.

44. Helen Mar Whitney, "The Last Chapter of Scenes in Nauvoo," *Woman's Exponent* 12 (1 November 1883): 81; also, Journal History, 4 February 1846.

45. Joseph Holbrook, "The Life of Joseph Holbrook," 75–76, Harold B. Lee Library, Brigham Young University.

46. Brigham Young, *The Journal of Brigham*, comp. Leland R. Nelson (Provo, Utah: Council, 1980), 129. This conclusion is also sustained by the report of Helen Mar Whitney, who described people removing the furnishings from the celestial room on 4 February 1845. "The Last Chapter of Scenes in Nauvoo," 81; and, Thomas L. Kane, *The Mormons: A Discourse* (Philadelphia: King and Baird, 1850), 21. If furnishings were indeed removed from ordinance rooms, then it raises questions about the full endowment ordinance being given after this date. The large numbers receiving ordinances after 4 February also indicate only a partial endowment being given.

47. Talmage, *Articles of Faith*, 444–46.

48. B. H. Roberts, *A Comprehensive History of the Church of Jesus Christ of Latter-day Saints* (Salt Lake City: Deseret News, 1930), 2:95.

49. Ibid., 2:102.

50. Ibid., 2:106.

51. Leonard Soby as quoted in Joseph Fielding Smith, *Blood Atonement and the Origin of Plural Marriage* (Salt Lake City: Deseret News, 1905), 96; also Nauvoo Expositor, 7 June 1844.

52. Helen Mar Whitney, "Scenes from Nauvoo and Incidents from H. C. Kimball's Journal," *Woman's Exponent* 12 (15 October 1883): 74.

53. Diary of Samuel Whitney Richards, 2:1–2, Harold B. Lee Library, Brigham Young University.

54. Richard O. Cowan, *Temple Building Ancient and Modern* (Provo, Utah: Brigham Young University Press, 1971), 29, quoting from a report prepared in 1912 (no source listed); also, Joseph Christensen (former Salt Lake Temple recorder) as quoted by J. Earl Arrington, "Story of the Nauvoo Temple," 24, LDS Church Archives.

55. Journal History, 30 October 1842.

56. Ibid., 23 October 1842. Charlotte Haven, in a letter to her mother dated 19 February 1843, described the seating arrangements used in subsequent meetings. "Some boards are placed for seats, but not half enough to accommodate the people; so men, women, and children, take with them chairs, benches, stools, etc." As quoted by Richard Neitzel Holzapfel and Jeni Broberg Holzapfel, *Women of Nauvoo* (Salt Lake City: Bookcraft, 1992), 87; also, George W. Givens, *In Old Nauvoo, Everyday Life in the City of Joseph* (Salt Lake City: Deseret Book, 1990), 145.

57. Journal History, 6 April 1843.

58. Jenson, *Historical Record*, 8 (June 1889): 864.

59. Roberts, *History of the Church*, 7:456.

60. George Whitaker as cited in Carol Cornwall Madsen, *Journey to Zion, Voices from the Mormon Trail* (Salt Lake City: Deseret Book, 1997), 51.

61. Jenson, *Historical Record* 7 (January 1888): 519.

62. Ibid., 7:555–56.

63. Ibid., 7:578.

64. Ibid., 7:594.

65. J. H. Buckingham, "Illinois as Lincoln Knew It," in *Papers in Illinois History and Transactions* (Springfield, Ill.: Illinois State Historical Society, 1938), 172.

66. Journal History, 30 June 1846; 31 July 1846; also, Roberts, *History of the Church*, 7:584.

67. Roberts, *History of the Church*, 7:542, 549, 555, 565.

68. Ibid., 7:567.

69. Ibid., 7:576.

70. Ibid., 7:577.

71. Helen Mar Whitney, "Scenes from Nauvoo and Incidents from H. C. Kimball's Journal," *Woman's Exponent* 12 (15 September 1883): 57–58; also, Roberts, *History of the Church*, 7:561–62.

72. Roberts, *History of the Church*, 7:566.

73. Diary of Samuel Whitney Richards, 1:2.

74. Ibid., 17–18.

75. *Valley Tan*, 15 February 1860.

76. Buckingham, "Illinois as Lincoln Knew It," 169.

77. James B. Allen and Glen M. Leonard, *The Story of the Latter-day Saints* (Salt Lake City: Deseret Book, 1976), 220.

78. Breck England, *The Life and Thought of Orson Pratt* (Salt Lake City: University of Utah Press, 1985), 108–9; also, Roberts, *History of the Church*, 7:554.

79. Helen Mar Whitney, "Scenes from Nauvoo," 58. 5

Photographic Reproduction of the Nauvoo Temple, daguerreotype, ca. 1846, Louis Rice Chaffin, International Society of Daughters of Utah Pioneers. This is the clearest daguerreotype print of the temple now available for study. It was taken by Louis Rice Chaffin with the camera facing in a northeastern direction. Because some of the temple windows are open, the daguerreotype is believed to have been taken sometime during the summer or warm weather months of 1846. Since Chaffin went west with the other exiled members of the Church, this daguerreotype would most likely have been taken prior to 17 September 1846, when the last Church members were driven from Nauvoo. What appears to be an angelic weather vane is clearly visible at the top of the spire.

Members of The Church of Jesus Christ of
Latter-day Saints look upon their temples
with great reverence. As set forth in scripture, a temple is a very sacred place, "a

CHAPTER FIVE

SPIRITUAL

BLESSINGS

house of prayer, a house of fasting, a house
of faith, a house of learning, a house of
glory, a house of order, a house of God"
(D&C 109:8). In the temple solemn
covenants are entered into and sacred
exalting ordinances received. These and all

other saving ordinances of the gospel are also vicariously performed by living patrons in behalf of individuals who died without receiving these ordinances while they lived in mortality.

It is the Lord's house, consecrated to be holy and sanctified, a place where God's glory rests upon his people. Those who enter worthily, who are spiritually prepared, and who come hungering and thirsting after righteousness acknowledge that the temple is God's house, sanctified by his Holy Spirit, a place of his holi-

sacrifices and hardships endured by its builders. That such blessings were realized is recorded in numerous journals of which the following serve as samples.

Joseph Fielding described his impressions of the temple in December 1845: "I entered it for the first [time] and I truly felt as though I had gotten out of this World and on Friday, the 12th I and my Wife received our Endowment having formerly received it in the Days of Joseph and Hyram [sic] but it is now given in a

The Spirit, Power and wisdom all felt satisfied that during t ments of the Saints, we wer

ness (D&C 109:8–22). Here, many people routinely enjoy sacred spiritual blessings such as personal revelation. Their minds are enlightened and their understanding quickened to more fully comprehend God's purposes and the divine plan of salvation. Here individuals may experience the sanctifying, cleansing influence of the Holy Ghost. They may be blessed with a sweet assurance of comfort and peace. This was what made the temple at Nauvoo worth all the

more perfect Manner because of better Convenience."[1] Erastus Snow summarized the feelings of many as he testified: "The Spirit, Power and wisdom of God reigned continually in the Temple and all felt satisfied that during the two months we occupied it in the endowments of the Saints, we were amply paid for all our labor in building it."[2] His sister Eliza R. Snow observed: "Thanks be to God for the holy ordinances of His house and how cheerfully grateful we ought to be that we are the happy participants of these great blessings."³

Fourteen-year-old Elvira Stevens, orphaned in Nauvoo and traveling west with her sister and brother-in-law, crossed back over the Mississippi three times to attend the Nauvoo Temple dedication. The strong spiritual impressions she experienced in this sacred building had a lasting impact on her life. "The heavenly power was so great, I then crossed and re-crossed to be benefited by it, as young as I

here say that the spirit of the Lord was poured out upon those that were attending to the Ordinances of the holy priesthood."⁶

In 1846 the total population of Church members living in and around Nauvoo was at the very most fifteen thousand to twenty-five thousand. This included both adults as well as children. Of this number 5,634 individuals received their endowments in the Nauvoo Temple.⁷ It is evident from these statistics that one out of every three or four members had partaken of

od reigned continually in the Temple and

vo months we occupied it in the endow-

ply paid for all our labor in building it.

was."⁴ Nancy Naomi Alexander Tracy explained that it was as difficult to leave the temple as it was to leave her own home. Writing to her children, she declared: "Through all my sufferings I never doubted, but felt to cling to the gospel." She went on to explain that the spiritual manifestations experienced in the Kirtland Temple and receiving her endowments in the Nauvoo Temple gave her the strength to endure.⁵ Perrigrine Sessions testified: "I will

these sacred temple ordinances. This unusually high percentage leads to the conclusion that the vast majority of adult members and a number of the teenagers leaving Nauvoo for the wilderness of the West had received their temple blessings.⁸

As the Saints journeyed on their westward trek into an unknown and uncertain future, these temple blessings for many made the journey of faith possible. Sarah Pea Rich expressed what this meant to her:

The work of giving endowments commenced. President Young chose many brothers and sisters to come to the Temple and assist in giving endowments. Among those chosen was Mr. Rich and myself. We were to be there in the morning and remain until work was done at ten or twelve o'clock at night if necessary. . . . We helped in the House of the Lord to give endowments for four months until the house was closed and we as a people commenced to prepare ourselves to depart to the Rocky Mountains.

Many were the blessings we had received in the House of the Lord which has caused us joy and comfort in the midst of all our sorrows, and enabled us to have faith in God, knowing He would guide us and sustain us in the unknown journey that lay before us. For if it had not been for the faith and knowledge that was bestowed upon us in that Temple by the influence and help of the spirit of the Lord, our journey would have been like one taking a leap in the dark, to start out on such a journey in the winter as it were, in our state of poverty, it would seem like walking into the jaws of death. But we had faith in our Heavenly Father and put our trust in him feeling that we were his chosen people and had embraced his gospel and instead of sorrow we felt to rejoice.[9]

These people made many sacrifices for their religion. One such story is told by John R. Young in his memoirs: "Orson Spencer was a

Figure 5.1 The Nauvoo Temple, tempura on muslin, ca. 1865, C. C. A. Christensen, courtesy Brigham Young University Museum of Art. All rights reserved. In the late 1870s, Christensen painted several panoramic murals. This section from one of the murals accurately portrays the completed Nauvoo Temple.

graduate from an eastern college, who having studied for the ministry, became a popular preacher in the Baptist Church. Meeting with a 'Mormon' elder, he became acquainted with the teachings of Joseph Smith and accepted them. Before doing so, however, he and his highly educated young wife counted the cost, laid their hearts on the altar and made the sacrifice! How few realize what it involved to become a 'Mormon' in those early days! Home, friends, occupation, popularity, all that makes life pleasant, were gone. Almost overnight they were strangers to their own kindred."[10]

Orson and Catherine Spencer were highly educated, capable individuals. Orson was later appointed, in 1849, as the first chancellor of the University of Deseret (forerunner of the University of Utah). Catherine was an accomplished, refined lady from an affluent family in the East.[11] They were among the first to receive their endowments in the Nauvoo Temple, receiving them on 11 December 1845, the second day these ordinances were available.[12] They were sealed to each other in an eternal marriage covenant on 15 January 1846.

The Spencer family along with other Church members became victims of the mobs. During the wintry month of February, they were driven from the protection of their home to privations and hardships on the open plains of Iowa. Catherine Spencer, slender and frail, suffered greatly from the severe difficulties of camping on the open plains. Her delicate frame could not endure the exposure to cold, wet weather and lack of sleep. As her health deteriorated, she sank rapidly under the ever accumulating hardships.

The sorrowing husband wrote imploringly to the wifes parents, asking them to receive her into their home until the Saints should find an abiding place. The answer came, "Let her renounce her degrading faith and she can come back, but never until she does."

When the letter was read to her, she asked her husband to get his Bible and to turn to the book of Ruth and read the first chapter, sixteenth and seventeenth verses: "Entreat me not to leave thee or to return from following after thee; for whither thou goest I will go, and where thou lodgest I will lodge. Thy people shall be my people and thy God my God." Not a murmur escaped her lips. The storm was severe and the wagon covers leaked. Friends held milk pans over her bed to keep her dry. In those conditions, in peace and without apparent suffering, the spirit took its flight and her body was consigned to a grave by the wayside.[13]

Like so many of their fellow exiles, these were not ignorant, gullible radicals led blindly by emotion or fanaticism. Rather, they were sensible, educated, skilled, and refined individuals, motivated by solid faith, spiritual knowledge, and deep conviction, all of which had been fortified by experiences and sacred covenants entered into in the temple at Nauvoo.

While most spiritual experiences connected with the temple were those of lasting impressions or witnesses to the souls of faithful members, there were others more striking in

nature. Samuel W. Richards reported that on 22 March 1846: "[I] went to my Quorum Meeting in the temple. The whole Quo. being present consisting of 15 members. . . . Dressing ourselves in the order of the Priesthood we called upon the Lord, his spirit attended us, and the visions of heaven were opened to our view. . . . I beheld other things which were glorious while the power of God rested down upon me. Others also beheld angels, and the glory of God."[14] John Pulsipher reported similar experiences. Summarizing his impressions of the temple, he stated: "It was accepted of the Lord, and His holy angels have ministered unto many therein."[15] Perrigrine Sessions recorded that both in the morning and also in the evening of 3 February 1846 he witnessed "a flaim of fier sean by many to rest down upon the Temple."[16] Thomas Bullock reported similar unusual spiritual experiences occurring on Sunday, 15 March 1846: "At sun down went to the Temple. 14 [fourteen people] partook of the Sacrament after which we had a most glorious time. . . . The power of the Holy Ghost rested down upon us. . . . And we continued our meeting until after midnight, which was the most profitable, happy, and glorious meeting I had ever attended in my life, and may the remembrance be deeply rooted in my soul for ever and ever."[17]

He recorded the events as they met again the next evening, Monday, 16 March: "Went to the Temple to pray. While there heard that last night Chester Loveland was called out of bed by his mother in Law stating that the Temple was again on fire. He dressed as quick as lightning and ran out of doors and saw the Temple all in a blaze. He studied it a few seconds, and as it did not appear to consume any, and as there was no others running, he was satisfied it was the glory of God, and again went to bed. Another brother saw the belfry all on fire at a 1/4 to 10. He ran as hard as he could, but when he came to the Temple he found all dark and secure. . . . Thus was the Spirit, power and glory to God manifest, not only at the Temple while we were there but also in our families for which my soul rejoices exceedingly."[18]

Impact on Doctrine and Practice

Revelation through the Prophet Joseph Smith concerning gospel principles and ordinances, much of which was closely associated with the temple, was the most important thing happening during the Nauvoo period of Church history. Doctrines of the Restoration had been revealed gradually to him, "line upon line and precept upon precept" (D&C 98:12). Under divine guidance, the Prophet gradually unfolded and taught those restored ancient doctrines and eternal truths to members of the Church as they became prepared to receive them. This was no easy task and a frustrating experience, as evidenced by his remarks and observations: "I have tried for a number of years to get the minds of the Saints prepared to receive the things of God; but we frequently see some of them, after suffering all they have for the work of God, will fly to pieces like glass as soon as anything comes that is contrary to their traditions: they cannot stand the fire at all. How many will be able to abide a celestial law, and go through and receive their exaltation, I am unable to say, as many are called, but few are chosen."[19]

On another occasion the Prophet declared: "I could explain a hundred fold more than I ever have of the glories of the kingdoms manifested to me in the vision, were I permitted, and were the people prepared to receive them. The Lord deals with this people as a tender parent with a child, communicating light and

While his mind was very much exercised with regard to religious matters, he had what he termed a vision, in which it was told to him, among other things, that the true church of Christ would soon be established on earth as it was anciently. A number of religious "reformers" came out from the churches about this time, claiming to be the true church. David investigated their claims, but none of them satisfied him. In the spring of 1830, he borrowed a Book of Mormon of a neighbor and read it carefully and tes-

The Lord deals with this communicating light and ways as they can bear it.

intelligence and the knowledge of his ways as they can bear it."[20]

The set ways and traditional thinking of some converts were difficult to overcome. The experience of David Foote as he investigated Mormonism was not unusual. Dissatisfied with the creeds of the various churches, he sought to find the true church of Christ as it existed in the days of the Apostles. A son told his father's story:

tified that it was a true record. But no Elder came to Dryden, and he knew nothing concerning the doctrine they preached. In the spring of 1832 he removed to Greenwood, Steuben county, N.Y. In the fall of 1833, two men professing to be 'Mormon' Elders came to Greenwood from Geneseo, Livingston county, N.Y. They held one or two meetings, and invited David and others to visit them at Geneseo. Accordingly, David and his brother-in-

law (Josiah Richardson), and his nephew (Moses Clauson), went to Geneseo in November, 1833, for the purpose of investigating the new religion. On arriving there, they found the large branch of the Saints somewhat divided, and some had been cut off from the Church, and among them the two Elders. . . . (The trouble in the branch arose with regard to the vision of Joseph Smith and Sidney Rigdon of the three glories. Some could not receive it as from the Lord.) After Elder Murdock [the branch president]

in scope by later revelations found in sections 88, 131, and 132. It was very difficult for some members to comprehend or accept any doctrine concerning life after death differing from their basic previous understandings of heaven and hell. A study of Church history reveals that they were not alone in their point of view. Temple ordinances and doctrines also became a great stumbling block for many members both in Nauvoo and also earlier at Kirtland, Ohio. As explained by Elder George A. Smith, the

ple as a tender parent with a child,

telligence and the knowledge of his

had expounded the gospel to David, to his satisfaction, he was baptized and returned home rejoicing that he had found the true Church of Christ, as it was promised in his vision several years previously.[21]

This concept of three degrees of glory, upsetting to some early members, was outlined in section 76 of the Doctrine and Covenants. The doctrine was further clarified and enlarged

temple ordinances, even as partially introduced in the Kirtland Temple, brought difficulties for some members. "Some apostatized because there was not more of it, and others because there was too much." He went on to explain, that "if the Lord had on that occasion revealed one single sentiment more . . . I believe He would have upset the whole of us."[22]

It was in Nauvoo—and directly related to the temple—that several doctrines, concepts,

and practices only partially revealed previously were now fleshed out and unfolded. Joseph Smith now taught them clearly to Church members through revelation and discourse. As Flanders noted: "The Nauvoo Temple was the focus of religious innovations which revolutionized Mormonism. Ordinances for the dead, as well as . . . ordinances for the living, including marriage for eternity, plural marriage, and other extraordinary familial arrangements, were introduced by Smith and Young in Nauvoo for temple observance. It is difficult to know which was conceived first—a temple needing special rites, or special rites needing a temple. At any rate the 'temple work' which became central to Mormon life in Utah had its beginnings in the Nauvoo Temple."[23]

Some resisted change and were unwilling to accept these expanding gospel concepts. This was a time of sifting. Those unable or unwilling to embrace the changes pulled away. Some dropped into inactivity, others left the Church, and still others openly opposed it. However, the vast majority of members accepted these doctrines, rejoicing in insights and understandings that greatly enriched their lives. They felt about them as Joseph Smith did when he declared: "This is good doctrine. It tastes good. I can taste the principles of eternal life, and so can you. They are given to me by the revelations of Jesus Christ; and I know that when I tell you these words of eternal life as they are given to me, you taste them, and I know that you believe them. You say honey is sweet, and so do I. I can also taste the spirit of eternal life. I know it is good; and when I tell you of these things which were given me by inspiration of the Holy Spirit, you are bound to receive them as sweet, and rejoice more and more."[24]

The sweeping doctrinal insights coming from the Nauvoo period and so closely interwoven with temple ordinances were numerous and varied. Though given on various occasions and at times under very trying conditions, they nevertheless emerged into a cohesive doctrinal plan of salvation and exaltation. Larry C. Porter and Milton V. Backman Jr., professors of Church history at Brigham Young University, observed: "As remarkable as the scope of the Nauvoo doctrines is their pattern. Where one might have expected disjointed results (given the press of time, leadership responsibilities, and persecution), there appears a pattern of profound consistency. Temple-related concepts dominate

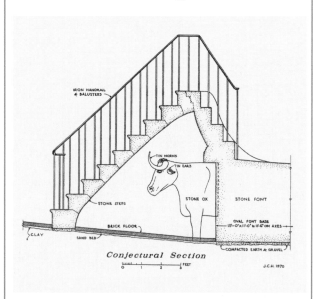

Figure 5.2 Conjectural Sketch of Stone Baptismal Font, drawing, 1970, LDS Church Archives. This sketch was produced by J. C. Harrington, who worked for Nauvoo Restoration, and was published in 1971 in his book, Rediscovery of the Nauvoo Temple, *which he coauthored with his wife, Virginia Harrington.*

and unify the Nauvoo doctrines as dramatically as the Temple dominated the Nauvoo landscape."[25] "The Nauvoo doctrine of Joseph Smith presents a clear and distinctive pattern, harmoniously drawing together perspectives on God, humankind, and the eternal elements and purposes of life. . . . All of these teachings were related to each other, particularly through the Temple. They stand as solidly at the core of the Prophet's revelations as the temple itself stood in Nauvoo."[26]

Some of those doctrines and practices revealed during the Nauvoo period, which are now such a basic part of the Church, are briefly summarized as follows.

Temple Ordinance Work

The performance of temple ordinances both for the living and in behalf of the dead was the main reason for building the temple at Nauvoo. It was also the reason why, in the face of increasing opposition and persecution, members remained in the city until the temple could be used for performing these ordinances. As Brigham Young explained, "The main and only cause of our tarrying so long, was to give the brethren those blessings in the Temple, for which they have labored so diligently and faithfully to build, and as soon as it was prepared, we labored incessantly almost night and day to wait on them until a few days prior to our departure."[27] Later the Church administered these same ordinances as temples were constructed in the West. Today these same ordinances are performed in temples throughout the world.

Family History Centers

Complementary and essential to the success of ordinances performed in numerous temples is the vast worldwide genealogical research effort being performed by thousands of Church members and Church service missionaries throughout the world. This and the hundreds of family history centers operating throughout the Church can all trace much of their beginnings to Nauvoo and the Nauvoo Temple.

Temple Ordinance Workers

Over one hundred temples are in operation throughout the Church with more in the process of construction, and many more planned or in various stages of development. These temples are staffed by ordinance workers who are called and set apart by their respective temple presidencies. In larger temples, hundreds of temple ordinance workers are required to administer and supervise the work. In addition to this, sealers are called and individually set apart by or under the direct supervision of the First Presidency of the Church. All of this had its beginning in connection with the Nauvoo Temple.

Certifying Worthiness to Use the Temple

In our day patrons who desire to participate in or receive the temple ordinances are carefully interviewed by a member of their bishopric and a member of their stake presidency. They are asked several questions to determine worthiness and readiness to enter the temple. A temple recommend is issued and signed by these leaders as well as by the individual. This recommend certifies to temple workers that this individual is a member of the Church who is in good standing and worthy to enter the temple.

The practice of certifying worthiness was in place at Nauvoo. Joseph Smith "had been strictly charged by the angel who had committed these precious things into his keeping that he should only reveal [the ordinances] to such persons as were pure, full of integrity to the truth, and worthy to be entrusted with divine messages."[28] As the temple came near to completion, Church leaders gave continual stress to the spiritual character and worthiness of each member. In preparation for receiving the blessings of temple ordinances, members were urged to "complete the Temple, and conduct yourselves worthy of the endowment."[29] The ordinances were to be bestowed upon "the members and elders who are prepared."[30] Church members were urged to "lay aside lightness and prepare themselves for these things."[31]

One basic requirement expected of all was the full and honest payment of tithing. Erastus Snow reported that the Prophet gave instructions that none should be allowed to participate in the privileges of the temple unless they could produce a certificate from the general Church recorder certifying that they had paid their tithing (see Figures 4.4 and 4.5).[32] The experience and report of George Whitaker was common with most members. "About the last of November the temple was so far along, having

the upper rooms finished, that they began to give endowments. Those [who] had paid their property tithing, that is, one tenth of the property they had brought with them, and also one tenth of their increase or labor, had the privilege of going through the temple. Everyone seemed to be trying to work and settle up their tithing that they might have the privilege of getting their endowments in the space of about ten weeks. I paid my property tithing and also my labor tithing and got my receipts for it, and had the privilege of going through the temple and getting my endowments a few days before they closed."[33]

When ordinance work commenced in December 1845, those allowed to participate came by special invitation of Church leaders. Personal invitations were extended to some, and apparently a list was posted, as noted by Warren Foote on 19 January 1846: "Our names was put down on the list today to receive our endowments."[34] No one was allowed into the building without an official invitation. Also, strict order and proper decorum were to be maintained within the sacred walls of the temple.[35] No records are available regarding any interviews to ascertain worthiness of participants prior to entering the temple. We do know that in the temple just prior to receiving their ordinances each member was examined or interviewed in rooms set aside for this purpose. Their commitment was determined, and it appears that each member was considered worthy if he or she "will walk according to the commandments, pay his tithing and seek after salvation."[36]

The Gathering

An essential part of the threefold mission of the Church is to testify of Christ and proclaim the gospel in all the world. It is an effort to bring all unto Christ and the fullness of his restored gospel. From its earliest beginnings, The Church of Jesus Christ of Latter-day Saints has been a missionary church. Today tens of thousands leave their homes each year for missionary service to most nations of the earth. This missionary effort is directly tied to the gathering of Israel in the latter days. An integral part in the Restoration of the gospel, this gathering is clearly prophesied in scripture (Deut. 30:1–3; Jer. 3:14–15; 16:14–16; 31:6–12; Isa. 2:1–4; 5:26; Micah 4:1–2; 1 Ne. 22:25; 2 Ne. 10:8; 21:12; 3 Ne. 20:18; 21:1). Gradually restored and unfolded, this fundamental gospel principle was first stressed less than six months after the Church was organized when the divine injunction was given "to bring to pass the gathering of mine elect" (D&C 29:7) "from the four quarters of the earth, even as many as will believe" (D&C 33:6). Six years later in the Kirtland Temple, Joseph Smith recorded that the essential keys of authority for this gathering were restored: "Moses appeared before us, and committed unto us the keys of the gathering of Israel from the four parts of the earth" (D&C 110:11). On 11 June 1843 a meeting was conducted in the Nauvoo Temple on the temporary floor of the first story. No roof was on the building at this time, and the walls were not yet up to the level of the second floor. In this setting Joseph Smith was inspired to proclaim some of the fundamental reasons why the gathering should take place.

Church members were urged to "lay aside lightness and prepare themselves for these things."

> This subject was presented to me since I came to the stand. What was the object of gathering the Jews, or the people of God in any age of the world? . . .
>
> The main object was to build unto the Lord a house whereby He could reveal unto His people the ordinances of His house and the glories of His kingdom, and teach the people the way of salvation; for there are certain ordinances and principles that, when they are taught and practiced, must be done in a place or house built for that purpose.
>
> It was the design of the councils of heaven before the world was, that the principles and laws of the priesthood should be predicated upon the

gathering of the people in every age of the world. . . . Ordinances instituted in the heavens before the foundation of the world, . . . for the salvation of men, are not to be altered or changed. All must be saved on the same principles.

It is for the same purpose that God gathers together His people in the last days, to build unto the Lord a house to prepare them for the ordinances and endowments.

These things are revealed in the most holy place in a Temple prepared for that purpose. . . . Why gather the people together in this place? . . . To receive the ordinances, the blessings, and glories that God has in store for His Saints.[37]

For over one hundred years, converts gathered to "Zion"—first to Kirtland, then to Missouri, next to Nauvoo, and then thousands left their native lands to gather in the valleys of the Rocky Mountains. It was predicted as early as 1833 that sometime in the future, emphasis would change from both a spiritual and a physical gathering in a central location to a spiritual gathering in stakes (D&C 101:20–21). This predicted change was implemented during the administration of President David O. McKay, as stakes were organized in several countries outside the United States. Members of the Church were told to remain in their native lands and build up the Church in their local areas.

This change of emphasis was explained by President Harold B. Lee: "Today we are witnessing the demonstration of the Lord's hand even in the midst of his Saints, the members of the Church. . . . Her boundaries are being enlarged, her stakes are being strengthened. In the early years of the Church specific places to which the Saints were to be gathered together were given, and the Lord directed that these gathering places should not be changed, but then he gave one qualification: 'Until the day cometh when there is found no more room for them; and then I have other places which I will appoint unto them, and they shall be called stakes, for the curtains or the strength of Zion.' (D&C 101:21)."[38]

Elder Bruce R. McConkie made some thought-provoking comments pertinent to this subject: "Now I call your attention to the facts, set forth in these scriptures, that the gathering of Israel consists of joining the true church; of coming to a knowledge of the true God and of his saving truths; and of worshipping him in the congregations of the Saints in all nations and among all peoples. . . . The place of gathering for the Mexican Saints is in Mexico; the place of gathering for the Guatemalan Saints is in Guatemala; the place of gathering for the Brazilian Saints is in Brazil; and so it goes throughout the length and breadth of the whole earth. . . . Every nation is the gathering place for its own people.[39] Elder McConkie explained later: "Whenever the growth of the Church in any area is sufficient, a stake of Zion is organized, thus making that area, in the general sense of the word, a part of Zion. The gathering of Israel . . . as of now is into the stakes of Zion wherever they may be. 'For Zion must increase in beauty, and in holiness' (D&C 82:14). . . . This process of gathering the

Figure 5.3 Nauvoo Temple on the Hill, detail copy of daguerreotype, 1846–47, LDS Church Archives. Charles W. Carter, a member of the Church and collector of early Church drawings and photographs, collected this old daguerreotype in the 1930s. This daguerreotype is believed to have been taken by Lucian Foster during the fall or winter of 1846–47. This detail from the daguerreotype shows the old armory next to the Nauvoo Temple. It is believed that several other daguerreotypes, including the Chaffin daguerreotype (see Figure 5.4) were taken from the second floor of this armory. This view looking toward the northeast shows mostly deserted homes and structures of old Nauvoo.

righteous together into the stakes of Zion will continue until stakes are organized in many nations."[40]

Today, the gathering has come full circle as stakes of the Church are organized in numerous countries, to be followed by the building of temples in those lands. These temples are built to bless the lives of those who have gathered with the fullness of gospel ordinances. The goal, as stated by President Gordon B. Hinckley, is that members throughout the

that clearly provides sensible answers to life's most basic questions. Many of these doctrines were partially revealed earlier in New York and Ohio. But it was in Nauvoo through revelations and discourses closely associated with temple ordinances that the Prophet Joseph Smith clarified and revealed those newly restored doctrines in their fullness. From descriptions and public statements made about the Nauvoo Temple ordinances, we learn that they offered understanding about the eternal origins,

Celestial marriage and tem ordinances. In the temp to each other for time an

entire world will have full access to all of the privileges and blessings of temple ordinances.[41]

Man's Destiny and Relationship to Deity

From childhood through old age, Latter-day Saints sing with deep feeling the hymns "O My Father," "I Am a Child of God," and "Families Can Be Together Forever."[42] These hymns and others like them express a comprehensive unifying philosophy of life based upon a theology

purposes, and destiny of human existence. Rising out of those concepts was an enlarged understanding of God the Father and his Son Jesus Christ, the character of God, our personal relationship with Deity as literal sons and daughters of God, and our ultimate potential to become like God our Eternal Father. As T. Edgar Lyon noted: "It marks a permanent theological landmark in the development of the doctrine of the Godhead among Latter-day

Saints and . . . has done much to clarify the understanding of the Saints and their relationships to their Eternal Father."[43]

These insights unfold light and understanding on the premortal existence of humankind, the creation of this earth, the Fall of Adam, the significance of the Atonement and the role of Jesus Christ in the plan of salvation, the nature and significance of covenants with God, and the ultimate destiny and possibilities of man. T. Edgar Lyon, commenting on the

the degrees of exaltation or damnation."[44]

Celestial marriage and temple sealings are the highest of temple ordinances. In the temple, husbands and wives can be married to each other for time and for eternity. Sealed together by divine authority, a married couple and the resulting family unit become eternal. As these illuminating concepts were explained and unfolded to Parley P. Pratt, he registered his feelings concerning the personal significance of these new understandings: "My dearly beloved brother,

e sealings are the highest of temple

usbands and wives can be married

r eternity.

Nauvoo sermons and writings of Joseph Smith, noted: "We might figuratively say that he took a huge canvas and on it, as would a master artist, painted a panorama of the pre-mortal life of man and his progress to a mortal existence, in which his preexisting spirit was clothed in a mortal body. Then he presented glimpses of the disembodied state following death, the re-embodiment of the spirit and body through the resurrection, and the various estates attained in

Joseph Smith, had . . . lifted a corner of the veil and given me a . . . glance into eternity."[45]

He taught me many great and glorious principles concerning God and the heavenly order of eternity. It was at this time that I received from him the first idea of eternal family organization, and the eternal union of the sexes in those inexpressibly endearing relationships which none but the highly intellectual, the refined and pure in heart,

*Figure 5.4   Photographic Reproduction of the Nauvoo Temple, daguerreotype, ca. 1846, Louis Rice Chaffin, International Society of Daughters of the Utah Pioneers.
This is the clearest daguerreotype print of the temple now available for study. It was taken by Louis Rice Chaffin with the camera facing in a northeastern direction.
Because some of the temple windows are open, the daguerreotype is believed to have been taken sometime during the summer or warm weather months of 1846. Since
Chaffin went west with the other exiled members of the Church, this daguerreotype would most likely have been taken prior to 17 September 1846, when the last Church
members were driven from Nauvoo. An angelic weather vane is clearly visible at the top of the steeple in enlarged copies.*

know how to prize, and which are at the very foundation of everything worthy to be called happiness.

Till then I had learned to esteem kindred affections and sympathies as appertaining solely to this transitory state, as something from which the heart must be entirely weaned, in order to be fitted for its heavenly state.

It was Joseph Smith who taught me how to prize the endearing relationships of father and mother, husband and wife; of brother and sister, son and daughter.

It was from him that I learned that the wife of my bosom might be secured to me for time and all eternity; and that the refined sympathies and affections which endeared us to each other emanated from the fountain of divine eternal love. It was from him that I learned that we might cultivate these affections, and grow and increase in the same to all eternity; while the result of our endless union would be an offspring as numerous as the stars of heaven, or the sands of the sea shore.

It was from him that I learned the true dignity and destiny of a son of God, clothed with an eternal priesthood, as the patriarch and sovereign of his countless offspring. It was from him that I learned that the highest dignity of womanhood was, to stand as a queen and priestess to her husband, and to reign for ever and ever as the queen mother of her numerous and still increasing offspring.

I had loved before, but I knew not why. But now I loved—with a pureness—an intensity of elevated, exalted feeling, which would lift my soul from the transitory things of this grovelling sphere and expand it as the ocean. I felt that God was my heavenly Father indeed; that Jesus was my brother, and that the wife of my bosom was an immortal, eternal companion; a kind ministering angel, given to me as a comfort, and a crown of glory for ever and ever. In short, I could now love with the spirit and with the understanding also.[46]

No individual can enter the highest degree of celestial glory alone.

Eternal Marriage and Equality of the Sexes

Joseph Smith confided to a group of close friends that "those who are married by the power and authority of the priesthood in this life, and continue without committing the sin against the Holy Ghost, will continue to increase and have children in the celestial glory."[47] During the Nauvoo period a revelation was received clearly explaining that no individual can enter the highest degree of celestial glory alone. One must be united with an eternal companion by entering into the new and everlasting covenant of eternal marriage (D&C 131:1–4; 132:4–24). From this revelation and the doctrinal understandings revealed through temple ordinances, we have received a clear understanding relative to the roles of men and women. Their roles are complementary and equal. As declared by Elder John A. Widtsoe: "The place of woman in the Church is to walk beside the man, not in front of him nor behind him. In the Church there is full equality between man and woman."[48] President Gordon B. Hinckley, describing the relationship that should exist between husband and wife, stated: "Marriage, in its truest sense, is a partnership of equals, with neither exercising dominion over the other, but, rather, with each encouraging and assisting the other in whatever responsibilities and aspirations he or she might have."[49] James E. Talmage explained how these insights came from the temple ordinances: "It is a precept of the Church that women of the Church share the authority of the Priesthood with their husbands, actual or prospective; . . . there is no grade, rank, or phase of the temple endowment to which women are not eligible on an equality with men. . . . The married state is regarded as sacred, sanctified, and holy in all temple procedure; and within the House of the Lord the woman is the equal and the help-meet of the man. In the privileges and blessings of that holy place, the utterance of Paul is regarded as a scriptural decree in full force and effect: 'Neither is the man without the woman, neither the woman without the man, in the Lord' (1 Cor. 11:11)."[50]

SPIRITUAL LEAVEN

So much of the rich, spiritual heritage enjoyed by present-day members of the Church, both in doctrine and devotion, has come from the Nauvoo period of their history. The revelations given at Nauvoo and contained in the Doctrine and Covenants (sections 124–32) are rich in content and doctrine. All of them are directly associated with the Nauvoo Temple and temple ordinances. These revelations, along with the ordinances and many discourses given by Joseph Smith, combine to make this a most important and fruitful period of doctrinal understanding. The impact of the Nauvoo Temple has been and continues to be very significant. As noted by President James E. Faust: "The spiritual leaven given in the Nauvoo Temple blesses us today in an ever-increasing measure. It spreads to every house of the Lord in the world so that all who hunger and thirst for the fullness of God's word may be filled."[51]

NOTES

1. Joseph Fielding, "'They Might Have Known That He Was Not a Fallen Prophet'—The Nauvoo Journal of Joseph Fielding," *BYU Studies* 19, no. 2 (winter 1979): 158–59.

2. Erastus Snow Sketch Book, 95, Harold B. Lee Library Special Collections, Brigham Young University.

3. Eliza R. Snow to Phebe Snow, 6 April 1868, Eliza R. Snow Papers, LDS Church Archives.

4. Elvira Stevens, as quoted by Carol Cornwall Madsen, *In Their Own Words: Women and the Story of Nauvoo* (Salt Lake City: Deseret Book, 1994), 23.

5. Nancy Naomi Alexander Tracy, as quoted by Madsen, *In Their Own Words*, 248.

6. Perrigrine Sessions, *The Diaries of Perrigrine Sessions*

(Bountiful, Utah: Carr, 1967), B–45.

7. B. H. Roberts, ed., *History of the Church of Jesus Christ of Latter-day Saints, Period 2: Apostolic Interregnum* (Salt Lake City: Deseret Book, 1932), 7:542–80. The number of endowments performed on each day are listed in these pages. Added together, these figures total 5,634. These ordinances even extended to some youth, as evidenced by the testimony of George Washington Bean: "Early in January, 1846, Ephraim K. Hanks, William Coray and I worked in the outer court of the Temple running a windlass, drawing up the wood and water needed to carry on, the endowments then being administered in the upper story of the Temple. We worked there for about six weeks, and then we workers received our endowments, although I was not yet fifteen years of age." *Autobiography of George Washington Bean,* comp. Flora Diana Bean Horne (Salt Lake City: Utah Printing, 1945), 23.

8. Bean, *Autobiography of George Washington Bean,* 23.

9. Sara Dearmon Pea Rich, "Reminiscences of Sara Dearmon Pea Rich," 65–66, LDS Church Archives.

10. John R. Young, *Memoirs of John R. Young, Utah Pioneer, 1847* (Salt Lake City: Deseret News, 1920), 17. Orson Spencer was a graduate of Union College and Baptist Literary and Theological Seminary in New York. In Nauvoo he was appointed as professor of foreign languages and was "well qualified to conduct his classes."

11. B. H. Roberts, *A Comprehensive History of the Church of Jesus Christ of Latter-day Saints* (Salt Lake City: Deseret News, 1930), 4:118.

12. Roberts, *History of the Church,* 7:543.

13. Young, *Memoirs of John R. Young,* 17–18.

14. Diary of Samuel Whitney Richards, 1:7–8, Harold B. Lee Library, Brigham Young University.

15. John Pulsipher, as quoted by E. Cecil McGavin, *The Nauvoo Temple* (Salt Lake City: Deseret Book, 1962), 95.

16. *The Diaries of Perrigrine Sessions,* 43.

17. Thomas Bullock, as quoted in Gregory R. Knight, "Journal of Thomas Bullock, 1816–1885," *BYU Studies* 31, no. 1 (winter 1991): 61–62.

18. Ibid., 62.

19. Joseph Smith, *History of the Church of Jesus Christ of Latter-day Saints,* ed. B. H. Roberts, 2d ed., rev. (Salt Lake City: Deseret Book, 1957), 6:185; Andrew F. Ehat and Lyndon W. Cook, eds., *The Words of Joseph Smith* (Provo, Utah: Religious Studies Center, Brigham Young University, 1980), 319.

20. Ibid., 5:402; also, Neal A. Maxwell, *Meek and Lowly* (Salt Lake City: Deseret Book, 1987), 74.

21. Andrew Jenson, *LDS Biographical Encyclopedia* (Salt Lake City: Western Epics, 1901), 1:374–75.

22. *Journal of Discourses* (London: Latter-day Saints' Book Depot, 1854–86), 2:215.

23. Robert Bruce Flanders, *Nauvoo: Kingdom on the Mississippi* (Urbana, Ill.: University of Illinois Press, 1965), 209.

24. Smith, *History of the Church,* 6:312; *Words of Joseph Smith,* 352.

25. Larry C. Porter and Milton V. Backman Jr., "Doctrine and the Temple in Nauvoo," *BYU Studies* 32, nos. 1–2 (winter and spring 1991): 43.

26. Ibid., 54.

27. Brigham Young to James Emmett, 26 March 1846, Brigham Young Papers, as cited in Richard E. Bennett, *We'll Find the Place* (Salt Lake City: Deseret Book, 1997), 20.

28. Elizabeth A. Whitney, "A Leaf from an Autobiography," *Woman's Exponent* 7 (15 December 1878): 105.

29. The Prophet, 22 February 1845.

30. *Times and Seasons* 6 (14 January 1845): 780.

31. Ibid., 6 (15 July 1845): 973.

32. *Journal of Discourses*, 19:337.

33. George Whitaker as quoted in Madsen, *Journey to Zion: Voices from the Mormon Trail* (Salt Lake City: Deseret Book, 1997), 52.

34. Autobiography of Warren Foote, 73.

35. Stanley B. Kimball, *Heber C. Kimball: Mormon Patriarch and Pioneer* (Urbana, Ill.: University of Illinois Press, 1981), 118.

36. Increase Van Deusen, *A Dialogue* (Albany: C. Killmer, 1847), 3.

37. Joseph Smith, *History of the Church*, 5:423–27; Words of Joseph Smith, 212–13.

38. Harold B. Lee, "Strengthen the Stakes of Zion," *Ensign*, July 1973, 4.

39. Ibid., 4–5, quoting Bruce R. McConkie.

40. Bruce R. McConkie, *A New Witness for the Articles of Faith* (Salt Lake City: Deseret Book, 1985), 578.

41. Hinckley, "New Temples to Provide 'Crowning Blessings' of the Gospel," 87–88.

42. *Hymns of The Church of Jesus Christ of Latter-day Saints* (Salt Lake City: The Church of Jesus Christ of Latter-day Saints, 1985), 292, 300, 301.

43. T. Edgar Lyon, "Doctrinal Development of the Church During the Nauvoo Sojourn, 1839–1846," *BYU Studies* 15, no. 4 (summer 1975): 438.

44. Ibid., 437.

45. Parley P. Pratt, *Autobiography of Parley P. Pratt*, ed. Parley P. Pratt Jr. (Salt Lake City: Deseret Book, 1938), 260.

46. Ibid., 259–60.

47. Joseph Smith, *Teachings of the Prophet Joseph Smith*, comp. Joseph Fielding Smith (Salt Lake City: Deseret Book, 1938), 301.

48. John A. Widtsoe, "Evidences and Reconciliations," *Improvement Era*, March 1942, 161.

49. "A Person's Behavior Governed by Beliefs, Pres. Hinckley Says," *Church News*, 14 March 1992, 11.

50. James E. Talmage, *The House of the Lord* (Salt Lake City: Deseret Book, 1969), 79.

51. James E. Faust, "Eternity Lies before Us," *Ensign*, May 1997, 20. 6

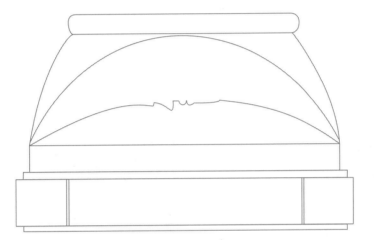

THE HOUSE OF THE LORD
Built by
THE CHURCH OF JESUS CHRIST
OF LATTER DAY SAINTS
Commenced April 6, 1841
HOLINESS TO THE LORD

West Elevation of the Nauvoo Temple, drawing, 2000, FFKR Architecture.

6

Travelers on the upper Mississippi in the mid 1840s could hardly escape viewing the prominent features of the temple as they approached Nauvoo. The city was located

CHAPTER SIX

EXTERIOR

FEATURES

on a horseshoe bend of the river, and the spire of its principal structure was visible from a distance of twenty or thirty miles.[1]

The building stood on the summit of a gently sloping bluff overlooking the lower town and the river. It was one of the choicest lots in the city. Charles Lanman, a western traveler, noted that "in the centre of this scene . . . stands the Temple of Nauvoo, which is unquestionably one of the finest buildings in this country."[2]

The temple faced to the west with its tower and main entrances on that end of the structure.[3] Frontage of the building was on what is now Wells Street, somewhere near the center of the block. The temple block was additionally bounded by what is now Bluff Street on the east, Mulholland Street on the south, and Knight Street on the north.

Nauvoo "was a prime attraction to Mississippi River tourist traffic . . . and the Nauvoo Temple [was an object] of particular interest."[4] It was reported that as early as mid-1843 four or five steamers a day would stop at Nauvoo.[5] A popular pastime with the citizens and visitors of the city was to climb either of the

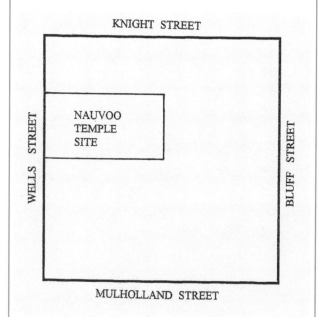

Figure 6.1 *Map of Temple Site, drawing, 2000, Don F. Colvin.*

winding stairways and behold the view afforded from the lofty tower of the temple. The view furnished from this vantage point was described with numerous adjectives by its patrons. The historian Thomas Gregg left this impression: "I took several occasions to look at the city and surrounding country from the top of the Temple. It is, indeed, a grand and imposing scene, and presents the most magnificent view to be found anywhere on the banks of the Mississippi."[6]

Another observer remarked: "The scene is rendered highly picturesque by being interspersed with large rolling praries, and relieved here and there, with groves of green wood, and tracts of woodland. Westward spreads 'the flat' all over which looms up the massive walls of hundreds of residences. . . . Beyond the river spreads the wood lands of Iowa, sprinkled here and there, with farm houses and cultivated fields. The little village of Montrose clusters upon the opposite bank."[7] In all, one could see for miles in all directions.

ARCHITECTURE

Probably no building in early America could be compared with the Nauvoo Temple as a prototype from which it had been copied. The building was a complexity of architectural designs, familiar and yet different from anything in ancient or modern history.[8] It was said to be "in style of architecture which no Greek, nor Goth, nor Frank ever dreamed . . . the style of architecture is exclusively the Prophet's own, and must be known as the Mormon Order."[9] Charles Lanman described it as "principally after the Roman style of architecture, somewhat intermixed with Grecian and Egyptian."[10] Joseph Fielding declared: "The Temple is indeed a noble Structure, and I suppose the Architects of our Day know not of What Order to call it Gothic, Dorick, Corinthian or What I call it Heavenly."[11]

The temple was a product of Joseph Smith, who planned its architecture in line with his concept of the building's purposes and supervised the project during much of its construction. The actual drawings were done by William Weeks, who drafted them under dictation of the Prophet.[12] Laurel Andrew explained: "Weeks' designs demonstrate his familiarity with the traditions of New England, but they are also a testament to the influx of modern ideas of the 1840's as transmitted primarily through the medium of architectural handbooks. His final plans do not depend on a specific source, and are novel in their . . . motifs, demonstrating, by comparison with the earlier plans, a greater proficiency in handling the architectural vocabulary."[13] Andrew goes on to explain that "the belief fostered by the Prophet that Weeks drafted the plans entirely under his dictation is no doubt true to a certain extent, but the building from its earliest stages clearly manifests a more sophisticated acquaintance with architectural styles . . . the most plausible assessment of each man's part in the building is to assign to Weeks those elements which are purely architectural, while crediting the determination of functional and symbolic requirements to the President himself."[14]

Source materials showing or describing the Nauvoo Temple are incomplete and sometimes contradictory. Surviving architectural sketches are few in number, and many of them are preliminary drawings. It is evident (based on comparison between daguerreotypes and architects' drawings) that changes and modifications were made in the final working plans and during construction.

Complete and accurate records were never made, or were not preserved, or else were lost due to the persecutions and forced exodus to the West. Various observations and reports are available, but these are not all consistent with each other. Available sketches and photographs are very helpful in determining external features of the building but not always satisfactory to verify the accuracy of written accounts regarding size, measurements of the building, some of its ornamental details, or its various parts.

Careful, detailed research, consultation with Church architects both past and present, and study and analysis of all available source materials lead to conclusions that provide the most likely and relatively accurate picture of what the temple was like. Future discovery of additional source material and data will either verify or cause revision of these impressions.

SIZE OF THE TEMPLE

Over the years, several different sets of external measurements have been reported, causing some confusion regarding the temple's size.[15] Measurements of the building's interior are clearly established and are consistent in the various written reports, along with architectural sketches and excavation reports. Internal measurements are uniformly shown to be 80 feet wide by 120 feet long. These figures are consistent on each floor level as explained with detailed verification in chapter 8. External dimensions of the building are most often described as either 88 feet by 128 feet[16] or 90 feet by 130 feet.[17] Both sets of figures are noted in several accounts and can be accepted as accurate depending on where (at what height) the measurements are taken. By adding the thickness of the walls to the well-established internal measurements, it is possible to determine the external dimensions, though it again depends on where the measurements are taken. It is most likely that the outside dimensions of the temple at the basement walls below ground level were 90 feet wide by 130 feet long.[18] The thickness of the walls is explained in the next section and can be studied by careful examination of Figure 6.2. The building was composed of a basement story, first story, second story, and a fully functional attic story. Each of the two main stories contained a mezzanine, or half-story, on each long side of the building in the recesses outside the central archway on each floor. Round windows in the half-stories made the structure look more like a four-story building with an "arrangement of two major and two minor divisions."[19] The attic story was divided into two parts—a regular sloping or gabled attic over the main part of the building and a rectangular boxlike structure on the west or front end of the building. Rising

from the center of this front attic section was the tower or steeple. At the top of the steeple the structure is described as rising to an overall height of 158½ feet.[20] A careful study of the original architectural plans and drawings establishes the height as 156 feet 5 inches from ground level to the top of the steeple.

The Walls

The walls of the temple represented a monumental task in building. They were an imposing work worthy of admiration. The building was mainly constructed of "fine white" native limestone, which resembled marble.[21]

Stones placed in the wall had been finished with great skill and were described as being "dressed with considerable neatness,"[22] and "worked and forced down to a perfect surface."[23] They "present a fine appearance when finished."[24] Archaeologists excavating the temple site in the 1960s found several pieces of stones in the rubble. They concluded that stones placed in the temple walls had been "given an overall tooled finish, and a border of about 1½ inches of channeling at right angles, or nearly so, to the edges. Stones used at corners could be identified by this finish on two adjacent sides."[25] A tooled 1½- or 2-inch border channeling was consistently used on stones at the corners of the building, at edges around window openings, and on the water table course of stones surrounding the entire building at the top of the foundation. Examples of these tooled borders can be viewed in Figure 6.5. The main wall panels between pilasters were believed to have been composed of stones having a vertical-striation textured finish, as shown in Figure 6.4. The pilaster shafts were composed of stones with a sanded or smooth untextured finish, while those used in the water table course of stones as well as those in the wall panels below them received a basket-weave textured finish enclosed within a channel-edged border (see Figure 6.5). Stones around the top arch of the large main windows, around all of the round windows, and surrounding the three arched entrances into the front vestibule all received a stipple-textured finish enclosed within a channel-edged border.[26] Stones in the frieze area (the 6-foot-high portion of the entablature) at the top of the walls appear to have received a rough or plain rustic finish. The tremendous effort, detail, and skill of the stoneworkers drew praise from viewers. One observer declared that the temple "is certainly an extraordinary specimen of human skill and industry."[27] Visitors impressed with both the exterior and the interior features of the temple were "continually astonished at the quality of material, and the accuracy and perfection exhibited in the completion of every part."[28]

The walls were strong and massive. They were made with an outer facing of heavier stones with rough, mostly irregular stones behind, all laid together with lime mortar. The procedure followed in laying the walls "was to lay the cut and tooled face stones first, which were of varying depth, into the wall; then to lay the backup or masonry in a solid mass behind

the face stones. Some face stones were much thicker than others, allowing bonding through the wall to form a unified mass."[29] The walls' thickness is variously described. One visitor to Nauvoo estimated them as 4 to 6 feet thick.[30] Another described them as about 3 feet thick in the basement by the baptismal font,[31] and still another as being at least 2 feet thick near the top of the walls.[32] One additional report described them as "of solid stone, four feet in thickness."[33] Accuracy on the thickness of the

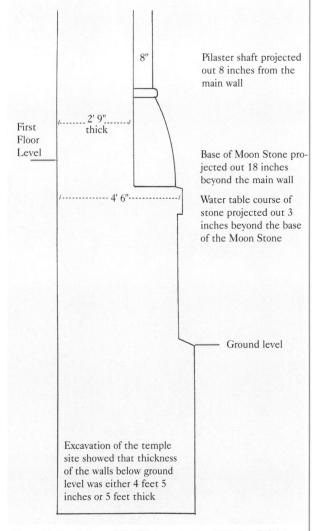

Figure 6.2 *Foundation and Wall Thickness, drawing, 2000, Don F. Colvin.*

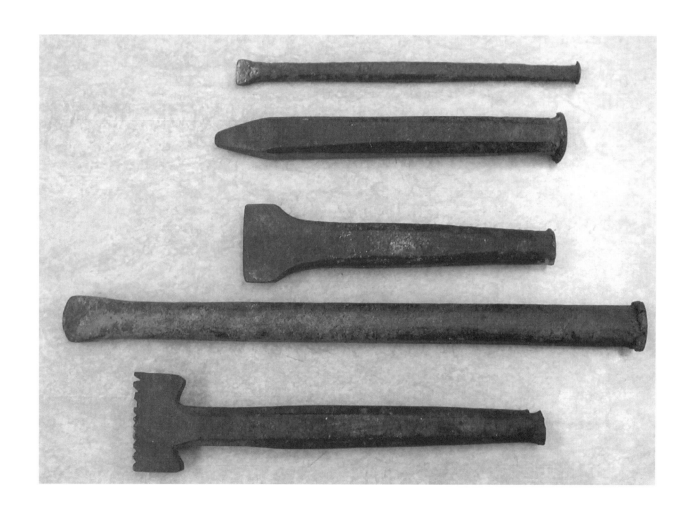

Figure 6.3 Alpheus Cutler's Stonecutting Tools, photograph, 18 August 2001, Don F. Colvin. Used by permission of the Community of Christ, World Headquarters, Independence, Missouri. Tools such as these were used by Alpheus Cutler, a member of the Nauvoo Temple Committee, and other stoneworkers for cutting, marking, forming, and texturing the rough limestone blocks that came from the quarry into finished stones, which were then placed in the walls of temple. The top tool is a 7½-inch-long flat chisel, ⅜-inch in diameter and ⅝-inch wide on the flat end. The second tool from the top is a 7½-inch-long pointed chisel, ¾-inch in diameter. The middle tool is a 6½-inch-long flat chisel, which is ¾-inch in diameter and 1½ inches wide on the flat end. The fourth tool down from the top is a 12-inch-long blunt-end chisel, which is ¾ inch in diameter. The bottom tool is an 8½-inch-long claw chisel, which is ¾-inch in diameter and 2 inches wide on the flat, claw-toothed end.

walls can now be established by examination of original architectural sketches and archeological evidence. The main outside stone walls are indicated by one preliminary drawing as being 2 feet 9 inches thick (see Figure 6.2). Another drawing, of an area around the main south front stairwell, shows the walls as 2 feet 10 inches thick (see Figure 7.11). The thickness of the walls was increased at the location of each of the thirty pilasters. The main shafts of these pilasters were 8 inches thicker than the wall panels between them. The sun stone or capital at the top of each pilaster extended out 17 inches, and the moon stones at the bottom of each pilaster shaft projected out 18 inches beyond the main wall. The thickest portion of the walls above ground level was where the water table course of stones encircled the building. This stone molding extended out an additional 3 inches beyond the bottom of each moon stone. The thickness of the walls in this area was 4 feet 6 inches. Each pilaster base (from ground level up to the water table stone molding) was either 19 or 20 inches thicker than the main wall, making the overall thickness of the walls at the pilaster base at least 4 feet 4 inches thick (see Figure 6.2). A close examination of the Chaffin daguerreotype (see Figure 5.4) indicates that the walls beneath the basement windows provided a sill, which appears to be part of a solid wall structure. This wall extended beyond the area under the window to cover the full space between pilaster bases. All of this leads to the conclusion that the walls of the temple from the footings up to the ground level were most like-

ly 5 feet thick. Walls under the front steps and in the corners of stairwells at the front of the building were easily 6 or more feet in thickness.

The size of the stones varied depending on their function. Most were uniform in size and shape, but others may have reached a reported weight of over four thousand pounds.[34] Some individual stones around each of the main windows on the outside wall bays are shown on sketches by the architect to be in courses of stone measuring 6½, 7½, and 10 inches in height. The length of stones in the wall bays also varies, but most appear to be about 24 inches long. Some stones taken from the temple ruins and used in other later buildings of Nauvoo have been measured as follows:

Length	Width	Thickness
2 feet	11 inches	10 inches
2 feet 11 in.	16 inches	12 inches
3 feet	16 inches	14½ inches
3 feet 8 in.	12 inches	13⅜ inches
4 feet	16 inches	8 inches
4 feet 4 in.	2 ft. 6½ in.	16 inches[35]

Rising from beneath the surface of the earth, walls at the square of the building were reported to have attained an overall height of some 60 feet above ground level.[36] This was up to the eaves of the second story and was as high as the stonework went, except for chimneys and possibly the railing piers of the balustrades. The stone walls started in the basement area 5 or 6 feet below ground level.[37] These foundation walls had no footings and commenced where large irregular loose stones were laid directly upon the native yellow clay of the basement excavation, cemented together with mortar.[38] Foundation walls were 12 feet high, having half of their elevation below the ground level.[39] They were apparently installed under the direction of the temple committee prior to the architect taking over full supervision of the project. This is the one area that Truman O. Angell described as "much botched" by them.[40]

Foundation walls were laid in March 1841, four months prior to the decision in July to build a font in the basement. When the baptismal font was constructed, more head room was required in the center of the basement at the font area. Rather than tear out basement walls and footings, they scooped out the center of the basement to accommodate the need for 4 additional feet of height. The floor of the basement was then sloped down from the sides and ends to the center at the font. This is explained in detail in chapter 8. Measuring from the floor to the crown of the arched ceiling, the inside height of the first story measured 25 feet (see Figure 7.1). The second story, largely a duplicate of the first, was of the same height (see Figure 7.1). Recesses between the arch and the outside wall on each of the two main floors made it possible to form or build a half-story at each level on both sides of the building (see Figure 7.1 and Figure 12.3). Preliminary architectural drawings have 30 feet penciled in on the plans for each of the two stories as well as 16 feet penciled in for the basement story (see Figure 7.1). We know for certain from archaeological excavation reports that even though the walls of the basement story remained at 12 feet, the floor area inside the walls was hollowed or scooped out in the center an additional 3 to 4 feet. This was done, as explained, to provide adequate head room above the baptismal font and resulted in increasing the basement height from 12 feet to 16 feet in the font area. It has now been established (by careful scaling of the daguerreotypes and study of billing records) that the penciled-in changes of height for upper portions of the building were never followed. The possible change in height may have been considered when Joseph Smith ordered that round windows be placed in the building to give light to the offices between stories.

> In the afternoon [5 February 1844], Elder William Weeks (whom I had employed as architect of the temple,) came in for instruction. I instructed him in relation to the circular windows designed to light the offices in the dead work of the arch between stories. He said that round windows in the broad side of a building were a violation of all the known rules of architecture, and contended that they should be semicircular—that the building was too low for round windows. I told him I would have the circles, if he had to make the temple ten feet higher than it was originally calculated; that one light at the centre of each circular window would be sufficient to light the whole room; that when the whole building was illuminated, the effect would be remarkably grand. "I wish you to carry out my designs. I have seen in vision the splendid appearance of that building illuminated, and will have it built to the pattern shown me."[41]

Figure 6.4 (Top) Stone with Vertical-Striation-Textured Finish, photograph, 7 April 2000, Ronald J. Prince, project manager, Nauvoo Temple Reconstruction Project, The Church of Jesus Christ of Latter-day Saints. This stone, typical of those used in main wall panels of the temple between pilasters, measured 8 inches in height by 23 inches in length. Buried for nearly 150 years, it was uncovered on 7 April 2000 as workers were clearing the site in preparation for rebuilding the temple. As a result of being covered and sheltered from the elements, it had been preserved in excellent condition. This stone had been given a vertical, striation-textured finish—sometimes referred to as an axe hammer strike—with fairly uniform vertical lines or grooves. Groove depth averaged no more than 3/32 of an inch and was generally spaced 3/8 of an inch from ridge to ridge on each side of the grooves.

Figure 6.5 (Bottom) Stone with Basket-Weave-Textured Finish, photograph, 7 April 2000, Ronald J. Prince, project manager, Nauvoo Temple Reconstruction Project, The Church of Jesus Christ of Latter-day Saints. This stone, believed to have been part of the water table course of stones, served as a corner base beneath one of the moon stones. A partial or broken piece of stone, it measures 10⅝ inches in height by 22 inches in length and is 13½ inches thick at its widest point. The front face of the stone has received a 2-inch-wide tooled border channeling on the top, bottom, and side edges. In the middle of this front facing, a 6-inch-high area was given a basket-weave finish consisting of horizontal lines (not over 1/16 of an inch in depth) crossed by very subtle vertical lines, creating a basket weave texturing of the stone face. The very top edge of the stone both on the front edge and the left end has a 3¼ inch tooled channeled finish, which tapers down ⅝ of an inch to facilitate moisture drainage from the walls. Having been buried for 150 years, this stone had suffered little or no weathering and provides a good illustration of the detailed stone texturing on many stones placed in walls of the temple.

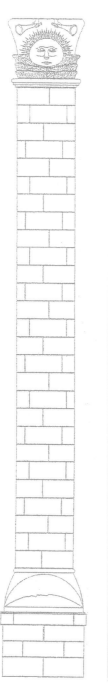

All documentary accounts, however, support the conclusion that the proposed changes were not required and windows were put into the building without adding any additional height. Careful examination of architectural sketches, and measurements of parts found in billing records, along with measuring and scaling of the various daguerreotypes, clearly support this view.

The Pilasters

The pilasters that formed a prominent part of the wall structure were a notable feature of the stonework. Jutting out from the wall surface, they numbered thirty in all, with nine on each long side and six on each end of the building.[42] Their design, including moon and sun stones along with the star stones immediately above them, was a remarkable feature of the temple. No clear explanations on the meaning or representation of these symbols on the Nauvoo Temple have been reported in the writings of the architect or early Church leaders. It has generally been accepted by Church members that these representations of the sun, moon, and stars gave emphasis to a theological concept symbolizing the three degrees of glory.[43] It is a religious concept fully embodied in the sacred purposes for which the building was erected. Commencing at their base below ground level, the pilasters ascended nearly to the eaves at the top of the wall. They were readily distinguished by the moon stone, located at the foundation level, and the sun stone, which was part of the capital or top of each pilaster. The total cost of each pilaster was estimated at three thousand dollars at a time when stone masons' pay was less than two dollars per day.[44]

Beneath each pilaster and commencing at ground level was a stone base 6 feet 2 inches wide.[45] This pilaster base column, 20 inches thicker than the main bays of the wall, was made up of several stones. Resting on top of each pilaster base and boldly projecting from it was a "water table" stone molding. This stone molding can be seen on the daguerreotypes projecting from the wall not only at the top of the pilaster base but also extending into the wall bays. According to architectural drawings and careful study of the daguerreotypes, this stone molding was about 11 inches in thickness or height and extended out 2 or 3 inches beyond the pilaster bases and wall bays (see Figure 6.2). This water table stone molding separated the pilaster base from the

Figure 6.6 (Top) Sun Stone, photograph, date, and photographer unknown, LDS Church Archives. This sun stone was originally part of the Nauvoo temple. Known as a capital, it was composed of five stones that combined together weighed over 4,000 pounds. A sun stone was placed at the top of each pilaster shaft. One of the sun stones being reproduced for the reconstructed temple required 358 man-hours with the use of modern powered chisels.

Figure 6.7 (Bottom) Moon Stones, photograph, date and photographer unknown, Utah State Historical Society. These stones were part of the original Nauvoo Temple. A moon stone formed the plinth or pedestal base for the pilaster shaft that rose above it. The moon stones for the reconstructed temple weigh approximately 4,000 pounds each.

plinth (moon stone) and pilaster shaft above. It provided a borderline course of stone surrounding the entire building, marking a division between the foundation and the rest of the building. As the walls were being constructed, it was reported that vertical recessions were placed "at regular intervals around the foundation to form the plinths or heavy stone bases, on the top of which rested the less heavy wall pilasters."[46] The plinth stones here mentioned were in reality the moon stones, which served as a solid support for the shaft of each pilaster. A representation of the pilasters is furnished in Figure 6.12.

Moon Stones, Sun Stones, and Star Stones

Moon stones, each carved from one piece of solid stone,[47] rested on top of the foundation at the commencement of the first story. They were a relief representation of a crescent moon with the crescent facing downward. Forming the plinth or base of each pilaster, they rested

on the water table course of stone and served as the bottom or pedestal support of each pilaster shaft. Each moon stone was 6 feet 2 inches in width at its bottom or base. It rose to a height of 3 feet 4 inches, where the width diminished to 4 feet 6 inches at the top of its juncture with the main shaft of the pilaster.[48]

Composed of many individual stones, each pilaster shaft measured 4 feet 6 inches wide, projected out 8 inches from the wall bays (see Figure 6.2),[49] and rose to a height of 50 feet from the ground level (including the base beneath the moon stone) to the top of the sun stone.[50]

On top of each pilaster shaft was a capital that included an image of the sun. Each capital was estimated to weigh over two tons and consisted of five different stones.[51] The bottom of each capital where it joined the main shaft of the pilaster was 4 feet 5 inches in width. The capital rose 4 feet 9 inches high and widened to a width of 6 feet at the top. It

Figure 6.8 Star Stone, photograph, date, and photographer unknown, LDS Church Archives. A star stone was situated within the frieze area of the entablature directly above each pilaster. These stones each measured 3 feet wide by 4 feet 4 inches high. The stars were composed of five rays with the bottom ray extended. This particular stone, originally part of the Nauvoo Temple, was removed from the ruins and taken to Keokuk, Iowa.

projected out 8 inches from the wall at its base and 17 inches at its crest.[52] The sun stones were part of the capitals that formed the top of each pilaster. These capitals were well described by Brigham Young on the occasion of laying the last capstone. He stated: "There are thirty capitals around the Temple, each one composed of five stones, *viz.*, one base stone, one large stone representing the sun rising just above the clouds, the lower part obscured; the third stone represents two hands each holding a trumpet, and the last two stones form a cap over the trumpet stone, and these all form the capital, the average cost of which is about four hundred and fifty dollars each. These stones are very beautifully cut, especially the face and trumpet stones, and are an evidence of great skill in the architect and ingenuity on the part of the stonecutters. They present a very pleasing and noble appearance, and seem very appropriate in their places."[53] The sun stone and moon stone can be examined by viewing Figures 6.6 and 6.7.

Above the pilaster system was the stone entablature that extended to the top of the wall and girded the building at its height. The entablature overhung the walls by 8 inches, matching the projection of the pilaster shafts below. This entablature was divided into an architrave "belt course of stone, and then six feet of plain cut stone."[54] Within this plain cut stone area were smaller round windows that provided light to the second half-story. Also in this area, a short distance above the capitals or tops of each pilaster and directly in line with them, were the star stones. The base or encasement of each star stone measured 3 feet 1½ inches wide by 6 feet high. The star stone itself measured 3 feet by 4 feet 4 inches and projected out 3 inches from the wall face (see Figure 6.9). The base itself appears to have projected out 6 or 8 inches from the wall. This symbolic decoration was composed of large stars with five spangles or rays, with the bottom ray elongated. They were positioned in the entablature just below a large, beautiful cornice, which ran around the eaves of the building. These star stones are easily visualized in the architect's drawing and in photographs (see Figures 6.8 and 6.9).

Cornice and Eaves

Above the stone walls were the eaves of the building, which projected at least 4 feet over the walls. An observer standing near the building looking up under the eaves could not help but be impressed by another symbolic decorative feature in the cornice area on the underside of the eaves. This cornice projection contained sixty stars, which were each placed within square mutules. These mutules are shown in Weeks's drawings to be 21 inches square, and they made up the largest part of the cornice area under the eaves. Close photographic analysis has proven that the cornice, eaves, and mutules were all built considerably larger than originally drawn by Weeks. The mutules as a part of the cornice were each "ornamented on the lower side with large stars," carved in wood or fashioned from hammered metal sheets (see Figure 6.10).[55] There was one of these stars directly above each of the small windows, as

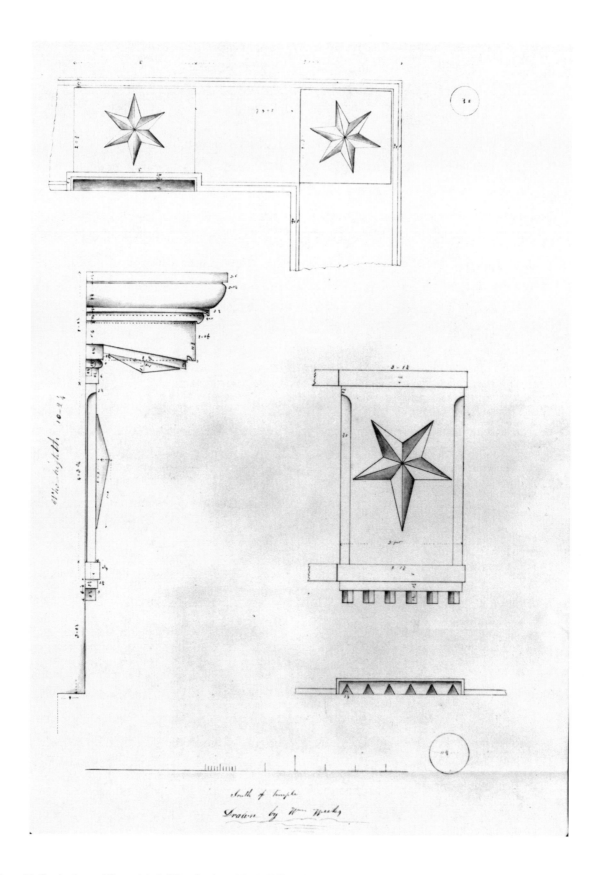

Figure 6.9 Cornice Area and Eaves of the Building, drawing, 1842–45, William Weeks, LDS Church Archives. This is an original architectural drawing by architect William Weeks. It contains three sections: section A, on the left side is a drawing of the cornice area under the eaves of the building; section B, the upper area at the top of the drawing shows the drawing of mutules—of which sixty with stars were placed under the eaves of the building—that were carved from wood or fabricated from metal; section C, on the right side is the drawing of a star stone, and there were thirty of these stones placed on the building in a direct line above each of the pilasters. A side view of these stones is shown in the left side of the drawing.

well as above each star stone and one at each corner of the cornice surrounding the entire building. Each star was in relief 3½ inches at the center, and the points receded in relief as they extended outward over the mutule surface (see Figure 6.9). Stars in this area were six pointed, as will be noted in the architectural drawings (see Figure 6.9). Several stars carved in wood or stone, or fashioned from metal, were also located on panels of the balustrades. An additional forty stars can be seen on the fascia at the top of the belfry. There is also some indication in enlargements of the Chaffin daguerreotype that additional stars may have been located on the fascia below the dome and just above the observatory level of the tower. These, along with the angelic weather vane, completed the placing of heavenly symbols on the exterior of the temple.

The Attic Sections

Above the stone walls on the west end of the building rose the front attic story, often referred to as the half-story. This boxlike rectangular attic section on the front of the building measured 86 to 87 feet long from north to south, essentially the same width as the main building. It extended back 36 to 37 feet in width and rose 16½ feet in height above the eaves of the main wall.[56] The roof of this section was relatively flat with a slight slope (see Figure 7.8). It was enclosed by a balustrade, or railing, of beautiful workmanship, which extended around the front of the structure.[57] This section of the building was lighted by eight rectangular windows about 4 feet wide and 5 feet high. There was room in the wall on the east side of this box attic for two more windows above the slope of the east attic roof; but it is not known if any windows were built in this area. Directly under the tower and on the front side of this attic section was an inscription in golden letters. It read:

This section of the building was lighted by eight rectangular windows.

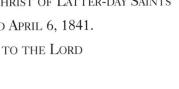

THE HOUSE OF THE LORD

BUILT BY

THE CHURCH OF JESUS CHRIST OF LATTER-DAY SAINTS

COMMENCED APRIL 6, 1841.

HOLINESS TO THE LORD

The entire attic story was constructed of wood and composed of two sections. The main attic section extended back to the east, stretching over the central part of the building. Inside it measured 88 feet 2 inches long by 56 feet 8 inches wide and was not quite as high as the west attic section.[58] The pitched roof structure of this main attic was pierced by two elegant chimneys on each side of the roof. They were made of hewn stone.[59] At the peak of this attic roof was a balustrade that enclosed a promenade on the decked roof of this area. The pitched roof of this attic was covered by white pine shingles "perfectly matched and laid in the neatest manner."[60] Light was provided to this east attic area by skylights in the roof along with a large window in the east end.

The Tower or Steeple

Rising with a telescopic effect above the front attic section of the temple was an octagonal tower. It added an attractive and imposing appearance to the building. The base section rose from the top of the 16½-foot-high attic, extending 12½ feet above it. This section along with its support structure in the attic section below measured 29 feet in diameter (see Figure 7.3). On the east side of this tower base, a small door opened onto the decked roof of the main or east attic section.[61] Above the tower base was the belfry section, somewhat narrower (22 feet in diameter) and rising 20 feet in height. In between the shuttered window openings and standing out from the outer walls of the belfry section were pillars or columns, which supported the well-decorated cornice and eaves above. This is clearly visible on the enlarged section of the Chaffin daguerreotype (see Figure 6.10). Next came the clock section (also 22 feet in diameter) rising 10 feet 8 inches above the belfry below. The last section (17 feet in diameter) was the observatory, which rose an additional 16 feet and provided a balcony for all-around observation purposes. The dome section added another 7 feet 10 inches to the height of the steeple and appears to be about 13 to 14 feet in diameter at its base. Divided into eight sections, it corresponded to the octagonal shape of the steeple (see Figure 6.10). Covered with tin or zinc, it was a "silvery capped dome."[62] Two openings in the top provided access to the rod at the summit of the steeple. A small ladder could be seen going up over the dome.[63] Coming out from the top of the dome was the ball and rod that rose 12 feet 8 inches higher, supporting an angelic weather vane.[64]

Plans were made early to have the ball and rod at the summit of the tower, ornamented by a horizontal figure of a flying angel. According to the sketches of the architect, it was to be about 5 feet long (see Figure 7.6). The installed angelic weather vane was described as being 7 feet in length and formed of some substantial metal, which some thought to be bronze but was more likely tin or zinc.[65] On 19 December 1845 the Tinners Association submitted a bill for labor on the temple. This bill included twenty-four days of labor for making the vane and nine days of labor making balls and ornaments for the spire.[66] The vane was

Figure 6.10 Detail of Chaffin Daguerreotype (see Figure 5.4).

SECTION OF THE TEMPLE WALL

FIGURE 6. 11 WINDOWS: WITHIN MAIN WALL PANELS BETWEEN PILASTERS

Historic Reconstruction Drawing, 2000, FFKR Architecture, Used By Permission of the LDS Church.

SMALL ROUND STAR WINDOW
[3 feet in diameter] There were 26 of these windows within the walls of the temple.

UPPER LARGE MAIN WINDOW
[10 feet 1 inch high by 4 feet 10 inches wide] There were 47 of these windows in the temple, 25 on this level and 22 on the lower level.

LARGE ROUND WINDOW
[4 feet 10 inches in diameter] There were 22 of these windows in the temple.

LOWER LARGE MAIN WINDOW
[10 feet 1 inch high by 4 feet 10 inches wide] There were 47 of these windows in the temple, 22 on this level and 25 on the upper level.

BASEMENT WINDOW [at ground level]
[4 feet 10 inches wide by 3 feet 11 inches high] There were 21 windows in the basement area.

FIGURE 6. 12 PILASTER

Historic Reconstruction Drawing, 2000, FFKR Architecture, Used By Permission of the LDS Church. The Walls of the Temple contained 30 pilasters which were described as 50 feet in height.

STAR STONE
Within the frieze area of the entablature above each pilaster there was a Star Stone which measured 3 feet wide by 4 feet 4 inches high.

CAPITAL or SUNSTONE
Measures 4 feet 5 and ½ inches high by 5 feet 11 inches wide at the top and 4 feet 6 inches wide at the bottom.

PILASTER SHAFT
Measures 4 feet 6 inches wide by 36 feet in length or height.

MOONSTONE [or Plinth]
Measures 3 feet 3 and ¾ inches high by 4 feet 6 inches wide at the top by 6 feet 2 inches wide at the bottom.

PILASTER BASE
The base was 6 feet 4 inches in height and consisted of several stones.

Figure 6.11 Windows: Within Main Wall Panels between Pilasters, drawing, 2000, FFKR Architecture, The Church of Jesus Christ of Latter-day Saints; hereafter cited as FFKR Architecture.

Figure 6.12 Pilaster, drawing, 2000, FFKR Architecture. The walls of the temple contained thirty pilasters that were described as being 50 feet in height.

attached in place at the top of the steeple on 30 January 1846.[67] It has been concluded that it was fastened in a position horizontal to the ground in such a way as to revolve in the wind.[68] Perrigrine Sessions reported: "On this day they raised the veign [vane] which is the representation of an Angel in his Priestly robe with the book of Mormon in one hand and a trumpet in the other which is over lain with gold leaf."[69] This angelic figure was described as being "gilded like burnished gold."[70] On 2 August 1845 the temple committee ordered from the firm of Bacon and Hyde, "60 books of gold leaf."[71] On 17 November 1845 the committee purchased from Amos Davis a "pack of gold leaf."[72] Part of these purchases may have been used to gild the angel weather vane as well as the balls ornamenting the spire. "The bronze ball [also apparently covered with gold leaf], and silvery capped dome" were described as "[appearing] like a blazing star in the firmament."[73]

Evidence that an angel was installed is plentiful. A person visiting the temple in 1846 described a glittering angel with a trumpet in his hand, near the top of the steeple.[74] This report is substantiated by the testimony of Thomas L. Kane, who likewise visited the building in 1846. He stated that the Saints had remained in Nauvoo and succeeded, in spite of opposition, in completing the temple, "even the gilding of the angel and trumpet on the summit of its lofty spire."[75] Another witness of the angel's existence was the Prophet's young son Joseph Smith III. He recorded that he watched the building rise from its foundation to the gilded angel that swung at the top of the spire."[76] Enlarged copies of the Chaffin daguerreotype show what appears to be the angelic weather vane in a horizontal position at the top of the spire. The most likely conclusion is that this photograph shows the angel or angelic weather vane in place at the top of the spire during the summer of 1846 (see Figure 6.10). The possible fate of this angelic weather vane is discussed in chapter 11.

Observers described the overall height of the building from ground level to the top of the rod at the summit of the steeple as 158½ feet.[77] A careful study of the original architectural plans and drawings establishes the height as 156 feet 5 inches.

The tower was richly ornamented with many cornices and one level of Corinthian pillars.[78] Emblems were carved on many of the different pieces of the tower, making this area a very attractive as well as functional part of the structure.[79] The tower itself was painted white except for the shutters, which were painted green.[80]

Windows

The building was well illuminated in the daytime by sunlight streaming in through its numerous windows. The basement story was lighted by windows in the form of a fanlight half-circle. Flat at the bottom, these semicircular windows were described to be about 5 feet wide and 5 feet high in the center of the arch.[81] More accurate figures (determined by study of architectural drawings) establish these windows as 4 feet 10 inches wide and about 3 feet 11 inches high. There were eight of these windows on each side with five more on the east end, making a total of twenty-one windows lighting the basement area (see Figure 6.11). These windows, containing twenty-one panes of glass, consisted of a fanlight upper portion with a single row of five panes below.

The first story was lighted by large triple-hung windows, with a fanlight window section at the top. An identical style and size of window was used to illuminate the second story. There were a total of forty-seven of these large main windows in the building.[82] The dimensions of these large windows are provided by preliminary drawings of the architect. These drawings indicate that openings in the stone walls to accommodate the windows were 4 feet 10 inches wide by 10 feet 1 inch high in the center at the top of the half-circle fanlight window (see Figures 6.11 and 7.7).[83] The window area was divided into three sections. Each lower and upper window or sash contained fifteen panes of glass. Each pane of glass measured 10 inches wide by 14 inches high.[84] The lower section or sash could be opened for ventilation, as can be seen by the open windows shown in the daguerreotypes. "The middle sash sections as well as the upper sash fanlight sections may also have been operable. There was room within the box frames on each side for sash weights. In 1842 the temple committee purchased sixty-four sash pulleys, which were probably used in these windows."[85] In the top sash section there were fourteen panes of glass

arranged in a fanlight pattern with the representation of an all-seeing eye located at the bottom in the center of this window (see Figure 7.7 for the architect's drawing of these windows). The fanlight window area measured 2 feet 5 inches high at the top of the arch, and the two lower sashes below totaled 7 feet 8 inches in height (see Figure 7.7).[86] The first- and second-story interiors were both well lighted by "a perfect flood of light from their sixteen large windows, eight on each side."[87]

Between these two rows of main windows, which provided light for the first and second stories, was a row of round windows. These round windows lighted rooms in the first half-story. There were twenty-two of these larger round windows, including eight on each side of the building, two on the front, and four more on the back or east end.[88] According to architectural drawings, these windows were 4 feet 10 inches in diameter and composed of thirty-six glass panes arranged in a wheel pattern (see Figure 6.11).

Located in the entablature above the capitals and between each of the star stones ran another row of smaller circular windows, furnishing light to rooms of the second half-story. These round windows show five-pointed star patterns in the window panes (see Figures 6.11 and 7.9). They were described as containing glass of "divers colors"[89] and as having "painted glass, the colors red, white and blue."[90] According to drawings of the architect, these windows were about 3 feet in diameter. Emil Vallet, a Frenchman belonging to the Icarian Society that purchased the standing walls of the temple after its destruction by fire, produced a painting of the temple in 1863. In his painting, he shows all the round windows and the fanlight portions of all other windows in the temple having red, yellow, and blue panes of glass. It is not known if he was taking artistic license or if he had received this insight from witnesses who had viewed the temple. A black-and-white copy of his painting can be viewed in Figure 3.6. There were twenty-six of these smaller round windows, with eight on each side and five on each end of the building.

At least eight rectangular-shaped, double-hung windows provided ample illumination to the west attic section.[91] These windows appear to be about 4 feet wide by 5 feet high. There were possibly two additional windows on the east side of this attic section. Temple account books contain information showing that panes of glass measuring 10 inches by 12 inches were placed in these windows.[92]

The east attic over the main building contained several skylight windows in the roof, as

Figure 6.13 Palladian, Venetian Windows, drawing, 1842–45, William Weeks, LDS Church Archives. This is an original architectural drawing by architect William Weeks showing one of the two large windows on the east or back end of the building. This window measured 9 feet 7 inches wide by 15 feet high. Placed in the center of the east wall on both the first and second story of the building, these windows provided illumination to the area directly behind the pulpits on each floor level.

will be detailed in the next section describing that area. Also in the center of the gable or east end of the attic was "constructed the frame of a window twenty and a half feet in the span, which forms four gothic windows, and three irregular triangles which partake of the eliptic and gothic."[93] A visitor to this attic area left this helpful description: "Coming down we were ushered into the Council Chamber, which is a large low room, lighted by one large half-circle window at the end and several small skylights in the roof."[94] No further descriptions or details can be found to determine the height or other features of this large end window.

There is clear evidence to indicate that skylights were constructed at the top and on each side of the decked roof over the east attic. If these reports are correct, then this main attic roof area contained a total of eighteen skylight windows. "Upon the top of the building, or deck . . . is constructed six octagon sky-lights through which light will be reached into the large room below."[95] This was the large central "council room" where the endowment ordinances were conducted. Lower on the roof on each side of the deck, there was a second set of six windows on each side of the roof. "In each of these roofs, is six square skylights through which, light will be reached into the small rooms immediately below."[96] These skylights provided light to each of the twelve offices on the sides of this east attic. Emily Austin, a non-Mormon who lived in Nauvoo and spent some fourteen years among the Latter-

ters or open louvers are located in the bell section of the tower, and windows were provided in the observatory and clock section. An enlargement of the Chaffin daguerreotype shows that diamond-shaped glass panes are visible in both levels of these tower windows.[98]

At the east end or rear of the building were two large venetian or palladian-style windows measuring 9 feet 7 inches wide and 15 feet high.[99] One of these windows was on the level of the first story and the other on the level of

The pitch of the roof was not sev

and companion walked all over

where, grasping one of the chim

day Saints, described this east attic roof area, having visited the temple as a youth. She reported, "We went into every part of the temple except into the endowment room. We were, however, on top of that, and removed some of the windows and looked in, as we did not intend to leave the place until our curiosity was perfectly satisfied."[97]

Additional long, narrow windows were located in the tower. What appear to be shut-

the second story. What appears to be the architect's drawing of these windows can be seen in Figure 6.13. The reconstruction drawings (see Figure 6.15) show a conceptual view of how the various windows may have appeared in both the walls and attic section of the temple's east end.

The Roof

The roof over the west front attic section had only a slight pitch and was covered with

white pine shingles (see Figure 7.8).[100] As can be seen from artists' sketches, daguerreotypes, and written descriptions, this attic section was enclosed by an artistic balustrade. The east portion of the attic over the main part of the building was enclosed by a pitched roof, which at its apex appeared to be near the same height as the west half-story front attic. This roof was made of "white pine shingles and [one inch] plank sheathing,"[101] having "an admirable system of joining and joint covering."[102] At the top

covered or sheeted with metal. He then went on to further describe the rest of the pitched roof: "At each side of the deck is a roof made of pine shingles perfectly matched and laid in the neatest manner."[104] Access to this roof area was made possible through a small door located on the east side of the steeple's base section.[105]

Near the bottom of the roof on each side were what were described as two elegant ornamental chimneys of hewn stone, running through each roof."[106] The pitch of the roof was

d was described as "so nearly flat that ourself

thout difficulty or danger, approaching the sides

, the sentries below looked like pigmies."

of this pitched roof there was a flatter area often described as a deck roof or promenade.[103] This deck roof was described in some detail by Lyman O. Littlefield: "We stand upon the top of the building, or deck, in which is constructed six octagon sky-lights through which light will be reached into the large room below. The deck is finished in the same manner that some of our eastern rooms is ceiled; or in other words in ceiling form, perfectly water tight," possibly

not severe and was described as "so nearly flat that ourself and companion walked all over it without difficulty or danger, approaching the sides where, grasping one of the chimneys, the sentries below looked like pigmies."[107]

The eave troughs at the edges of the roof were reported to have been lined or "sheeted with sixty-five hundred pounds of lead" and capable of holding "thirty barrels of water."[108] It had been planned to run rain water from the

troughs of the eaves "into a large reservoir at the east end of the building from which the baptismal fount will be supplied with water."[109] No reports can be found to describe this reservoir unless it was the water storage tank located in the east end of the basement as described in the excavation reports.[110] Due to the early exodus from Nauvoo, it is likely that the proposed reservoir was never constructed.

Part of the roof had been covered by sheet lead as an experiment. As the *Times and Seasons* reported: "The *first* roof of the Temple, has been made of white pine shingles and plank. The *second,* (for a building which will cost about *two millions*) most probably, will be constructed of zinc, lead, copper, or porcelain. An experiment of sheet lead, covering a portion of the shingles, has already been made."[111]

A balustrade was built along the sides of the east attic, matching the one around the west attic. It appears that an additional matching balustrade was constructed at the ridge level of the pitched roof (around or enclosing the deck roof) over the main attic. This type of roof adaptation is visible in daguerreotypes of the building and is most clearly visualized in the Easterly daguerreotype (see Figure 3.7).

Front of the Temple

Entrance into the building was gained by passing through one of three large open archways into what might be called the outer court or front vestibule of the temple. This main front entrance was located on the west end of the building. The outer court was reached by climbing a flight of eight stone steps (each with an 8-inch rise), that ascended to a height of 5 feet 4 inches above ground. Inside the semicircular arched entrances were two additional steps (each with a 6-inch rise) that brought one to the level of the first story, some 6 feet 4 inches above ground level (see Figure 2.3). The steps and the front entrance can be seen clearly in Figure 2.3. The arched entrances were described as being 9 feet 7 inches wide and 21 feet high.

The open vestibule area measured 43 feet long from north to south and 17 feet wide or deep. On the inside, near each end of this outer court or vestibule were two large doors.[112] Passing through these, a person would then be in the first story of the building. The three central wall bays between pilasters at the front of the building were wider than similar bays on the sides of the building. This became necessary in order to accommodate the large entryways into the front vestibule. It also served as "a visual relief. This technique was employed by the early Greeks; it was called *entasis*."[113] "It is a characteristic employed anciently in Greek orders of architecture and in many examples of American Greek revival architecture of the 1820s through the 1840s."[114] A fairly accurate view of the front of the temple can be obtained by studying and comparing four sources: (1) the preliminary sketch by the architect (Figure 2.3); (2) the architectural rendering attributed to Baird and Nauvoo Restoration (Figure 1.2), which is an excellent work and the most accurate artistic reproduction of the temple (this

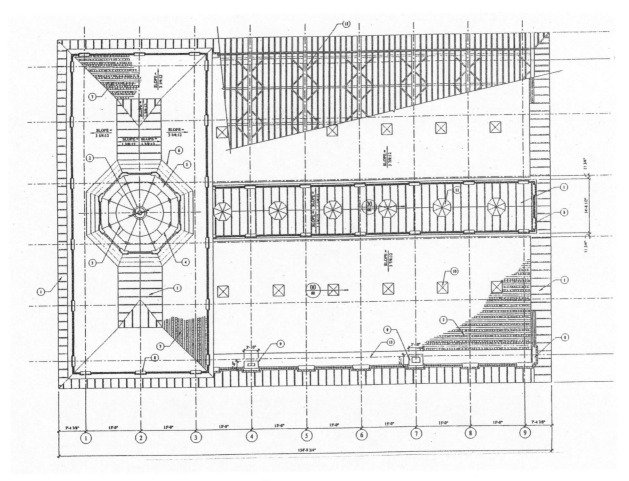

Figure 6.14   Roof Plan of the Temple, drawing, 2000, FFKR Architecture.

sketch is correct except for the top of the steps, of which two were inside of the arched entrances; and the color of the dome, which was silver in color rather than gold); (3) the Chaffin daguerreotype, which is the best available photograph of the building (Figure 5.4); and, (4) the tintype photograph of the front ruins taken about 1850 (Figure 11.2).

East End of the Building

There are no known photographs or confirmed historical sketches of this section of the building. Sources providing data on this portion of the structure furnish only minimal informa-

tion and are limited to descriptions of some windows. These have been detailed and illustrated in the section above describing the various windows of the building. From these we know that on each of the two main stories there was a large venetian-style window, at least one of which measured 9 feet 7 inches wide by 15 feet high.[115]

The three central wall bays were of necessity wider than those on the sides. This would be essential in balancing the overall width of the east wall and to accommodate the large venetian windows in the center on each floor level. In the east end of the attic story there

Figure 6.15 East Elevation of the Nauvoo Temple, drawing, 2000, FFKR Architecture.

was also a large window 20½ feet in width.[116] Figure 2.2 shows William Weeks's preliminary conception of how both ends of the building were to look prior to his revised design that changed the front gable to a rectangular boxlike front attic. It is believed that the east end of the building retained the same gable design and wide elliptical windows as earlier designed for both ends.[117] This area of the temple can be visualized by studying the historical reconstruction drawing (Figure 6.15).

The Grounds

The level terrain of the temple block posed few problems in construction or landscaping. The grounds were intended for beautification and as a site for additional Church structures. No mention is made of landscaping in the available records, but the ground was cleared around the temple in June 1845.[118] Owing to the practice of the Saints to beautify their residences with flowers and shrubs, it is safe to conclude that some efforts were made to enrich the beauty of the temple grounds. It is questionable that extensive work was undertaken, however, or it would have been recorded; and if intended, it may have been set aside because of the exodus to the West. Had the Church been allowed to remain in Nauvoo, the grounds around the temple undoubtedly would have been covered with trees, flowers, and shrubbery similar to Church temple sites today.

Of particular interest is a project commenced in the spring of 1845. Part of a planned improvement of the grounds, it was announced in the *Times and Seasons:* "A trench is being excavated about six feet wide and six feet deep, around a square of about six or eight acres, which will be filled with stone, and upon which will be placed an iron fence for the security of the Temple, and Tabernacle."[119] As reported by Brigham Young in late June 1845, the project was to be an iron picket fence 8 feet high, with a 5-foot-thick foundation at the base. He stated that the wall on the north side was nearly complete at that time.[120] A letter of Brigham Young published 15 July 1845 in the *Millennial Star* stated that the fence would also enclose the block west of the temple.[121] This massive project would also have been completed and made its contribution to

The level terrain of the temple block posed few problems in construction or landscaping.

the beauty of the grounds had the Saints been permitted to stay in Nauvoo to enjoy their city and temple. As guards were placed around the temple for security purposes, a watch house was built near the southwest corner of the building. This can be viewed by examining daguerreotypes of the building (Figures 5.4 and 8.13). Pine torches and lanterns were utilized to illuminate the temple grounds at night. The builders had "4 large lanterns made for the purpose and placed 25 feet from each corner of the Temple to keep a light by night."[122]

Church leaders recognized that the temple would accommodate only a small portion of the growing congregation, so an effort was made to provide additional meeting space. Prior to his death, Joseph Smith counseled the Saints to erect a tabernacle on the temple block.[123] Consequently, Brigham Young appointed Orson Hyde to chair the project, raise the required funds, and purchase the materials. This action was taken in June 1845. The structure was to be made of canvas and would cost between one and two thousand dollars.[124] Hyde went east to purchase the four thousand yards of cloth, and an Elder Egan went to St. Louis to purchase 125 dollars worth of hemp for making rope.[125] Orson Pratt described Hyde's mission and the proposed tabernacle: "Pres. Orson Hyde . . . is now in the east. His mission is to collect tything for the purpose of purchasing 4000 yards of canvas in this city. It is intended to erect a tabernacle of canvas in front of, and joining the Temple on the west. The form of this tabernacle will be that of an ellipse; its longer axis running north and south, parallel to the front of the Temple. Its height will be 75 feet in the centre; its sides sloping at an angle of 45 degrees. The area of its base will be sufficient to contain eight or ten thousand persons; its seats will gradually rise one above another in the form of an amphitheatre. This will be intended for preaching to the vast congregation; while the temple will be used for the meeting of councils and quorums, and the administrations of ordinances and blessings, and preaching to smaller congregations."[126]

It is estimated that "the Nauvoo Tabernacle would have been approximately 250 feet long and 125 feet wide."[127] Hyde's mission was successful. Visiting the main branches of the Church in the East, he succeeded in raising the required funds. He purchased the canvas and had it shipped to Nauvoo.[128] On Saturday, 18 October, Heber C. Kimball reported that Orson Hyde had "returned home from the east and brought five thousand yards of topsail Russia duck."[129] Since an exodus had been announced and was being planned for the following spring, use of the canvas was now diverted for tents and wagon covers.[130] Some of it was utilized in the attic story of the temple to partition the large council room of the east attic for performance of the endowment ordinances.[131] This canvas was later removed from the temple when ordinance work ceased and was likely utilized for tents and wagon covers.

A Work of Love

The exterior features of the temple seem to have been completed in every particular.

The detail and excellence exhibited in carvings, polishing and texture, finishing of stonework, and painting of woodwork was widely praised. In light of conditions existing during construction, Church leaders could easily have opted for a course of expediency. They would have been justified in slapping together a utilitarian structure to get by until circumstances would allow building a better, more permanent building. Instead, and in spite of all obstacles, they chose to build as if they would live there for generations. It was from beginning to end a work of love, dedication, reverence, and highest quality. No effort was spared in producing the finest building possible. Only limited shortcuts were taken. As Tim Maxwell explains:

Figure 6.16 West Elevation of the Nauvoo Temple, drawing, 2000, FFKR Architecture.

> Shortcuts that may have been taken were only those that in fact improved the purpose or functions of the Temple. Around the second floor windows, sixteen-inch-high courses of stone were used consistently, where courses averaging eight inches had predominated in the courses below

that. This is very apparent in a 16 by 20 enlargement of the Chaffin daguerreotype. From my experience as a youth in helping to open a stone quarry, and later in laying stone, I believe those in the Nauvoo quarry may have reached a better stratum of stone that was as easy to remove in large pieces as smaller. Less blasting powder would have been required for which the Temple accounts report they were paying $4.50 per bag. That compared to $2.50 per bag of white lead for paint. Fifty feet of "fuse rope" cost 75 cents. These were items that took scarce cash out of the community. It takes a little less labor to cut a large stone than to cut two smaller ones that total the same weight. Although larger stones must have given some inconsistent appearance to the facade, it actually improved quantity and performance of those courses.

The courses in the frieze appear in the daguerreotype to have been of rustic texture. While this was somewhat less time-consuming than many of the textures used lower on the

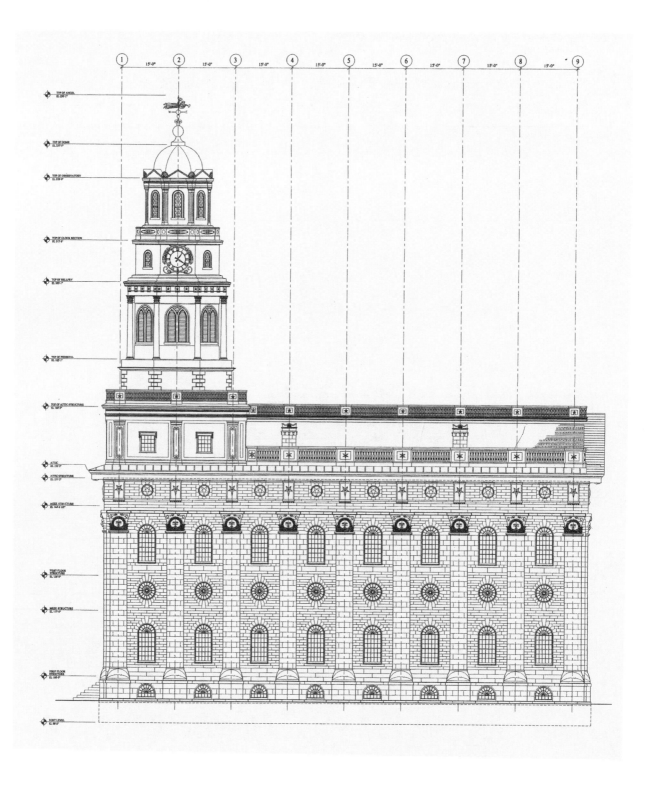

Figure 6.17 South Elevation of the Nauvoo Temple, drawing, 2000, FFKR Architecture.

building, it was an esthetic improvement, helping to emphasize the capping of the walls, and enhancing the shadow effect under the eaves.[132]

For six eventful years, Church members had shared a focus on building the temple and looking forward to its use and the blessings it would bring. After all this sacrifice and toil, one can only imagine the emotions they felt as they left this magnificent building to depart into the wilderness. It was for many as hard to leave their beloved temple as it was to leave behind their comfortable homes. Priddy Meeks reflected the feelings common to many: "While crossing over a ridge seven miles from Nauvoo, we looked back and took a last sight of the Temple we ever expected to see. We was sad and sorrowful. The emotions of our mind at that time I cannot describe."[133] A typical last look back by departing exiles is recorded by Lewis Barney: "On reaching the summit between the Mississippi and Des Moines Rivers the company made a halt for the purpose of taking a last and peering look at the Nauvoo Temple. The spire of which was then glittering in the bright shining sun. The last view of the temple was witnessed in the midst of sighs and lamentations all faces in gloom and sorrow bathed in tears at being forced from our homes and Temple that had cost us so much toil and suffering to complete its erection."[134]

NOTES

1. *Hancock Eagle*, 24 April 1846.

2. Charles Lanman, *A Summer in the Wilderness* (New York: D. Appleton, 1847), 31.

3. Journal History, 12 June 1844, LDS Church Archives, citing *Saint Louis Gazette* and *Nauvoo Patriot*, 8 December 1856; also, *Deseret News*, 20 February 1937.

4. James L. Kimball Jr., "Nauvoo Restoration Pioneer: A Tribute," *BYU Studies* 32, nos. 1–2 (winter and spring 1991): 96.

5. Dennis Rowley, "Nauvoo: A River Town," *BYU Studies* 18, no. 2 (winter 1978): 258.

6. Thomas Gregg, *Missouri Republican*, as cited in David R. Crockett, *Saints in the Wilderness* (Tucson: LDS Gems, 1997), 186.

7. *New-York Messenger* 2 (30 August 1845): 68.

8. *Hancock Eagle*, 24 April 1846; also, Journal History, 15 June 1843.

9. Journal History, 12 June 1844.

10. Lanman, *A Summer in the Wilderness*, 31.

11. Joseph Fielding, "The Nauvoo Journal of Joseph Fielding," ed. Andrew F. Ehat, *BYU Studies* 19, no. 2 (winter 1979): 158.

12. John W. Gunnison, *The Mormons, or, Latter-day Saints in the Valley of the Great Salt Lake* (Philadelphia: J. B. Lippincott, 1856), 116; also, Jenson, *Historical Record* 8 (June 1889): 858.

13. Laurel Andrew, "The Nineteenth-Century Temple Architecture of the Latter-day Saints" (Ph.D. diss., University of Michigan, 1973), 90.

14. Ibid., 90–91.

15. Stanley B. Kimball, "The Nauvoo Temple," *Improvement Era*, November 1963, 982.

16. *New-York Messenger* 2 (20 September 1845): 93; also, *The Prophet*, 30 November 1844; also, Journal of

William Clayton, "History of the Nauvoo Temple," 6, LDS Church Archives; *Times and Seasons* 5 (1 January 1845): 759; W. W. Phelps to William Smith, 25 December 1844, LDS Church Archives; also, Frederick Hawkins Piercy, *Route from Liverpool to Great Salt Lake Valley*, ed. James Linforth (London: Latter-day Saints' Book Depot, 1855), 67.

17. Virginia S. Harrington and J. C. Harrington, *Rediscovery of the Nauvoo Temple* (Salt Lake City: Nauvoo Restoration, 1971), 17; also, William A. Gallup Journal Entry, 1848, LDS Church Archives; also, a writer for the *Peoria Democratic Press* of 29 May 1844, "claimed to have seen a 'diagram model' of the temple which was shown to him by Joseph Smith [and which] gives the dimensions as 130 by 90," as cited in Kimball, "The Nauvoo Temple," 982.

18. Harrington and Harrington, *Rediscovery of the Nauvoo Temple*, 17.

19. Andrew, "Temple Architecture," 102.

20. *New-York Messenger* 2 (30 August 1845): 68; and *Nauvoo Neighbor*, 30 July 1845.

21. *Deseret Evening News*, 7 March 1876, citing an article from the *Cincinnati Times*, n.d.

22. *Deseret News*, 30 September 1857.

23. *Chillicothe Advertiser* 16 (25 July 1846): 1, as cited in J. Earl Arrington, "Story of the Nauvoo Temple," 37, LDS Church Archives.

24. *Liberty Hall and Cincinnati Gazette* 40 (19 October 1843): 1, as cited in Arrington, "Story of the Nauvoo Temple," 37.

25. Harrington and Harrington, *Rediscovery of the Nauvoo Temple*, 13.

26. Jerry McElvain and Tim Maxwell, telephone conversation with author, 7 June 2000. Jerry McElvain and Uriel Schlair served as consulting architects on the Nauvoo Temple reconstruction project with special assignment to stone anchoring and quality characteristics of stone used in the temple. They carefully studied and examined 100 to 150 stones that were part of the original Nauvoo Temple. These studies provided clear evidence regarding finish and texturing used on stones in various parts of the structure. Tim Maxwell is an architect who worked on the Nauvoo Temple historical reconstruction drawings, as well as plans for the reconstructed temple at Nauvoo. He spent several years working with Nauvoo Restoration, and he studied extensively other stonework in old Nauvoo as well as other buildings of that time period.

27. *Hancock Eagle*, 8 May 1846.

28. *New York Herald*, 6 September 1846.

29. Tim Maxwell, personal communication.

30. Lanman, *A Summer in the Wilderness*, 32.

31. *Nauvoo Neighbor*, 1 May 1844.

32. *Hancock Eagle*, 24 April 1846. See also The Missouri Reporter, 5 (2 May 1846): 2, as cited in J. Earl Arrington, "Story of the Nauvoo Temple," 3.

33. *The Prophet*, 5 April 1845.

34. B. H. Roberts, ed., *History of the Church of Jesus Christ of Latter-day Saints, Period 2: Apostolic Interregnum* (Salt Lake City: Deseret Book, 1932), 7:323.

35. Arrington, "Story of the Nauvoo Temple," 37a. During 1946 Arrington measured stones that had been taken from the ruins of the Nauvoo Temple and used in other buildings then standing.

36. *Nauvoo Neighbor*, 30 July 1845.

37. A report in the *Liberty Hall and Cincinnati Gazette* 40 (19 October 1843): 1, as cited in Arrington, "Story of the Nauvoo Temple," 10, describes the temple basement as "about 12 feet in the clear, half of which is underground." Harrington and Harrington, Rediscovery of the Nauvoo Temple, 16, confirms that the foundation walls of the

excavated basement were about 5 feet below the ground level. The floor of the first story was 6 feet 4 inches above ground level. This level of the first story floor would include the 12 feet of the basement walls, plus the 1-foot-thick beam supporting the first floor. The original basement floor at the outside walls was somewhere between 5 feet 8 inches and 6 feet 8 inches below the ground level.

38. Harrington and Harrington, *Rediscovery of the Nauvoo Temple*, 16.

39. *Liberty Hall and Cincinnati Gazette* 40 (19 October 1843): 1, as cited in Arrington, "Story of the Nauvoo Temple," 10.

40. Truman O. Angell to John Taylor, 11 March 1885, as cited in Andrew, "Temple Architecture," 88. "A ground plan must have been worked out and drafted in some detail during the latter part of 1840 so that initial preparation of the grounds could commence that fall. . . . Stone quarries were located and initial excavating commenced at the temple site. While quarry work proceeded slowly that winter, in February the foundation was laid out by the temple committee and digging of the cellar commenced. By March, cellar walls were started and foundation stones were being set. The walls were high enough by 6 April for a special cornerstone laying ceremony. William was present, he marched in the parade, and he then helped lower the first cornerstone into place. J. Earl Arrington, "William Weeks, Architect of the Nauvoo Temple," *BYU Studies* 19, no. 3 (spring 1979): 343.

The temple committee had evidently begun the construction of the temple, which was to be similar to Kirtland, but the basement was "much botched" by them. Truman O. Angell to John Taylor, 11 March 1885, LDS Church Archives. Joseph Smith's history does not mention the name of the architect until 1843. But from the context it is clear that this person had been the temple

architect for some time and was given total control over the building as a result of the "spoiling of the foundations." "In consequence of misunderstanding on the part of the Temple committee, and their interference with the business of the architect, I gave a certificate to William Weeks to carry out my designs and the architecture of the Temple in Nauvoo, and that no person or persons shall interfere with him or his plans in the building of the Temple." Smith, *History of the Church*, 5:353.

41. Smith, *History of the Church*, 6:196–97; and Joseph Smith, *Discourses of the Prophet Joseph Smith*, comp. Alma Burton (Salt Lake City: Deseret Book, 1977), 267.

42. *New-York Messenger* 2 (30 August 1845): 68; also, 2 (20 September 1845): 93.

43. Doctrine and Covenants 76. The sun, represented by the sun stones, symbolizes the celestial degree of glory. The moon, represented by the moon stones, symbolizes the terrestrial degree of glory. The stars, represented by star stones and carved wooden stars, symbolize the telestial degree of glory.

44. *Journal of History* 3 (April 1910): 163 as quoted in *Saints' Herald*, 26 September 1949; and Josiah Quincy, *Figures of the Past* (Boston: Roberts Brothers, 1883), 389.

45. These figures correlate with width measurements of the moon stones, which were 6 feet wide at their juncture with the pilaster base. Measurements were taken by Arrington as reported in "Story of the Nauvoo Temple," 4, 39. The pilaster bases were the same height as the foundation walls.

46. *Liberty Hall and Cincinnati Gazette* 40 (19 October 1843): 1, and *Universalist Union* 9 (June 1844): 407, as cited in Arrington, "Story of the Nauvoo Temple," 2. A plinth is defined as "a square vertically faced member immediately below the . . . base of a column in classical architecture, . . . the lowest member of a pedestal."

Webster's Third New International Dictionary (Springfield: Merriam-Webster, 1986) s.v. The plinths were put into the wall at just the time and in the same location (height) where the moon stones would have been placed. The first plinth was put in place on 11 June. By October the walls were up to the window sills, which were then all in place including the large sill on the eastern Venetian window. At this time there were two courses of stone on the plinths. Journal History, 11 October 1842. The daguerreotypes show that this would be at the level of two courses of stone above the moon stones. This establishes the plinths and the moon stones as one and the same. The plinths were cut by several individuals, and account books listed payment for four plinths to Pulaski Cahoon and two to George Ritchie, all at forty-five dollars for each plinth. "Nauvoo Temple Building Committee Records," 5 September 1842, LDS Church Archives.

47. *New-York Messenger* 2 (30 August 1845): 68.

48. Arrington, "Story of the Nauvoo Temple," 39.

49. *Missouri Reporter* 5 (2 May 1846): 2, as cited in Arrington, "Story of the Nauvoo Temple," 3.

50. Ibid.

51. Roberts, *History of the Church,* 7:323.

52. Arrington, "Story of the Nauvoo Temple," 39.

53. Roberts, *History of the Church,* 7:323.

54. *Warsaw Signal,* 11 September 1844.

55. *New-York Messenger* 2 (30 August 1845): 68.

56. *Journal of History,* 2 (1909): 464–65.

57. *Iowa Territorial Gazette and Advertiser* 9 (18 April 1846): 1, as cited in Arrington, "Story of the Nauvoo Temple," 49.

58. Brigham Young, *The Journal of Brigham,* comp. Leland R. Nelson (Provo, Utah: Council, 1980), 112.

59. *New-York Messenger* 2 (30 August 1845): 68.

60. *Times and Seasons* 6 (1 August 1845): 983; also,

New-York Messenger 2 (20 September 1845): 93.

61. Journal History, 9 October 1848, citing an article in the *Nauvoo Patriot,* of the same date.

62. *New-York Messenger* 2 (8 November 1845): 152.

63. "The Old Temple," *Nauvoo Independent* 17 (20 December 1889): 7.

64. *Iowa Territorial Gazette and Advertiser* 9 (18 April 1846): 1, as cited in Arrington, "Story of the Nauvoo Temple," 51.

65. Ibid., also, *Carthage Republican,* 25 February 1864, as cited in E. Cecil McGavin, *The Nauvoo Temple* (Salt Lake City: Deseret Book, 1962), 95.

66. Newell K. Whitney, Whitney Collection, Box 3, Folder 1, Harold B. Lee Library, Brigham Young University.

67. Journal History, 30 January 1846.

68. *Iowa Territorial Gazette and Advertiser* 9 (18 April 1846): 1, as cited in Arrington, "Story of the Nauvoo Temple," 51. Arrington makes this conclusion based on this and other reports describing the angelic weather vane.

69. Perrigrine Sessions, *The Diaries of Perrigrine Sessions* (Bountiful, Utah: Carr, 1967), 43–44.

70. *Iowa Territorial Gazette and Advertiser* 9 (18 April 1846): 1, as cited in Arrington, "Story of the Nauvoo Temple," 516.

71. Whitney Collection, Box 3, Folder 6.

72. Ibid., Box 3, Folder 1.

73. *New-York Messenger* 2 (8 November 1845): 152.

74. *Deseret Evening News,* 7 March 1876, citing an article from the *Cincinnati Times,* n.d.

75. Thomas L. Kane, *The Mormons: A Discourse* (Philadelphia: King and Baird, 1850), 20.

76. Joseph Smith III, *Joseph Smith III and the Restoration,* ed. Mary Audentia Smith Anderson

(Independence, Mo.: Herald House, 1952), 100.

77. *New-York Messenger* 2 (30 August 1845): 68; and *Nauvoo Neighbor*, 30 July 1844.

78. *New York Herald*, 6 September 1846.

79. *New-York Messenger* 2 (30 August 1845): 67–68.

80. Ibid. (8 November 1845): 152.

81. *Liberty Hall and Cincinnati Gazette* 40 (19 October 1843): 1, as cited in Arrington, "Story of the Nauvoo Temple," 30.

82. *New-York Messenger* 2 (30 August 1845): 68.

83. The original drawing has measurements along the side that provide clear evidence on the size of these windows.

84. Account books for the temple show quantity purchase of window panes measuring 10 by 14 inches. This size fits consistently with measurements of these large main windows. Account books are found in LDS Church Archives. They have been microfilmed and fill five full reels. Glass purchases, along with blasting powder, fuse, and iron, are periodically cited throughout all of the building committee account books.

85. Tim Maxwell, personal communication, from extensive research in Nauvoo Temple architectural drawings, account books, and billing records.

86. The original drawing has measurements along the side that provide clear evidence on the size of these windows.

87. Charles A. Dana, *The United States Illustrated* (New York: H. J. Meyer, 1855), 1:39–40, as cited in Arrington, "Story of the Nauvoo Temple," 32.

88. *New-York Messenger* 2 (30 August 1845): 67–68.

89. *Illinois Journal*, 9 December 1853, as reprinted in *Journal of Illinois State Historical Society* 38 (1945): 483; also, *New-York Messenger* 2 (30 August 1845): 68.

90. Emily M. Austin, *Mormonism; or, Life among the Mormons* (New York: AMS, 1971), 201.

91. Ibid.

92. Maxwell, personal communication.

93. *New-York Messenger* 2 (30 August 1845): 68.

94. Ibid., 67–68.

95. Ibid., 68.

96. Ibid.

97. Austin, *Mormonism; or, Life among the Mormons*, 201, 202.

98. Maxwell, personal communication. Observations made after careful study of an enlarged copy of the Chaffin daguerreotype.

99. *New-York Messenger* 2 (30 August 1845): 67–68. No definitive records have been found to indicate how many of these windows were placed in this end of the building. However, careful study of the back end of the Kirtland and St. George Temples leads to the conclusion that the same general pattern was followed in Nauvoo as was used in these temples. They each had one large window on each level. William Weeks may have studied the Kirtland Temple plans; his assistant, Truman O. Angell, who was the architect of both the St. George and Salt Lake Temples, seems to have followed much of the general pattern of Nauvoo as he constructed the temple in St. George. Documentation on the numbers of main and larger circular windows also supports the conclusion of just one large venetian-style window on each main story.

100. The span of the roof was 38-40 feet with a rise in the center of the pitched roof of 4 feet 6 inches. This would be a rise of less than 3 inches per foot.

101. *New-York Messenger* 2 (20 September 1845): 93; also Times and Seasons 6 (1 August 1845): 983.

102. *New York Herald*, 6 September 1846.

103. *Maysville Eagle* 12 (26 October 1846): 2, as cited in Arrington, *Story of the Nauvoo Temple*, 5.

104. *New-York Messenger* 2 (30 August 1845): 68.

105. Journal History, 9 October 1848, citing an article in the *Nauvoo Patriot* of the same date. "On Monday (October 9th) our citizens were awakened by the alarm of fire, which, when first discovered, was bursting out through the spire of the temple, near the small door that opened from the East side to the roof, on the main building."

106. *New-York Messenger* 2 (30 August 1845): 68.

107. Mr. Davidson, editor of the *Carthage Republican*, as cited in E. Cecil McGavin, *Nauvoo the Beautiful* (Salt Lake City: Stevens and Wallis, 1946), 39.

108. *New-York Messenger* 2 (30 August 1845): 68.

109. Ibid.

110. Harrington and Harrington, *Rediscovery of the Nauvoo Temple*, 32.

111. *Times and Seasons* 6 (1 August 1845): 983.

112. *New-York Messenger* 2 (30 August 1845): 67.

113. Steve Goodwin, personal communication, from extensive research in Nauvoo Temple architectural drawings and study of Greek Revival architecture. He is an architect who worked on the plans for the reconstruction of the Nauvoo Temple.

114. Maxwell, personal communication.

115. *New-York Messenger* 2 (30 August 1845): 67–68.

116. Ibid., 68.

117. Maxwell, personal communication.

118. Roberts, *History of the Church*, 7:431.

119. *Times and Seasons* 6 (1 April 1845): 856.

120. Roberts, *History of the Church*, 7:427, 431.

121. *Millennial Star* 6 (15 July 1845): 43.

122. Hosea Stout, *On the Mormon Frontier, the Diary of Hosea Stout 1844–1861*, ed. Juanita Brooks (Salt Lake City: University of Utah Press, 1964), 1:64.

123. Roberts, *History of the Church*, 7:427.

124. Ibid.

125. Ibid., 431, 427.

126. *New-York Messenger* 2 (30 August 1845): 67.

127. Elden J. Watson, "The Nauvoo Tabernacle," *BYU Studies* 19, no. 3 (spring 1979): 420.

128. Roberts, *History of the Church*, 7:482–83.

129. Helen Mar Whitney, "Scenes in Nauvoo and Incidents from H. C. Kimball's Journal," *Woman's Exponent* 11 (15 May 1883): 186.

130. Watson, "Nauvoo Tabernacle," 421.

131. Catherine Lewis, *Narrative of Some of the Proceedings of the Mormons* (Lynn, Mass.: Catherine Lewis, 1848), 7–8.

132. Maxwell, personal communication.

133. *Priddy Meeks Journal*, 22 October 1879, LDS Church Archives.

134. Lewis Barney, *The Life of Lewis Barney as Written by Himself* (Duncan, Ariz.: Clifford Page Sanders, 1988), 28. 7

Detail of Architectural Drawing No. 2 of the Nauvoo Temple (see Figure 2.3), drawing, 1842 or 1843, William Weeks, LDS Church Archives. This is an original architectural drawing by architect William Weeks. This enlarged photograph shows details of the angelic weather vane placed at the top of the steeple.

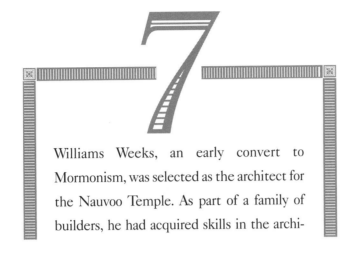

Williams Weeks, an early convert to Mormonism, was selected as the architect for the Nauvoo Temple. As part of a family of builders, he had acquired skills in the archi-

CHAPTER SEVEN

EARLY SKETCHES AND ARCHITEC-

TURAL DRAWINGS OF WILLIAM WEEKS

tecture of New England while working with his father. Examination of his work indicates that he was an architect of the Greek Revivalist school. The excellence of his drawings demonstrates both skill and competence. Laurel B. Andrew, after studying his

sketches, observed: "The evolution of the Nauvoo Temple as seen in these drawings offers a unique opportunity to study the coming of age of a frontier builder-architect as he worked towards a satisfactory accommodation of architectural tradition with a desire for original expression. Weeks's designs demonstrate his familiarity with the traditions of New England, but they also record the influx of modern ideas from the 1840s as transmitted primarily through the medium of architectural hand books. His final plans do not depend on a specific source and are novel in their adaptation of architectural motifs. They demonstrate by comparison with the earlier plans a greater proficiency in handling the architectural vocabulary."[1]

A number of William Weeks's temple drawings still exist and are in the possession of the Church. They are available for careful examination. Though some are preliminary sketches, they still furnish valuable insights into the size and features of the building. By permission of The Church of Jesus Christ of Latter-day Saints, they have been reproduced in this book. The drawings have been used throughout the book and are found in chapters 2 (Figures 2.1–2.3), 4 (Figures 4.2–4.3), 6 (Figures 6.9, 6.13), and 8 (Figures 8.8–8.9). Additional Nauvoo Temple architectural drawings are included on the pages that follow (Figures 7.1–7.11).

NOTE

1. Laurel B. Andrew, *The Early Temples of the Mormons* (Albany: State University of New York Press, 1978), 62.

Figure 7.1 Cross-Sectional View of the Temple Framework, drawing, 1840s, William Weeks, LDS Church Archives. This is an original architectural drawing by architect William Weeks showing the structural framework of the temple. It clearly shows the half-story mezzanines at the sides of the arch on both the first and second story levels.

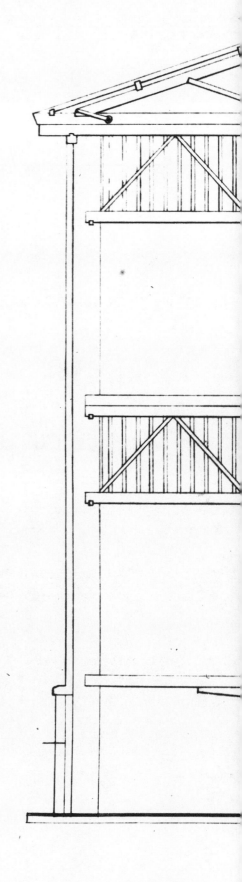

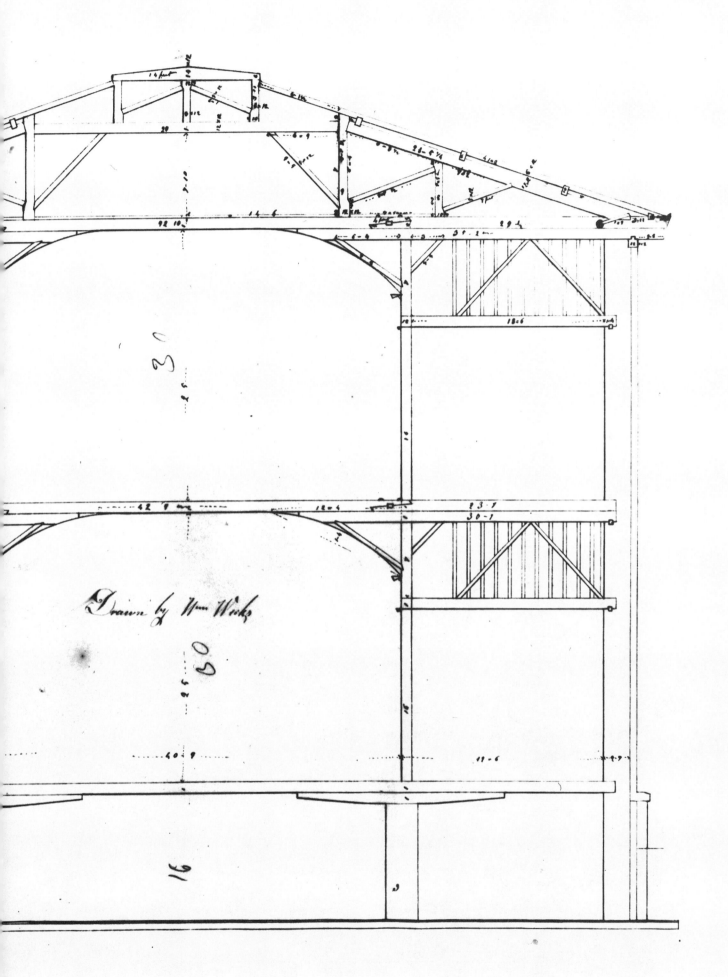

Drawn by Wm Wicks

Tower Dimensions Based on Original William Weeks Drawings (see Figure 7.4 at right)

Section	Height	External Diameter
Base or pedestal up to belfry	29 feet	29 feet wide
below attic roof	16 feet 6 inches	
above attic roof	12 feet 6 inches	
Belfry up to clock	20 feet	22 feet
Clock up to observatory	10 feet 8 inches	22 feet
Observatory up to dome	16 feet	17 feet
Dome	7 feet 10 inches	13 feet or 14 feet at base
Rod, ball, and angel (weather vane)	12 feet 8 inches	Angel was 7 feet long?
Total overall height	96 feet 2 inches	

Figure 7.2 (Top) Stone Coursing around Top of Main Windows, drawing, 1840s, William Weeks, LDS Church Archives. Notice the detailed stonework, which is remarkable even by today's standards.

Figure 7.3 (Bottom) This is a summary of tower dimensions taken from careful examination of drawings by architect William Weeks.

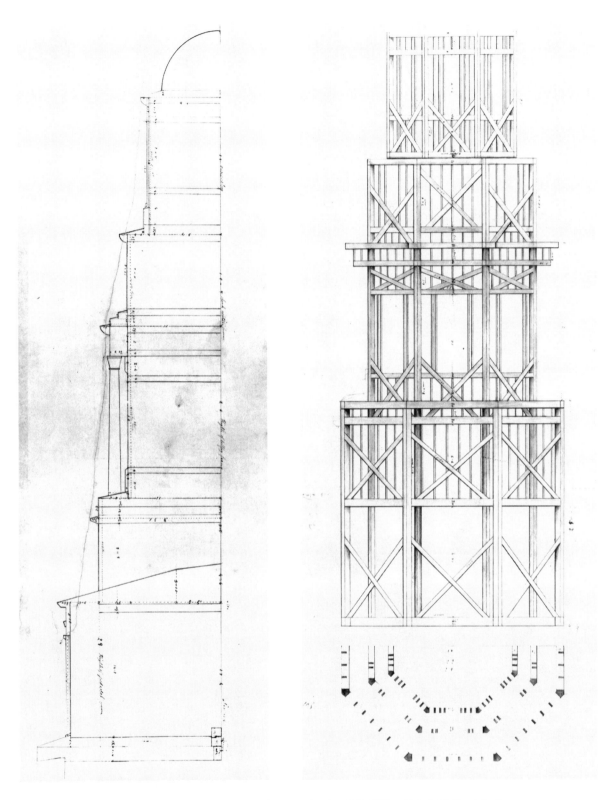

Figure 7.4 (Above left) Half-Sectional View of Tower Structure, drawing, 1840s, William Weeks, LDS Church Archives.

Figure 7.5 (Above right) Structural Framework of the Temple Tower, drawing, 1840s, William Weeks, LDS Church Archives.

Figure 7.6 (Next page) Proposed Angelic Weather Vane, drawing, 1840s, William Weeks, LDS Church Archives.

for a Temple

Figure 7.7 Design of the Main Windows, drawing, 1840s, William Weeks, LDS Church Archives. It shows the design for the placement of the forty-seven main windows in the walls of the temple. These windows were divided into three sections, a lower sash, an upper sash, and a fanlight section at the top. The windows were 10 feet 1 inch in height and 4 feet 10 inches wide.

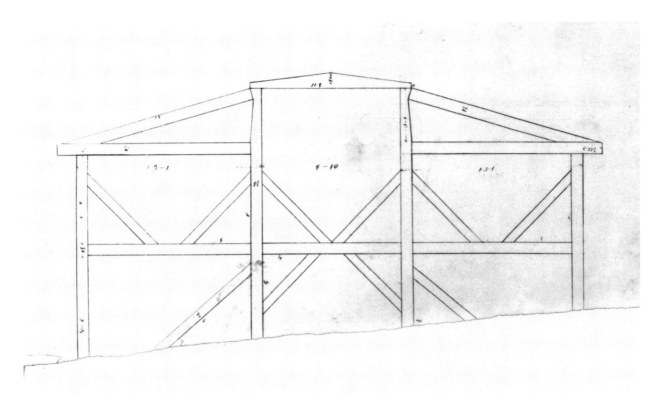

Figure 7.8 (Top) End Framing for West Front Attic, drawing, 1840s, William Weeks, LDS Church Archives. This drawing shows a detail of the framing and roof line of the west front attic section.

Figure 7.9 (Bottom) Small Round Star Window and Star Stone, drawing, 1840s, William Weeks, LDS Church Archives. This is an original architectural drawing by architect William Weeks. This drawing clearly shows the design of the small round star windows that furnished illumination for the second-story mezzanine. It also provides a clear drawing of the star stones that were placed above each pilaster.

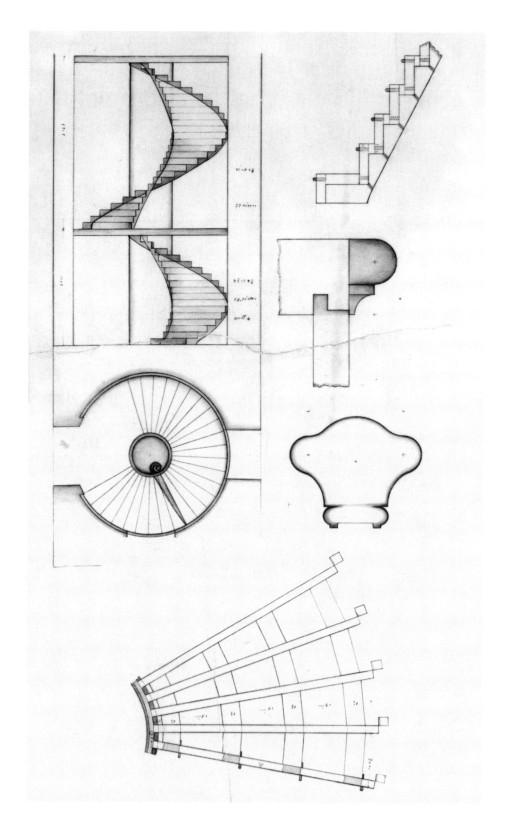

Figure 7.10 Design of Circular Stairways, drawing, 1840s, William Weeks, LDS Church Archives. This is an original architectural drawing by architect William Weeks. The open area of the stairway was 6 feet across.

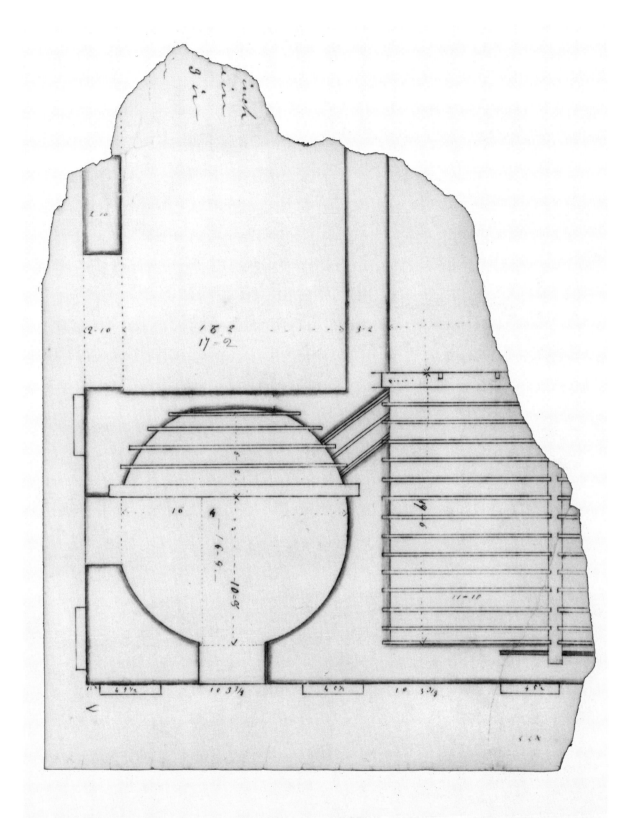

Figure 7.11 Fragment of Design for Southeast Stairwell at Level of First Mezzanine, drawing, 1840s, William Weeks, LDS Church Archives. This is an original architectural drawing by architect William Weeks. It provides helpful information on measurements and is a good illustration of how floor joists were designed for and used in the building.

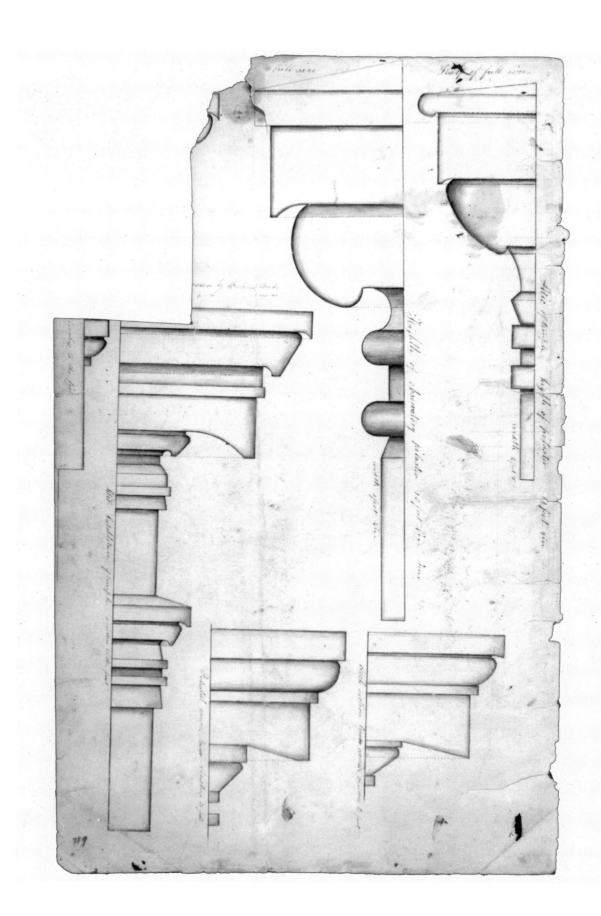

Attic Entablature, drawing, 1840s, William Weeks, LDS Church Archives.

Evidence concerning the building's interior comes from a few architectural drawings, eyewitness descriptions, archaeological evidence, and lists of materials in account

CHAPTER EIGHT

INTERIOR

FEATURES

books. Other than the Henry Lewis sketch of the baptismal font (Figure 4.1), there are no artist's sketches or photographs of the temple's interior available for analysis.

Over the years uncertainty has existed regarding the extent of completion in

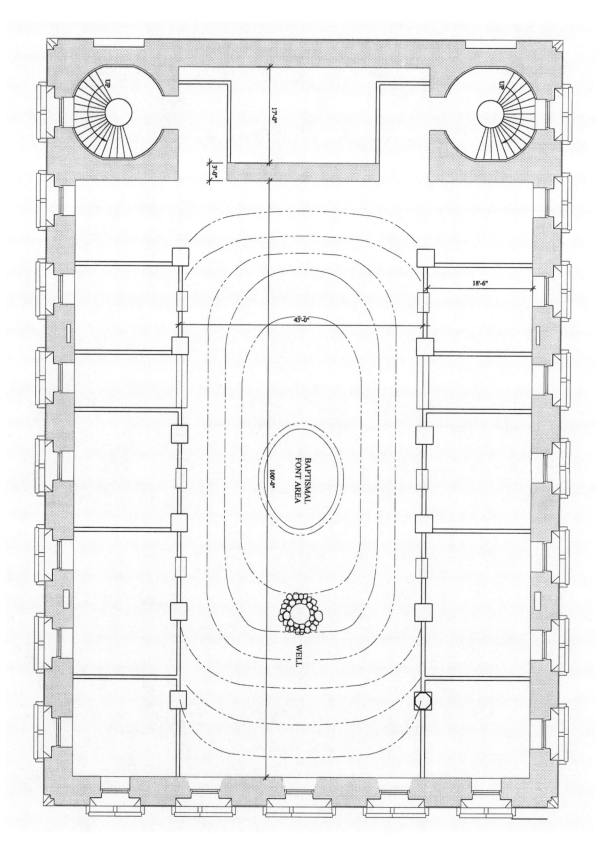

Figure 8.1 Basement Floor Plan, drawing, 2000, FFKR Architecture. These drawings were modified and adapted from historic reconstruction drawings at the request of the author by Steve Goodwin, an architect working on the Nauvoo Temple reconstruction project (see description of this area in chapter 8).

various interior sections of the temple. Careful examination of each floor level and section of the building, along with consideration of all available evidence, will shed some light on this issue.

THE BASEMENT STORY

Work on the original basement excavation started in the fall of 1840. It was probably done by pick and shovel along with teams of oxen and scrapers to drag out the earth. Archaeological excavation shows that the cut into the earth was nearly vertical and that foundation or basement walls were laid against it except for a 30-foot space on the south side of the building, which is thought to "have been where the excavated earth was dragged or otherwise removed from the basement"[1] (see Figure 9.1).

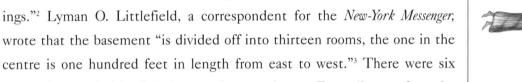

Rooms

A letter from the Twelve Apostles to all Church members explained that "upon each side of the font there will be a suite of rooms fitted up for the washings."[2] Lyman O. Littlefield, a correspondent for the *New-York Messenger*, wrote that the basement "is divided off into thirteen rooms, the one in the centre is one hundred feet in length from east to west."[3] There were six rooms along each side of the large main central room. Extending out from the walls and dividing the side rooms from each other were thick stone partitions that varied from 19 to 23 inches in thickness.[4] These heavy partitions provided additional strength to the outside walls and added support for floors above the basement. "The interior super structure was supported by 12 piers, 6 on each side, spaced at 15 foot intervals, center to center." Each heavy stone "pier was 4 feet square, built on a subpier 8 feet square and approximately 4 feet deep."[5] These piers provided the main support for beams, columns, and floors above the basement. They ran along each side of the large main room and had stone partitions running between them that separated the side rooms from the main hall. These side rooms were each 18 feet 6 inches wide but varied considerably in length. The last rooms on the west were open, lacking partitions separating them from the main hall (see Figures 8.1 and 8.2). The central room was 40 feet wide by 100 feet long.[6]

Additional temporary rooms may have been curtained off on the east end of this main hall to provide more space for patrons changing clothes to participate in baptisms.[7]

On the west end of the basement was the vestibule area. It was separated from the main hall by a 3-foot-thick stone wall that, except for two 6-foot-wide passageway exits, extended the full width of the basement. This heavy vestibule partition wall continued above the basement, through the first and second stories to the top of the stone walls. It provided stability to the building and direct support for the attic and steeple.

Access to the basement was through the stairwells and vestibule on the west end. It is logical to consider that another entrance may have been constructed on the east end or north side of the building, but there is no record of any kind to indicate that such existed.

The vestibule area was taken up by one large room or area about 16 or 17 feet wide by 30 to 32 feet long. From all available evidence, this area was walled off by a wooden partition with no doors or access into it.[8] This area seems never to have been developed or utilized. On each corner of the west end were stairwells with stairs providing access to each level of the building. "The stairwells were not true circles, as expected, but each was 16 feet east to west and 17 feet north to south. Rather than their perimeters being a continuous curve, there was a flattened space on each of the four sides, one of which was the entrance to the passageway"[9] (see Figures 8.1 and 8.2). These stairwells at

their base opened toward the center of the vestibule area into a 6-foot-wide open hallway or passageway that then led east into the large main basement room. The entire vestibule area and stairwells can be seen in Figure 8.1.

All rooms of the basement were used extensively. In the baptismal font—both the earlier wooden and later stone font—thousands of ordinances were performed. Rooms on the sides were used as dressing rooms for patrons utilizing the font. Additional rooms were used by clerks appointed to keep records of all ordinances performed. Others were no doubt used for confirmation ordinances. The open side rooms on the north and south sides may have been used by the recording clerks or as a reception area for patrons waiting their turn to participate in the ordinances. There is no record available to indicate that any parts of the endowment ordinances were conducted in this part of the building.

Dimensions

The total inner dimensions of the basement area were the same as those of the first and second stories above. All are found to be 80 feet wide by 120 feet in length.[10] By adding the breadth of the 40-foot-wide main room in the basement plus a room on each side of 18 feet 6 inches, along with stone partitions on each side of 18 inches, we come to an overall width of 80 feet. The main hall was 100 feet long and had on its west end a 3-foot-thick wall, and beyond this the vestibule and stair wells were 16 or 17 feet wide. Adding these together, we come to a total interior length of 120 feet. The overall layout of the basement story floor plan can be seen in Figure 8.1.

The walls of the building in the basement area were either 4 feet 5 inches or 5 feet in thickness (see Figure 9.3). [11] They were composed of large irregular blocks of stone laid directly on the clay floor of the excavation, without footings, and cemented together with lime mortar.[12] The total outside dimensions in this area could very likely have been 90 feet wide by 130 feet in length.[13]

Depth

The sides and ends of the basement floor level were 5 or more feet below ground level.[14] Excavation of the temple site revealed that in the center of the basement where the baptismal font was located, the floor level was deeper. Here it ranged from 3 feet 3 inches to 4 feet 2 inches below the level of the outside walls (see Figure 9.1). It is not certain when this change of depth in the basement was implemented; it may have been done partially or even totally as the wooden font was constructed. Available evidence, however, leans in favor of this change being done at a later date.[15] Without question, the increased depth added to the basement floor level was done to accommodate the need for more headroom above the font. The wooden font was 7 feet high.[16] Without this change, headroom would have been at most only 5 feet from the rim of the font to the ceiling.[17] The stone font, which stood either 7 feet 7 inches or 8 feet high, would have had even more severe problems.[18] Without this change, headroom of the stone font would have been at most only 4 feet above the rim of the font. The entire basement area was scooped out to accommodate those working in the font and was inclined down to the center. Rooms on the sides were affected less than the main room.

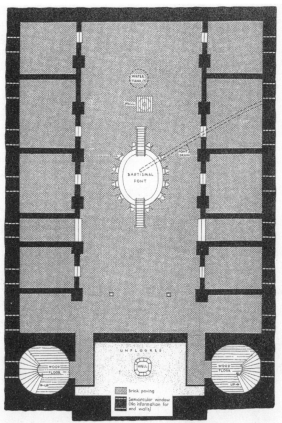

Figure 8.2 Conjectural Reconstruction of Basement Floor Plan, photograph of drawing, 1970, LDS Church Archives. This floor plan produced by Nauvoo Restoration is based primarily on archaeological findings of Nauvoo Restoration as they excavated the site in the 1960s.

the baptismal font was located, the floor level was deeper. Here it ranged from 3 feet 3 inches to 4 feet 2 inches below the level of the outside walls (see Figure 9.1). It is not certain when this change of depth in the basement was implemented; it may have been done partially or even totally as the wooden font was constructed. Available evidence,

They were sloped 4 to 6 inches down from the outside wall to the inner partition wall. The large interior room was sloped down from 3 feet 3 inches on each end and 2 feet 9 inches on each side to the font at the center of the room. These grade levels can be examined by study of Figure 9.1. Steps were placed at the entrances of side rooms to lessen the slope of the grade on each side of the main room, as can be noted in Figure 8.2. Figure 9.9 shows how these steps were constructed. The problem of inadequate headroom may have been why Truman O. Angell felt that the temple committee had "much botched" some aspects of the basement area.[19] The committee had the walls in place in April before they made a decision in July to build the font. Since it was then impractical to start over, they must have opted to incline the floor to pick up additional height.

The Baptismal Font

Dominating the central hall of the basement was the baptismal font. It was placed beneath ground level by direct command of the Lord "to be immersed in the water and come forth out of the water is in the likeness of the resurrection of the dead in coming forth out of their graves. . . . Consequently, the baptismal font was instituted as a similitude of the grave, and was commanded to be in a place underneath where the living are wont to assemble, to show forth the living and the dead, and that all things may have their likeness" (D&C 128:12–13; see also Rom. 6:3–5).

There were really two fonts used in the temple, the original wooden one and its replacement, a permanent font made of stone. Both were located in the same spot. Joseph Smith provided a detailed description of this temporary wooden font:

> The baptismal font is situated in the center of the basement room, under the main hall of the Temple; it is constructed of pine timber, and put together of staves tongued and grooved, oval shaped, sixteen feet long east and west, and twelve feet wide, seven feet high from the foundation, the basin four feet deep, the moulding of the cap and base are formed of beautiful carved work in antique style. The sides are finished with panel work. A flight of stairs in the north and south sides lead up and down into the basin, guarded by side railing.
>
> The font stands upon twelve oxen, four on each side, and two at each end, their heads, shoulders, and fore legs projecting out from under the font; they are carved out of pine plank, glued together, and copied after the most beautiful five-year-old steer that could be found in the country, and they are an excellent striking likeness of the original; the horns were formed after the most perfect horn that could be procured.
>
> The font was enclosed by a temporary frame building sided up with split oak clapboards, with a roof of the same material, and was so low that the timbers of the first story were laid above it.[20]

An observer pointed out that the carved wooden oxen were "so perfectly cut out of timber," and looked so similar as to cause visitors "to look with surprize, resembling the living animal."[21] Another, commenting on the joining work, said that it was done with "a fidelity and perfection of detail difficult to surpass."[22] The oxen "were painted as white as snow."[23] It is reported that panels on the sides under the surface of the basin had "various scenes, hand-somely painted."[24]

Though the decision to replace the wooden font was made during the winter of 1843, it was not until 15 January 1845 that a formal announcement was made to members of the Church. They were then informed that "as soon as the stone cutters get through with the cutting of the stone for the walls of the Temple, they will immediately proceed to cut the stone for and erect a font of hewn stone."[25] Stonecutters and carvers worked steadily, and by the end of June, Brigham Young was able to announce that "the new stone font is mostly cut." At 4 P.M. on 27 June "the first stone was laid," and it was expected that "in about five or six weeks . . . the font will be all finished."[26] President Young declared in July 1845: "We have taken down the wooden fount that was built." He went on to explain that Joseph Smith had said to him, "We will build a wooden font to serve the present necessity." It is also evident that some very real problems had developed with this temporary font in trying to keep it clean. As President Young explained, "we will have a fount that will not stink and keep us all the while cleansing it out."[27] On 20 August it was observed that the new font was "in an advanced state of completion."[28]

Visitors viewing the stone font might conclude that the stone oxen supported the font basin resting upon their backs, but this was not the case (see Figure 9.4). The stone basin "rested on a foundation of its own, composed of the heavy blocks of stone closely joined togeth-

Figure 8.3 Brick Floor Pattern, drawing, 1970, LDS Church Archives. This drawing, based on archaeological findings, was produced by Nauvoo Restoration and was published in 1971 in the book Rediscovery of the Nauvoo Temple, *written by J. C. and Virginia Harrington. The drawing shows the herringbone pattern of brick paving laid on the basement floor of the temple. It also shows how bricks would be cut diagonally along foundation walls and partitions.*

er and fashioned in the form of a circle. The oxen were not fully developed but resting on their forefeet, the middle of their bodies was firmly cemented to that circular foundation and thus the basin seemed to rest on their backs."[29] The oxen were further secured in position by having their front feet cemented in place by "Roman cement."[30]

The architectural drawings of William Weeks indicate that the stone font was designed to stand upon an oval-shaped stone base 12 feet long by 8 feet wide.[31] There is, however, substantial evidence to indicate that changes were made during construction to increase the base size by 3 feet in each direction to dimensions of 15 feet long by 11½ feet wide.[32] Following these proportions, the stone font basin above this base had an outside dimension of 18 feet 5½ inches by 14 feet 3½

Figure 8.4 *Remains of Brick Floor, photograph, 1960s, LDS Church Archives. This shows remains of the brick floor paving (after cleaning) that were found in the area east of the well during the excavation of the temple site. The bricks were laid in approximately two inches of sand without mortar. It is believed that the temple committee may have sold many of the bricks to defray costs as they left the temple.*

inches (see Figure 12.4). The depth of the font basin is difficult to determine. It could have been 3 feet 7 inches deep, as indicated by the architect's drawings. This is a shallow basin and if the width and length were altered, then it is very possible that some depth may have been added in the stone basin. The overall height of the font was 7 feet 7 inches.[33] It could have been even taller if changes were added. A circular iron railing around the font added beauty and served the purpose of keeping the curious away from the oxen and font itself.[34]

Access to the font was provided by "a flight of stone steps with iron railing on each side

[that] led up to the font and a similar flight on the other side descended therefrom"[35] (see the Henry Lewis sketch of the font in Figure 4.1 as well as the reconstruction drawings, Figure 12.3). Littlefield explained that "the fount will be entered by a flight of steps in an arch form at each end."[36] In contrast to the earlier wooden font, the stone replacement had its stairs located on the east and west ends of the oval basin.[37] Each of the stone steps leading up to the font had a 9-inch rise with an 11-inch tread.[38] Remains of these steps were found during the archaeological excavation and can be examined in Figure 9.6. One end piece of a stair tread con-

tained two sockets that showed a baluster spacing of 5½ inches.[39] The steps down into the font were carved into the bowl itself on both ends of the stone basin. They consisted of three steps on each end, having a 10-inch rise for each step with an 8-inch tread (see Figure 12.3).

The basement level where the font stood, as well as the area close around it, was level. "To the east and west of the font the slope rises only 6 inches in the first 10 feet presumably to the bottom of the font stairs, and then goes up more steeply to reach a level of 2.9 feet above the center to the west, at the vestibule wall, and 3.3 feet at the east wall."[40]

The oxen were each carved from solid blocks of stone.[41] William W. Player was called upon to supervise the construction of the font, and a master stone carver (as yet unidentified) was engaged to guide the creative hands of workers carving the oxen. The challenge of the stone carvers was to create from solid blocks of stone twelve identical oxen about the size of living natural animals and to duplicate the wooden oxen that preceded them. From the reports of most observers, they were successful in their task.

The editor of the *Hancock Eagle,* somewhat startled when first viewing the baptismal font, declared that "the beholder is lost in wonder at the magnitude of the design and the extraordinary amount of labor that must have been expended in the direction of the work."[42] Upon viewing the work, Charles Lanman described the "Baptismal Font, supported by twelve oxen," large as life, the whole executed in solid stone.[43] Emily Austin described the "oxen of white lime

stone, very natural, and twelve in number, all perfectly executed, so that the veins in the ears and nose were plainly seen. The horns were perfectly natural, with small wrinkles at the bottom."[44] According to the Lewis sketch and other descriptions, there were four oxen on each side of the font and two at each end.[45] Another observer explained that the oxen "were well executed and with their bright eyes of glass and well formed ears, looked exceedingly life like and altogether presented a very handsome appearance.[46] The oxen [had] tin horns and tin ears.[47] The ends of the horns were tipped with a metal resembling gold.[48] There were negative reports and critical observations, but most observers were pleased with the oxen and stone baptismal font.

It was decided on 15 March 1845 to "build a drain for the font."[49] Evidence confirming the existence of this drain was uncovered during the archaeological excavation (see Figure 9.7). They found that "the drain was constructed of large slabs of stone, laid without mortar, to make a channel roughly 12 inches square. . . . It runs from the east end of the font in a southeasterly direction . . . then under the south wall in the direction of the ravine south of Mulholland Street. . . . The bottom of the drain channel is 9 feet below the existing ground level. . . . When the drain was first uncovered in 1962 a plumber's flexible rod was able to probe 35 feet to the southeast."[50]

Water Supply

Joseph Smith explained that water for the font "was supplied from a well thirty feet deep

in the east end of the basement."[51] The well was apparently dug early in the construction of the temple by Hiram Oaks and Jess McCarrol. Hiram Oaks's granddaughter described the project: "They had to penetrate through ten feet of solid rock before they struck water. When they struck water, they lost the drill and water spirited up with great force. Grandfather put his hat over the hole until Jess could get a block of wood to stop the water."[52] This deep well with its reliable flow of water seems to

ordinance work was being conducted, priesthood assignments were issued and men "were appointed to see to the fires."[54]

An additional well came to public attention during the occupation of the temple by mob forces in September 1846. A newspaper correspondent reported: "On Saturday, there was quite an excitement in the camp and the city, created by the discovery of a dry well under the floor of the portico of the Temple, about fifteen feet deep, and situated in a room to which there

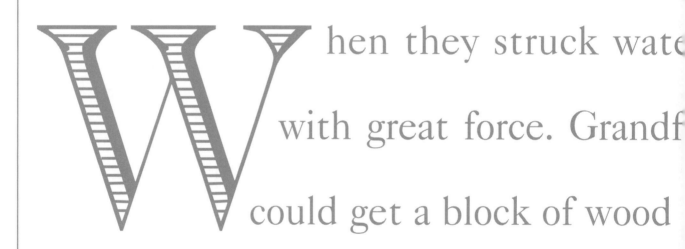

When they struck wate with great force. Grandf could get a block of wood

have supplied the baptismal font adequately as well as all other needs of the temple. Designated by Nauvoo Restoration as Well B, this traditional well can be viewed much as it existed during 1846 in Figure 9.2. It was lined with stone and probably fitted with a pump to draw water for its various uses.

Water from the well was quite cold, so "arrangements were made to heat the rooms and the water in the baptismal font."[53] When

was no entrance except by an opening made in the floor; there were various surmises as to the purpose for which it had been made, but the most reasonable one is, that it had been used as a cistern whilst the temple was being built."[55]

This abandoned shallow well was rediscovered during archaeological excavations of the temple site in 1969.[56] An ordinary stone-lined well that was apparently dry during most of the year, it was walled off and never put to use.

When and why it was dug, and for what purpose, remains unanswered. It may have been used as a drainage well to take water from the font before the southeasterly underground drain was built. If this is true, then it may be that this drainage well could not percolate the water away fast enough, and it became necessary to build the permanent drain.

During site excavation a 7-foot-wide square of brick paving was discovered near the east end of the basement (see Figure 8.4). Archaeologists

and dressing rooms. If this were not the case, they would have had to walk on the slippery clay floor of the basement, which would have been hazardous and dirty. A reporter who toured the temple in August 1845 found that the basement "floor was not yet paved, which I was informed however would be shortly done."[58] Another observer reported on 29 December 1845 that the basement floor was almost finished.[59] William Mendenhall recorded in his journal that he was laying brick in the temple in late March

...ey lost the drill and water spirited up ...er put his hat over the hole until Jess ...op the water.

believe that a water tank or boiler stood on this spot. This tank may have been utilized for storing water, or it may have been connected to a water heating device for the font.[57]

The Basement Floor

This area of the temple was not completed until the spring of 1846. Some type of temporary walkway or flooring was likely put in place for patrons utilizing the wooden baptismal font

and early April 1846.[60] His effort may have been to assist in finishing the main floor or laying brick wall bases in side rooms in preparation for the temple's dedication. An eyewitness who visited the temple shortly after the dedication in May 1846 was pleased "to perceive how much had been accomplished in a month. The appearance of the basement hall has been entirely changed by a laborious use of the trowel." He described that the "animals" now showed to great advantage "in contact with the tiled floor" that had apparently just been laid. This observer went on to declare that "the basement floor is now considered finished."[61] Charles Lanman, who toured the temple during the summer of 1846, described the font as located "in the basement room, which is paved with brick, and converges to the centre."[62] Also in the summer of 1846, Hiram G. Ferris commented on the basement: "The floor of this room is made of brick and has a gradual descent from the sides and ends [to] the font."[63]

When the temple site was excavated in 1968, considerable evidence was found to confirm that most, if not all, of the basement area had been covered with about two inches of clean sand, and the sand then covered with "specially selected brick, larger than usually found in Nauvoo buildings of the period, and of a uniform red color." Of some one hundred whole bricks, "over three-fourths of the bricks measured 9 [inches long] by 4½ [inches wide] and 2½ inches [thick]."[64] The bricks were laid in a herringbone pattern as shown in Figures 8.3 and 8.4. There is strong evidence indicating that the sand layer and red brick paving were put in place between the late fall of 1845 and the dedication in the spring of 1846.[65]

Windows

The basement was illuminated by twenty-one windows, eight on each side and five on the east end.[66] Some artists' sketches and paintings show two more basement windows at the front of the building, one on either side of the entrance steps. Architectural drawings plus photographic evidence in the 1865 Tintype (see Figure 11.2) clearly show that there were no basement windows on the front (west) end of the building. All basement windows were formed in a half circle described to be "about 5 feet high and as many wide."[67] A more accurate identification of the size of these windows, derived from a study of the architectural drawings and daguerreotypes, would be 4 feet 10 inches wide (same as windows in the walls above them) and about 3 feet 11 inches high. They matched the large windows in a direct line above them. A reporter by the name of Hiram Ferris described rooms in the basement, observing: "these small rooms on the sides are lighted by windows in the shape of an oblong semi-circle."[68] These windows were composed of several panes of glass in a fanlike pattern with what seems to be a row of upright window panes at the bottom (see Figure 6.11). "The lower sash probably opened in hopper fashion to ventilate the basement."[69]

Doors

It is apparent that some rooms on each side of the basement were fitted with doors. A visitor described these rooms "all with doors from within."[70] Another observer declared that each room "has one door opening into the large, or central room. But the end room [the walled off, enclosed area, under the front vestibule] has neither any visible door or window. It is directly under the entrance."[71]

Figure 8.5 Diagonally Cut Bricks, photograph, 1960s, LDS Church Archives. This shows diagonally cut bricks from the original herringbone floor, still in place against the stone partition. A stone step to one of the south rooms is shown at the right.

Overall Extent of Completion

The basement area of the temple was probably used more extensively than any other portion of the building. Baptisms for the dead were conducted here beginning on 21 November 1841.[72] These ordinances took place in the wooden font and later in the stone font. Though the stone font was not totally finished by the winter of 1845–46, it was nevertheless considered usable. Baptisms for the dead were regularly conducted there in December 1845[73] and continued until ordinance work ceased on 7 February 1846. It was recorded that 15,626 baptisms for the dead were completed in Nauvoo, almost all of which were done in the temple.[74] The font was completely finished prior to the dedication of the building in the spring of 1846. The basement area was used regularly by the police, who held meetings to regulate assignments for guarding the temple and other sites in Nauvoo.[75] During the summer of 1845 it was observed that the basement was temporarily used as a storage area. "Large piles of ornamental carpenter work is heaped in different parts of the room designed for the finishing of different parts of the Temple. Curious devices or emblems are wrought or carved upon many of the different pieces."[76]

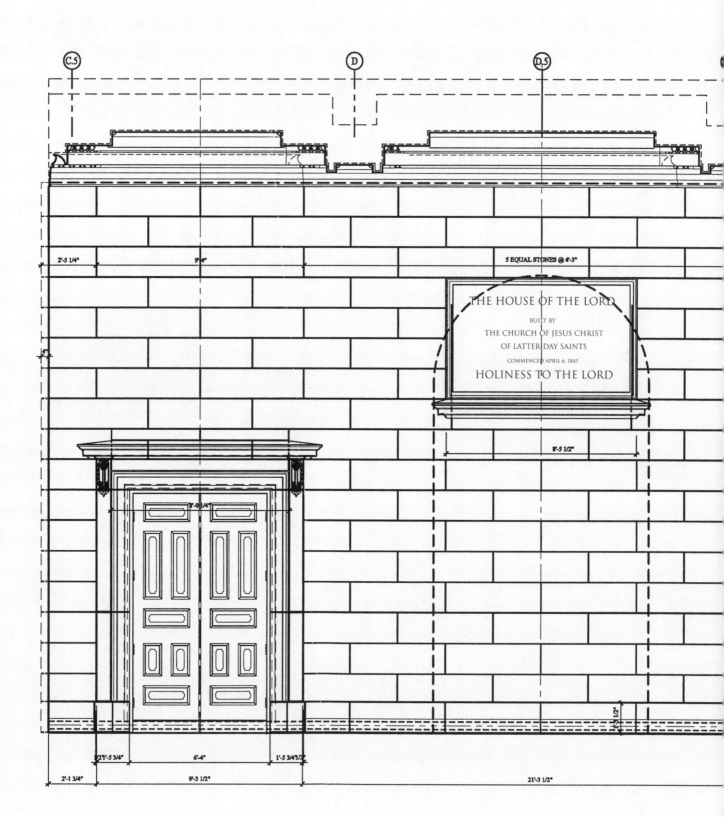

THE HOUSE OF THE LORD

BUILT BY
THE CHURCH OF JESUS CHRIST
OF LATTER-DAY SAINTS

COMMENCED APRIL 6, 1841

HOLINESS TO THE LORD

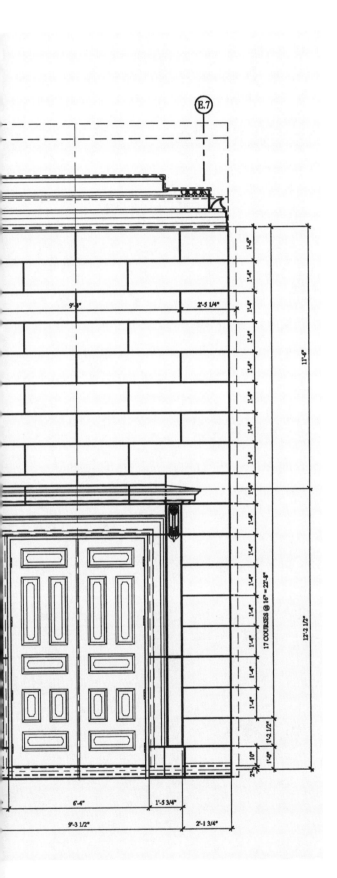

E.7

9'-3"   2'-5 1/4"

1'-5"
1'-4"
1'-4"
1'-4"
1'-4"
1'-4"   11'-5"
1'-4"
1'-4"
1'-5"

17 COURSES @ 16" = 22'-8"

1'-4"
1'-4"
1'-4"
1'-4"   12'-2 1/2"
1'-4"
1'-4"
1'-4"
1'-4"
1'-5"
1'-2 1/2"
1'-5"
10"
2'-1"

6'-4"   1'-5 3/4"

9'-3 1/2"   2'-1 3/4"

Upon entering the vestibule, one's attention was quickly drawn to the dedication plaque centered high on the interior wall.

Figure 8.6 Inside Stone Wall of the Vestibule, drawing, 2000, FFKR Architecture. The dotted lines in the center indicate the center of the three openings into the vestibule. The floor of the vestibule was most likely stone.

Excavation of the temple site revealed that plaster was "found in place on several of the basement piers and partition remains."[77] Prevailing archaeological evidence indicates that the stone walls in the basement were plastered. There is no physical evidence to indicate whether or not these walls were painted. In the winter of 1846 several purchases of white lead, linseed oil, turpentine, and even "shelack" (shellac) were made for the temple. Some of this may have been used for the window frames, but some may also have been for areas of the basement. This wintertime purchase of paint was probably not used on the first or second stories, since at the time neither story was far enough along in completion. It is also possible that the basement walls were covered with lime whitewash.[78] As previously noted, doors and windows had been finished and used in this area of the building. There is also no question that the stone baptismal font had been finished and used prior to the exodus. No record is found of any permanent seating in basement rooms. It is assumed that benches, chairs, and stools were placed in the rooms or brought in by patrons.

T he basement story of the temple was finished in 1846.

Some questions have been raised relative to the completion of the basement floor. The only area of the basement that may have been left unfinished was the floor. Buckingham, who visited the temple in 1847, described the basement as unpaved.[79] His observation is in direct conflict with reports cited above that this area of the temple was paved with brick. Those who excavated the temple site in 1968 reported "it seems safe to conclude that brick paving was planned for the entire basement area, and had probably been laid in most if not all the rooms."[80] It is now evident that when Buckingham visited the building in 1847 the brick paving in existence in 1846 had been carried away. Since the bricks were laid in sand and not set in mortar, they could be removed easily. Because funds were scarce, it is possible that the temple committee had these bricks taken up following the temples dedication. They may have been sold to purchase badly needed supplies for the western exodus. It is also possible that local citizens appropriated them for construction purposes.

Had the Saints remained in Nauvoo, some additional finer finish may have been added to the basement area. There is, however, clear evidence to indicate that this area of the temple was completed, functional, and heavily utilized. This is confirmed by the report of John Taylor in the summer of 1846, when he declared that "the basement story of the temple is finished."[81]

THE FIRST STORY

The first story could properly be called the main floor of the temple. It was here that general conferences and other important Church meetings were held. This was also the place where the formal dedication services were conducted.

The Front Vestibule

Entrance from outside the temple was gained by climbing a flight of ten steps. As Littlefield entered the building in 1845, he left this observation: "Now let us examine what is properly called the first story. . . . We enter this at the west end, passing through either of three large open doors or arched pass-ways, each of which is nine feet seven inches wide and twenty one feet high. Passing through these we are standing in a large outer court, forty-three feet by seventeen feet wide."[82] The area from the floor to the ceiling was 25 feet in height, identical to the main interior area of the first story (see Figure 7.1). On each end of this 43-foot-long outer lobby were stairwells, each 17 feet deep and 18 feet 6 inches long. These areas were separated from the open court by stone partition walls. Each wall had doors that opened into the large spiral staircases. Adding together the spacious outer court along with the stairwells on each side (43 feet plus 18½ and 18½) results in a total interior width dimension of 80 feet (see drawing of the first story floor plan and vestibule area, Figure 8.7).

Upon entering the vestibule, one's attention was quickly drawn to the dedication plaque centered high on the interior wall (see Figure 8.6). It reads the same as its larger duplicate located on the outside of the front attic.

THE HOUSE OF THE LORD
BUILT BY
THE CHURCH OF JESUS CHRIST OF
LATTER-DAY SAINTS
COMMENCED APRIL 6, 1841.
HOLINESS TO THE LORD

No account has been found to describe the floor of this open exposed vestibule area. There is some evidence and good reason to conclude that it was a stone floor. Temple committee records show entries for flagging stones being produced in large quantity.[83] These flagging stones were likely about 4 inches thick and could have been laid over wooden beams. In this open, exposed area, this flagstone-type flooring would certainly have offered much greater protection from the elements than a wooden floor.

The Spiral Staircases

Enclosed within the solid stone stairwells "were winding stairs which led from one story to another until the top of the building was reached."[84] These stairs were built of wood in a spiral fashion. Fortunately, five drawings made

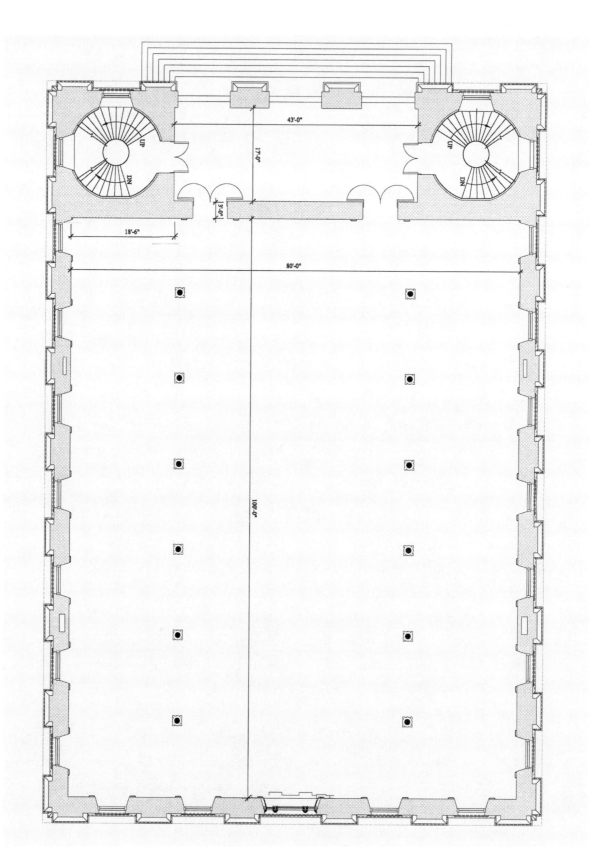

Figure 8.7 The First Story Floor Plan, drawing, 2000, FFKR Architecture. This drawing was modified and adapted from historic reproduction drawings by Steve Goodwin, an architect working on the Nauvoo Temple reconstruction project, at the request of the author. This story contained large, four-tiered pulpits on each end of the central floor area. At the sides of these pulpits were galleries for choirs and musicians. Permanent seats were placed in the main hall with backs that could be repositioned, allowing patrons in the audience to move and view either end of the hall. Permanent seats on each side of the main hall (behind the support columns) all faced to the center. This plan provides for temporary cloth partitions that divide off seven rooms on each side of the main hall. These rooms would likely have been used for small group meetings and instruction. No record is available to indicate that these plans were ever carried out. (For information on support columns, see the explanation in Figure 8.8.)

by the architect have been preserved, furnishing a rather clear picture of these spiral staircases. To design and build such stairs was a significant engineering achievement. The architectural drawings clearly show that each step had a rise of 7 inches. As indicated by the drawings, there were thirteen risers or steps from the basement to the level of the first floor, a total rise of 11 feet 8 inches. The drawings show twenty-seven risers or steps from the first floor level to the first mezzanine, a total rise of 17 feet 1 inch. The heights for each of these areas are consistent with other architectural plans or drawings as well as the photographic evidence available for study. Detailed drawings of the stairs above the first mezzanine are not available. Both spiral staircases were well lighted, especially in the daytime, by the large windows as well as the circular windows located in the corners of the building. The spiral stairs left an open well area 6 feet in diameter at the middle of each spiral stair.[85] This may have been used as a location for a winch and pulley system to aid in getting firewood, coal, and water up to the level of the attic. A large amount of stove coal was purchased, as evidenced by entries found in the Building Committee account books." This also is supported by the description of George Washington Bean, who explained: "I worked in the outer court of the Temple running a windlass, drawing up the wood and water needed to carry on the endowments."[86] If so used, it was probably the north stairwell that was utilized for this purpose.

Stairs in the southwest stairwell were considered finished and used extensively by patrons who came for their temple ordinances. The stairs on the northwest stairwell were used consistently by workers during construction, but evidence indicates that these stairs had only a rough finish. Joseph Smith III, who visited the temple on several occasions, claimed that "the stairway in the northwest corner was not finished. Rough inch boards [steps] were laid over the risers so that the workmen could pass up and down."[87] Account books indicate that some hardwood was used in finishing the temple. There are purchases for cherry wood, oak, and walnut.[88] Some cherry wood was used for doorsills, but no other indication is given as to where these types of wood were used.[89] It is very possible that some hardwood was utilized in the stairs. Archaeological excavation found in the charred fragments "of the north stairwell, a small piece of walnut, possibly from the steps or handrail."[90]

The Main First-Floor Area

The large assembly hall of the first story was entered by the main entrance on the west end through one of two large doors coming off the outer court. This story was planned to be divided into fifteen rooms. The large room running through the center was 100 feet long from east to west and 50 feet wide.[91] The fourteen rooms on the sides of this main hall (seven on each side) were never permanently partitioned. There is also no record of any division into various-sized rooms by the planned temporary cloth partitions.[92] If such a division were to have taken place, the most common dimension of these rooms would probably have been 15 feet by 15 feet.

The overall dimensions of the first floor are easily determined. Architect's drawings provide a cross-sectional drawing with an arched central ceiling over the main hall of 40 feet 9 inches (see Figure 7.1). On each side of this arched ceiling there were six support posts 12 inches in diameter, each of which was sheathed with twenty fluted staves, making them into rounded 18-inch-diameter columns. Beyond these support columns on each side of the building was an area 18 feet 6 inches in width (see Figure 8.7). Adding these figures together brings an internal width of 80 feet. Overall internal length of the first story was 120 feet: 100 feet in the main hall plus a 3-foot-thick dividing wall between the main assembly hall and the vestibule plus a 17-foot outer court vestibule or portico area. This area can be examined by study of the first-story floor plan (Figure 8.7).

The permanent wood floor was finished or put in place by New Year's Day of 1846.[93] No written descriptions of this floor have been provided. There is a possibility that the finished flooring was laid over the top of a rough subfloor, or it may have been only a finished 1- to 2-inch tongue-and-groove floor (1-inch thickness was common in other Nauvoo buildings). Support for the floor was provided by heavy stone columns or piers in the basement (see Figure 9.3). There were six of these 4-foot-square columns on each side of the basement, each set at 19 feet from the outside walls. Over the center of these columns were six heavy timber beams running the whole width of the temple, which were set on 15-foot centers. These heavy 12-inch-diameter pine timbers or beams were anchored or inset 16 inches into the stone walls of the temple (see Figure 7.1). The timbers may have been one long pole or beam 82 to 83 feet long but more likely were sectioned into three pieces, with the middle section being fit into place having a beveled edge, as shown in Jackson's drawing (see Figure 8.12). These beveled endpieces would likely have been nailed or bolted together by strong boards on one or both sides of the beam at the joint area. Between these timbers, floor joists were placed on 14-inch centers to provide stability and support for the flooring placed upon them. In all likelihood these floor joists were 3-by-12-inch boards, approximately 14 or 15 feet in length. A drawing showing this type of floor joists can be viewed by examination of the fragment showing some of the south stairwell (see Figure 7.11). Billing records also support these measurements.

As the temple neared completion, permanent bench seats were installed in the center hall and along each side. Buckingham reported that in the "grand hall" of the first floor "seats are provided in this hall . . . and they are arranged with backs, which are fitted like the backs to seats in a modern railroad car, so as to allow the spectator to sit and look in either direction, east or west."[94] Another observer reported that the benches in the central hall under the arch were "constructed with backs that turn either way so as to admit of the

Figure 8.8 Support Columns, drawing, 1843–45, William Weeks, LDS Church Archives. This is an original architectural drawing by architect William Weeks. Both the first and second story of the temple contained a large central hall covered by an arched ceiling that ran the full 100-foot length of the hall. Supporting this semicylindrical arch were twelve support columns (six on each side of the building) on each floor level. These columns were composed of a 12-inch-diameter support post surrounded at the bottom by a 3½-foot-high, wood-paneled pedestal base. Above the pedestal base the posts were encased by fluted staves, making them into attractive round columns 18 inches in diameter. At the top of each column (as it reached the cornice area at the bottom of the arch) wooden capitals were intricately carved in a rising sun motif. Similar columns were found in the east attic section of the building. Additional similarly designed external columns can be seen surrounding the clock section of the tower as shown in daguerreotype photographs of the temple.

Figure 8.9 Wood Paneling and Inside Wood Casements around Main Windows, drawing, 1840s, William Weeks, LDS Church Archives. This is an original architectural drawing by architect William Weeks. This drawing shows the design of a 3-foot-high wood panel wainscoting, which was placed under each window. There was also a 3-foot-high wood panel wainscoting such as this at the base of the walls around the entire first floor of the temple. This drawing also shows designs of wood casements on the inside of the building around each of the forty-seven main windows. In the upper right of the drawing, it also shows a detail section of a very decorative wood carving used on both sides of each window showing the sun rising above foliage.

audience being seated facing either end of the room."[95] One additional witness who toured the building declared: "The benches under the arch face each other in pairs." He then added: "Those at the sides all face the center."[96] No reliable figures are available on the seating capacity of the first story. Some attendance figures were reported for the October conference of 1845, but these seem to be inflated.[97]

The first story of the Nauvoo Temple had "a large arch over its entire length."[98] Supporting this semicylindrical arch and the

second floor above were twelve posts of round timber, each 12 inches in diameter. There were six of these posts on each side. The support posts were 24 feet in length rising from the level of the first floor to the bottom of the sleeper under the long timber beams supporting the second floor (see architect's sketch of this area in Figure 7.1). Where exposed to view, each post was covered to 3½ feet by an ornamental wood-paneled pedestal. Above this pedestal each post was encased by fluted staves, making attractive columns. These round columns, each 18 inches in diameter, rose above the pedestals to the bottom of the first mezzanine.

As noted by Tim Maxwell, an architect working on the Nauvoo Temple reconstruction project, "240 tapered staves 11 feet long are listed in the carpentry shop records. Also listed are 330 15-inch-long staves, evidently for carving the capitals. The number 330 is consistent when it is considered that one capital consisting of 30 staves may have been carved as a pattern prior to the 330 in the list. The 20 long staves and 30 short staves, when assembled in circles of the size pieces listed, both perfectly surround a 12 inch center. These dimensions and arrangement also confirm the fluted column and half sun-face capital found in William Weeks's drawing that in the past was dismissed as only early discarded studies by Weeks."[99]

The columns supported an entablature and cornice running along the inner base of the arch. The entablature, frieze, cornice, soffits, and support columns were all places for special finish. Building records indicate considerable detailed wood carving and ornamentation in these areas. Ceilings on the sides under the mezzanines were flat.

Plans were made to subdivide the whole floor of the main hall by the use of "three great veils of rich crimson drapery."[100] These were to be suspended overhead from the ceiling and lowered into place when the occasion determined such a division. However, no record has been found to indicate that these plans were ever carried out.

The permanent floor was being laid in November 1845, making it possible to construct permanent tiered pulpits. In December Brigham Young, along with other leaders, "went down to the lower room and counseled on the arrangement of the pulpits."[101] On 1 January 1846 leaders found "the floor is laid, the framework of the pulpits and seats for the choir and band are put up; and the work of finishing the room for dedication progresses rapidly."[102] On this same date one year earlier a letter written by W. W. Phelps to William Smith was published in the *Times and Seasons*. It described features to be constructed in the interior of the temple. "The two great stories will each have two pulpits, one on each end; to accommodate the Melchisedek and Aaronic priesthoods; graded into four rising seats: the first for the president of the elders, and his two counsellors; the second for the president of the high priesthood and his two counsellors; the third for the Melchisedek president and his two counsellors, and the fourth for the president over the whole church, (the first president) and his two counsellors. . . . The Aaronic pulpit at the other end the same."[103]

J. H. Buckingham, who visited the temple a year after its dedication, left this description of the first story interior: "At the east and west end are raised platforms, composed of series of pulpits on steps one above the other. The fronts of these pulpits are semi-circular and are inscribed in gilded letters on the west side: PAP, PPQ, PTQ, PDQ, meaning, as the guide informed us, the uppermost one,

President of Aaronic Priesthood; the second, President of the Priests' Quorum; the third, President of the Teachers' Quorum; and the fourth and lowest, President of the Deacons' Quorum. On the east side the pulpits were marked PHP, PSZ, PHQ, and PEQ, and the knowledge of the guide was no better than ours as to what these symbolic letters were intended for."[104] The meaning of this last set of letters is explained in the previous paragraph except for the letters PSZ. They may

Buckingham but offers no clarification. Further confirmation of the accuracy of this designation is provided by the same lettering being used on the Melchizedek Priesthood Pulpits in the St. George Temple (see note 104). Other descriptions show that each pulpit unit "was graded into four rising seats"[106] and was wide enough "to accommodate three persons each."[107] Each pulpit had its own decorative lettered insignia identifying its occupants.

On the wall in back of the highest pulpit on

On the wall in back of the high... tion in large gold letters SACRIFICE: COME AFTER US."

have stood for President of the Seventy in Zion, but that is only conjecture.

James A. Scott, a member of the Church of Jesus Christ of Latter-day Saints who attended the temple dedication on 1 May 1846, recorded the following description: "Inscriptions on the seats of the priesthood. Me P. highest seat PHP, 2nd PSZ, 3rd PHQ, 4th PEQ. A. P. highest seat PAP, 2nd PPQ, 3rd PTQ, 4th PDQ."[105] Scott confirms the PSZ lettering noted by

the east end was "an inscription in large gold letters,"[108] which read "THE LORD HAS BEHELD OUR SACRIFICE: COME AFTER US."[109] An observer declared that these "two grand pulpits at the East and West ends gave to the whole an appearance of Oriental Magnificence."[110]

For conference meetings in the fall of 1845, temporary pulpits and seating were in place. At the west end of the large main hall "was constructed a large box for the use of the choir and players on instruments."[111] This may have been the area referred to as the galleries by L. O. Littlefield. Reporting his attendance at the conference, he stated: "I found a seat in the north gallery and had a commanding view of the congregation which spread out itself below and around me. . . . On either side ranged a solid phalanx of seated males, and all were o'er-topt with down-gazing auditors that crowded the galleries."[112]

moment's notice."[113] This described gallery may have been included as part of the large choir section that was built. Then again, due to the forced exodus these galleries may never have been constructed. There is no report of galleries being present as the first floor was finished. Another possibility is that for this fall conference temporary galleries were provided above the first floor in the unfinished first mezzanine. This area could have been open on the sides at this time and utilized as galleries to provide

pulpit on the east end was "an inscrip-

hich read "THE LORD HAS BEHELD OUR

It is possible that temporary galleries or balconies had been constructed to provide additional seating at this conference. If so, these would have been taken down during the following month as the temporary floor was replaced. There is a single reference describing some type of gallery to be constructed on the permanent floor. "The gallery is to consist of different chambers, . . . which are all to be separated by veils, which can be drawn or withdrawn at a

additional seating. Further explanation of this possibility is pursued in the next section.

Extent of Completion

The first story of the temple was completed with careful attention to detail and the highest quality of workmanship. It was described as "worthy of the attention of all architects who delight in originality and taste. It has been thronged with visitors from abroad since its

completion, and excites the surprise and admiration of every beholder."[114] The vestibule entrance was complete, secured with doors and locks. Inside, the permanent wood floor was laid, and attractive decorated pulpits were in place along with large galleries for the choir and musicians. Visitors found "the inner temple an artistic work in the medium of wood, stone and glass."[115] One observer who visited the building in the fall of 1846 noted "the immense audience chamber . . . with its pews and changing backs, its immense altars and oratories, its gorgeous tapestry and motes in gold and silver, its ponderous chandeliers and innumerable columns and frescoes that elsewhere bewildered the eye with their gorgeous beauty."[116]

Another observer commented that "the work is of the best character . . . the carving both in wood and stone evinces great taste and ingenuity."[117] Much of the detailed finish work was completed as the exodus from Nauvoo was under way. Church leaders and many members had already gone west. In spite of this, the temple was pushed to completion. It was an unselfish act of love and devotion to God. Under the circumstances that existed, it is most significant to note the detail, artistry, and quality that was put into the efforts of these builders. Observers entering the main hall found that "the woodwork of the doors and windows was composed of beautifully carved work," the tops of the door jambs being "ornamented with Corinthian capitals of the most exquisite workmanship!"[118] There was "beautiful vine work," along with "delicately executed leaf and bud." Bills for these artistically finished windows and door casings include orders for several pieces of door and window jambs, rails, pilasters, pedestals, capitals, sills, panels, sash, architraves, crown fillets, crown molds, and other items or pieces.[119] These were not simple, plain, or crude frames—they were works of art. Figure 8.10 illustrates the highly decorated woodwork around each window of this main floor. From descriptions and bills of materials it is evident that the same kind of work was put around each doorway as well.

Wooden panels of varying lengths were used as part of a 3-foot-high wainscoting at the base of walls around the entire floor. There were panels under each window, in between windows and in between doors. Illustration of this

The carving both in wood and stone evinces great taste and ingenuity.

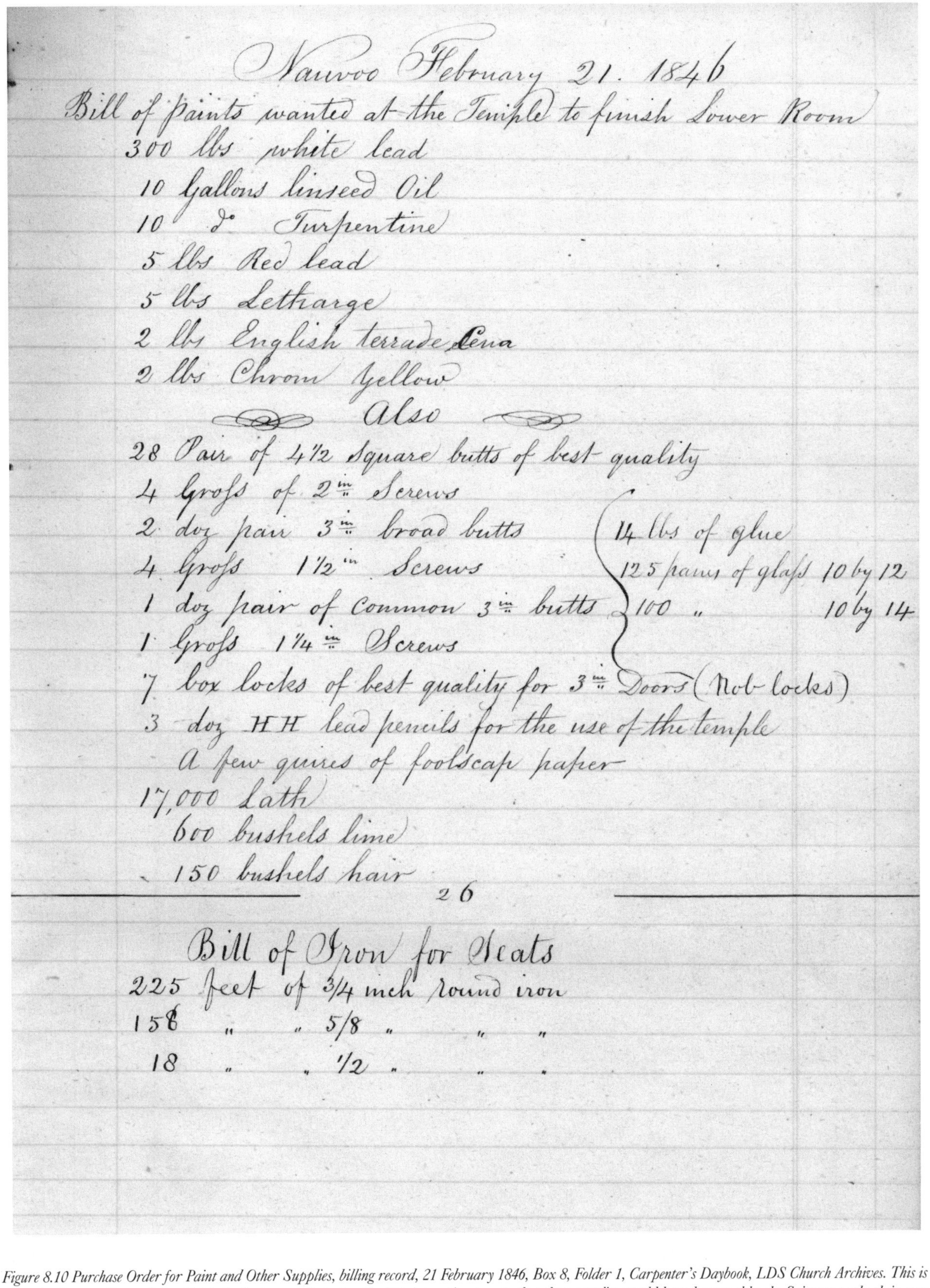

Nauvoo February 21. 1846

Bill of Paints wanted at the Temple to finish Lower Room

300 lbs white lead

10 Gallons linseed Oil

10 do Turpentine

5 lbs Red lead

5 lbs Letharge

2 lbs English terrade Siena

2 lbs Chrom Yellow

Also

28 Pair of 4½ Square butts of best quality

4 Gross of 2in Screws

2 doz pair 3in broad butts

4 Gross 1½in Screws

1 doz pair of Common 3in butts

1 Gross 1¼in Screws

14 lbs of glue

125 pains of glass 10 by 12

100 " 10 by 14

7 box locks of best quality for 3in Doors (Nob locks)

3 doz H H lead pencils for the use of the temple

A few quires of foolscap paper

17,000 Lath

600 bushels lime

150 bushels hair

26

Bill of Iron for Seats

225 feet of ¾ inch round iron

158 " " 5/8 " " "

18 " " ½ " " "

Figure 8.10 Purchase Order for Paint and Other Supplies, billing record, 21 February 1846, Box 8, Folder 1, Carpenter's Daybook, LDS Church Archives. This is an order for supplies needed to finish the first story of the temple. It is interesting to note that these supplies would have been used by the Saints to make their own paint.

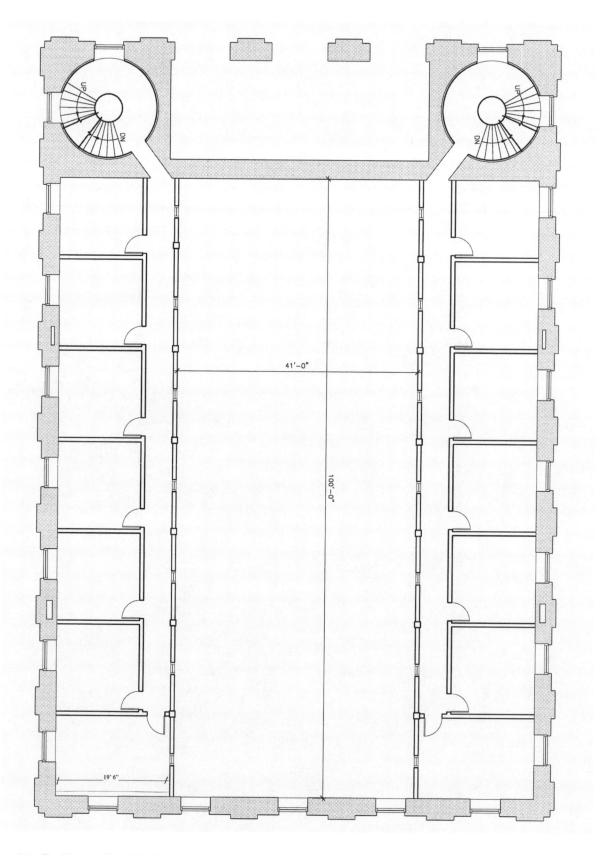

Figure 8.11   First Mezzanine Story Floor Plan, drawing, 2000, FFKR Architecture. This drawing was modified and adapted from historic reconstruction draw-
ings by Steve Goodwin, an architect working on the Nauvoo Temple reconstruction project, at the request of the author. The rooms were planned for offices on each
side of the building in this half-story mezzanine. The size of these offices is not known, and there is no clear indication or description providing evidence that they were
ever partitioned off or finished. This area may have been utilized in its unfinished state as a temporary open gallery providing additional seating for the conference
held on the temporary floor of the first story in October 1845.

paneling and wainscoting (under the windows) can be examined by study of Figure 8.9. Bills for this wainscoting furnish valuable insight into the details of this woodwork. An example of one of these bills is as follows:

A BILL OF WAINSCOTING FOR NORTH AND SOUTH SIDES

24 Pieces	6 feet	11 long	x 5 1/2	1 1/2
24 Pieces	2 feet	11 long	3 1/2	1 1/2
24 Panels	6 feet	8 long	1 1/2	1

86 FEET FOR WEST END WAINSCOTING

43 feet of panels	x	14	1
43 feet of fillet	x	3 7/8	1 1/4
43 feet of crown mold	x	1 3/4	1[120]

The arched semicylindrical ceiling over the main hall as well as the flat ceilings on the sides were all plastered and finished. A bill for this work was submitted on 21 February 1846; it included "17,000 lath 600 bushels lime and 150 bushels hair" (see Figure 8.10).

The first floor was predominantly white. Ceilings were plastered white, the stone walls were grayish white, and the woodwork was painted white or a light tan color. A bill of paints for the first floor included "300 lbs. white lead, 10 gallons linseed oil, 10 gallons turpentine, 5 lbs. red lead, 5 lbs. letharge, 2 lbs. English terra cena and 2 lbs. chrome yellow."[121]

The woodwork of the columns and cornice area around the bottom of the central arch was also specially finished. Bills of materials call for 205 feet each of crown molds, crown fillet, fascia, architraves, frieze, and other items, along with 214 mutules and mutule caps.[122] This was without question a place of extensive artistic detail.

After the dedication, many of the religious and decorative furnishings were removed from the temple. As noted by one observer, "When finished it was profusely ornamented on the inside, and dedicated by the most solemn services; these over, it was despoiled of its ornaments and abandoned." He also noted: "The walls within the Temple were bare, the only ornaments being those cut in the wood or stone."[123]

THE FIRST MEZZANINE HALF-STORY

Recesses on the sides of the arch made it possible to construct a half-story on each side of the building between the first and second floors. The length of the recesses or half-stories was 100 feet. This created two side halls that were long but low and narrow.[124] These 100-foot-long hallways were each 18 feet 6 inches wide and 7 feet high (see architectural drawings, Figure 7.1 and 8.11). It was intended that these areas be divided into seven rooms on each side of the building. Each room was to be lighted by one of the lower round windows. No record has been found to determine if the partitions and rooms were actually constructed. This area would have consisted of a long hallway some 3 to 5 feet wide, along with seven rooms approximately 14 feet square on each side of the building. Some may have been built due to the intent of conducting endowment ordinances at this location. Brigham Young once stated, "In the recesses, on each side of the arch, on the first story, there will be a suit of rooms or ante-chambers. . . . As soon as suitable number of those rooms are completed we shall commence the endowment."[125] Since the endowment ordinances were moved to the main attic area, records are absent on any use of the first mezzanine. Layout of the floor plan for this first mezzanine can be studied by examining Figure 8.11.

There is some possibility that on a temporary basis this mezzanine was used as a gallery overlooking the main hall below, which is supported by the report of one observer who described having "a seat in the north gallery and had a commanding view of the congregation which spread out itself below and around me."[126] If temporary galleries were used here in the fall of 1845, they probably lacked tiered seating. This would mean that most of those seated there would have been unable to see the pulpits. Unfinished at this date, the first mezzanine could have been open on the inner sides, thus allowing such usage.

THE SECOND STORY

As interior floors of the temple were under construction, observers could view "range upon range of massive timber," and one visitor expressed being impressed with "the stupendous height of the ceiling, and the massiveness and quality of the timber."[127] Richard Jackson, a retired Church architect, noted an interesting possible method of construction used in building this floor and other floors of the temple. Jackson also served a Church mission in Nauvoo and has carefully studied the architecture and construction of the Nauvoo Temple. He notes that two very old photographs of the building show

the fifth window from the front on the third floor [second story] not yet having a sill in one and a modified sill in the other. In both it is obvious that the window opening extended down to what would probably have been the floor level, most likely to allow roof and floor framing members to be brought into the building for installation in the middle bay. A gin-pole would have been mounted on the top of the outside wall with a swinging boom-arm with a pulley on the end [see Figure 8.13]. The member would be raised to the level of the third floor [second story] by a horse pulling on a rope through a pulley on the ground. At the floor level, the member would be pulled into the building and unloosed. It would then be picked up with a similar pulley system mounted on top of the intermediate column supports and from there elevated or lowered into the desired position in the middle bay [see Figure 8.13]. When the work was finished the window opening would have been closed with matching material but the material lines show.[128]

Jackson's observations are sustained by the earliest known daguerreotype of the building (see Figure 8.13), which indicates that this particular window area was indeed open and could easily have been utilized in the manner that he explained. Permanent stone steps in front of the building were not completed until late in the building's construction. It is most likely that this opening and another like it on the north side were needed for bringing construction materials into the building. It would not be practical to bring everything in through the front entrances. Heavy beams and timbers used in construction would have been too cumbersome to move by hand. The floor of this story was supported by six 12-inch-diameter posts on each side of the building, along with the timbers and joists just like that of the first story.

The second story was designed to be an exact duplicate of the first. It was, however, 20 feet longer than the first story in consequence of running out over the top of the front outer court or vestibule. This additional open space was marked by a stone arch which spanned 41 feet and served as support for the tower. An excellent view of this arch can be seen by examining Figure 11.3. This artist's sketch has some discrepancies in that it shows no access to the mezzanine levels and has another problem, as cited by Tim Maxwell: "The arch must have been the artists attempt to picture one that had in fact already collapsed at the time of the drawing. The arch pictured is far too thin over the top to have carried the tremendous dead weight and wind loads of a 90-foot-high tower. More likely the arch masonry was 8 to 12 feet deep at the thinnest point over this span."[129]

The room of the second story is described by Lanman as being in every particular precisely like that of the first story.[130] It was well lighted by large windows on both sides and both ends of the building. On 20 January 1846 it was

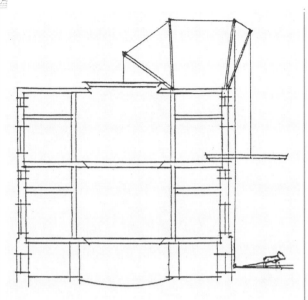

Figure 8.12 Sketch of Roof and Floor Framing Construction Process, drawing, 1960s, Richard Jackson. This drawing shows how beams and other materials were likely brought into the building during construction through the opening in the walls, which is visible in Figure 8.13.

announced in the *Times and Seasons* that "the floor of the second story is laid."[131] After the floor was laid, this hall was used on many occasions. Strong and substantial, this floor supported large crowds of people as they gathered here for the various meetings conducted in this part of the building. Typical of these meetings is the following, as Hosea Stout observed: "Went to the Temple to a public meeting in the Second Story but the congregation was so numerous that it would not contain them."[132] Brigham Young reported that on 24 January he "attended a general meeting of the official members of the church held in the second story of the Temple, for the purpose of arranging the business affairs of the church prior to our exit from this place."[133] Another example of such meetings is the report of Sunday services or a "public" meeting conducted in the second story of the temple on 1 February 1846.[134]

This area of the temple was said to have been "partially finished, having benches and temporary pulpits which could be used in case of necessity."[135] These pulpits and seating were probably the same ones used on the first floor for the October 1845 conference. Some office rooms may have been constructed along the sides of the main hall. Doors for those offices were ready by midsummer 1845, and bills of materials call for locks, hinges, etc.[136] Since they were ready this early, it is likely that some of them were put in place. A reporter from the *Illinois Journal* wrote that there were "small rooms eight or ten feet square on either side."[137] A description of these rooms and their exact location is uncertain. They may have been on the second floor level or on the level of the second mezzanine half-story. The floor was described as having a rough finish but was reportedly used for dances throughout the winter of 1845–46.[138] The room was also used for other recreation purposes following the exodus of the Mormons from Nauvoo. No record seems to be available describing the plastering or painting of this section of the building. Available evidence leads to the conclusion that this area, though not totally finished, was functionally completed and extensively used. A layout of the second story is found in Figure 8.15.

THE SECOND MEZZANINE OR UPPER HALF-STORY

There is very little information on this area of the temple. It was planned to be identical in size and configuration with the lower mezzanine half-story. The only basic difference between the two was the size of the round windows. Smaller round windows providing illumination to this mezzanine section had a star shape configuration in the window panes (see Figures 6.9 and 7.9). The panes were colored glass or were painted in colors red, white, and blue.[139] From November 1845 through April 1846, heavy emphasis and urgency was given to work on the second story and the completion of the first story. It is therefore very likely that both the lower and upper mezzanine half-stories were only roughed in and never finished. No record has surfaced describing rooms, floors, extent of finish, or usage for this upper mezzanine section of the building. A layout of this second mezzanine and the proposed design of its rooms is found in Figure 8.14. It should be noted that a set of stairs was installed providing access between this mezzanine and the east attic area above it. This is explained in greater detail later in this chapter in the section describing the east main attic of the building.

THE FRONT ATTIC SECTION

A boxlike rectangular attic or half-story spanned the width of the stone walls on the west end at the top of the building. This front attic section was 86 to 87 feet long. Extending back from the front, it had a depth of 37 feet (see Figure 7.8). It was described as being 16½ feet in height.[140]

The inside of this front attic was described as containing "two or three large square rooms."[141] A nearly square room on the south end measured about 27 feet north to south and about

Figure 8.13 An Early Daguerreotype of the Nauvoo Temple, daguerreotype, ca. 1845, photographer unknown, LDS Church Archives. This may be the earliest photographic reproduction of the Nauvoo Temple. The large upper middle window on the south side of the building lacks a window sill and part of the wall below this window opening. This would indicate that this open space may have been used for taking materials into the building during construction as illustrated in Figure 8.12. The bottom of this opening would fit well with the level of the second story. There is no angelic weather vane on the steeple in this daguerreotype, but instead what appears to be a retouched vane of some sort added to the daguerreotype. This daguerreotype was very likely taken in the fall of 1845 at the time when the building was fully enclosed and all outside work was nearly completed. It was clearly taken before the weather vane was installed on the steeple on 30 January 1846. Later photographs show this open wall section filled in and an angelic weather vane in place at the top of the steeple (see Figure 5.4).

36 feet east to west. Nearly one quarter of this room was taken up by the southwest corner stairwell, as it rose from the basement to this level (see diagram of this floor level, Figure 8.17). The rest of this room was an assembly or waiting room area for those coming to receive their endowments (see note 142 for justification of this conclusion).[142] In the center of this attic area was "a massive pine frame, from the centre of the roof from which rises the tower."[143] This

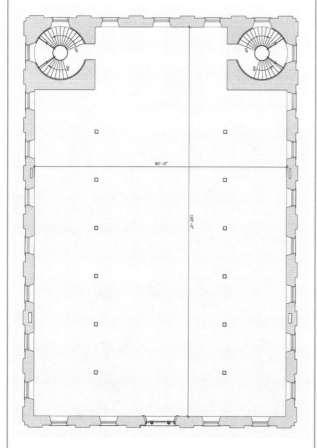

Figure 8.14 Second Story Floor Plan, drawing, 2000, FFKR Architecture. This drawing was modified and adapted from historic reproduction drawings by Steve Goodwin, an architect working on the Nauvoo Temple reconstruction project, at the request of the author. The six support columns on each side of this story had a square pedestal base from which rose the 18-inch round columns that provided support for the second mezzanine and the attic story. This second story was to be an exact duplicate of the first story except that it was 20 feet longer due to extending out over the front vestibule. Permanent rooms were planned for the sides, but there is no clear definition on any construction of these rooms. This area of the temple was used extensively but was given only a rough finish.

large supporting timber frame was octagonal in shape and 29 feet in width. On the west side of this framed area between it and the outside wall was a narrow space only 2½ to 3 feet wide (see diagram in Figure 8.17). On the east side between this steeple base and the wall between the two attics was another narrow space of the same width. Open passageways are believed to have led into the interior of this framed tower base area. Here stairs could be accessed leading to the tower sections above. Access may also have been gained to the large room on the north end and also into the main east attic (see Figure 8.17). On the north end of this front attic was a room known as the "pantry" or "dining room," identical in size to the south room. It had the same space taken up by a stairwell as the stairs rose to this level in the northwest corner of the building. This room was widely used by Church authorities, construction workers, temple ordinance workers, and patrons to eat and store food.[144] This was an essential accommodation necessitated by nearly round-the-clock temple ordinance work during December 1845, through January and early February 1846.

The front attic section was well illuminated during daylight hours by eight rectangular windows. Some seating may have been provided in the reception or assembly room, but no reference verifying this has been found. It is also likely that seating and tables were located in the pantry room, but again no information has surfaced to validate this conclusion. There appears to be no documentation as to whether or not this area was finished. However, it is likely that the area was plastered and painted at the same time as the east or main attic. Had it remained unfinished, it would most likely have been noted by observers.

Tower or Steeple Section

From the center of the front attic section rose an octagonal tower. Its timber framework was massive, containing posts, beams, braces, and supports (as can be observed by examining Figure 7.5). Inside the framework of this tower was "a series of steps which were very steep."[145] Climbing up from the attic one could "ascend to the bell room of the steeple, thence to the clock room, at last to the observatory."[146] One who climbed the full height of this stairway described having "to ascend 15 flights of steps to reach the top."[147] This description may have also included the flights of stairs below the attic level.

The tower consisted of various sections. As the tower rose in height, those sections diminished in width, creating a telescopic effect. The base or pedestal section was 29 feet in diameter. It started on the floor of the attic and rose another 12½ feet above the attic roof. At the roof level on the east side of this octagonal base was a small doorway that provided access to the deck roof over the top of the main east attic.[148] The section above the base or pedestal narrowed to 22 feet in diameter. It was composed of the belfry and, directly above it, the clock section. The belfry had eight openings, each with two louvered Gothic shutters. The openings were about 4 feet wide and 10 feet tall. The louvers of the

shutters were painted green. It is not clear as to whether any glass windows were put in the belfry section, but it likely remained open to the air. The belfry housed a large bell.

The clock section was designed to have a clock on the four different faces of the tower. In between each of the clock facings were small windows. No descriptions have been found of this section's interior. Above the clock section was the observatory, which diminished in size to a diameter of 17 feet. This area had eight windows, and it is likely that these windows had glass in them and could be opened to permit observation. Careful examination of the Chaffin daguerreotype (see Figure 5.4) indicates partially open windows in this section of the tower. It also shows that these had diamond-shaped, leaded glass panes. Rising above the observatory was the dome, said to be diminished in size to about 13 or 14 feet at its base. There are reports of visitors writing their names on the ceiling inside the dome.[149]

There is a bill in the temple billing records calling for 2,225 feet of floor to be used in various sections of the tower and its stairways.[150] The stairs were described by an observer who noted that some of the finishing work was not done, "the inside of this was not entirely finished," making it possible for visitors "to observe the massive strength of the frame-work, and perceive the solidity and view the durability, with which it was constructed. The bare timbers presented a never-ending system of braces, each supporting the other successively."[151]

The Main East Attic Area

Brigham Young clearly described the layout and dimensions of this area:

> The main room of the attic story is eighty-eight feet two inches long and twenty-eight feet eight inches wide. It is arched over, and the arch is divided into six spaces by cross beams to support the roof. There are six small rooms on each side about fourteen feet square. The last one on the east end on each side is a little smaller.
>
> The first room on the south side beginning on the east is occupied by myself, the second by Elder Kimball, the third by Elders Orson Hyde, Parley P. Pratt and Orson Pratt; the fourth by John Taylor, George A. Smith, Amasa Lyman and John E. Page; the fifth by Joseph Young and Presidents of Seventies; the sixth, a preparation room.
>
> On the north side, the first east room is for Bishop Whitney and the lesser priesthood, the second is for the high council, the third and fourth for President George Miller and the high priests' quorum, the fifth the elders' room, and the sixth the female preparation room.[152]

Rooms on the sides were all numbered, those on the south having odd numbers and those on the north even numbers.[153] These numbered rooms and assignments can be viewed by examining Figure 8.17.

Access into the east attic section of the building was gained by going either through the tower support structure or the narrow 2½- to 3-foot-wide space on the east side of the tower base to a door located at the center in the west end of the large main east attic council room. This can be visualized by examining Figure 8.18. Another entrance and exit to this attic area was noted by Catherine Lewis. She commented that there were those who entered the attic from the west and then went "out a different way."[155] As the second floor of the temple was under construction (in late December 1845), plans were made to build a stairway into Heber C. Kimball's room.[156] His journal reports that on 23 December, "A staircase has this day been put up by which we can pass out through Elder Kimball's room which has been converted into an office for the convenience of transacting business with persons from without."[157] His journal entry for 26 December reports that Sheriff Backenstos came to the temple and was admitted to this office (No. 3) by the back stairs.[158] This back stairway most likely led down from Kimball's office (Room 3) to the floor of the second mezzanine. From here someone using this access could pass through the south second story mezzanine to the front of the building. One could then go down the stairs in the southwest corner stairwell and exit the building. It is also possible that a temporary construction stairway may have been in place on the outside of the building that was used as an access to the building. Buckingham referred to the large central room of this east attic as the "council chamber," describing it as a long, low room.[159] The room was designated by William Clayton and Brigham Young as the "main room"[160] and by Heber C. Kimball as the "big hall."[161] No description is available on its height, but it was 28 feet 8 inches wide by 88 feet

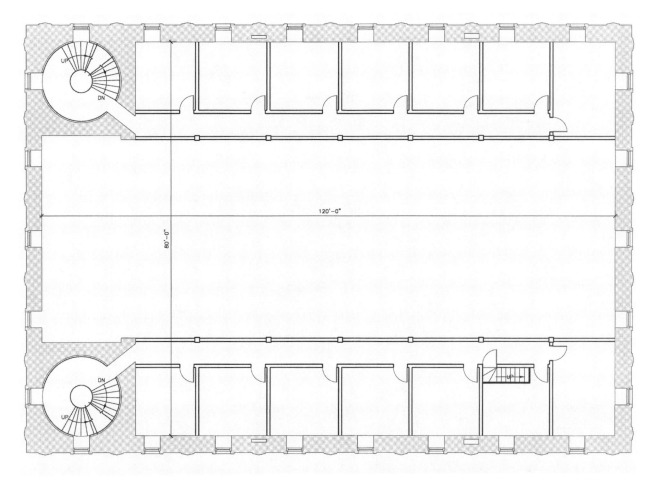

Figure 8.15 Second Mezzanine Floor Plan, drawings, 2000, FFKR Architecture. This drawing was modified and adapted from historic reproduction drawings by Steve Goodwin, an architect working on the Nauvoo Temple reconstruction project, at the request of the author. Rooms were planned for offices on each side of the building on this floor level. The size of these offices has not been found and there is no clear indication or description providing evidence that this area was or was not partitioned. There is clear evidence that a stairway was constructed between this level and the attic, near the east end of the building up into room 3, the office used by Heber C. Kimball. Indications lead to the conclusion that this mezzanine section of the building was given only a rough finish.

2 inches long.[162] The main room was well lighted from above during daylight hours by the six sky-lights located in the deck roof.[163] An additional abundance of light came from the large 20½-foot-wide Gothic-styled window of the east end.[164]

The central hall was "divided into six spaces by [five] cross beams to support the roof."[165] These cross beams and the arch over the council room were held in place by a queen-post truss.[166] The ten posts supporting these trusses (five on each side) were covered with a wood casing, making them into attractive composite columns, described by a reporter from the *Illinois Journal* as a "double row of Composite columns, of excellent workmanship."[167] There was a door at the main entrance on the west end of the large council room. Each of the twelve side rooms also had a door, each of which was described as having a "massive lock."[168]

Rooms on the sides of this attic diminished in height due to the slope of the roof. Historical reproduction architectural drawings indicate that the outer or back ends of these rooms would have been only 5 feet 8 inches high. This

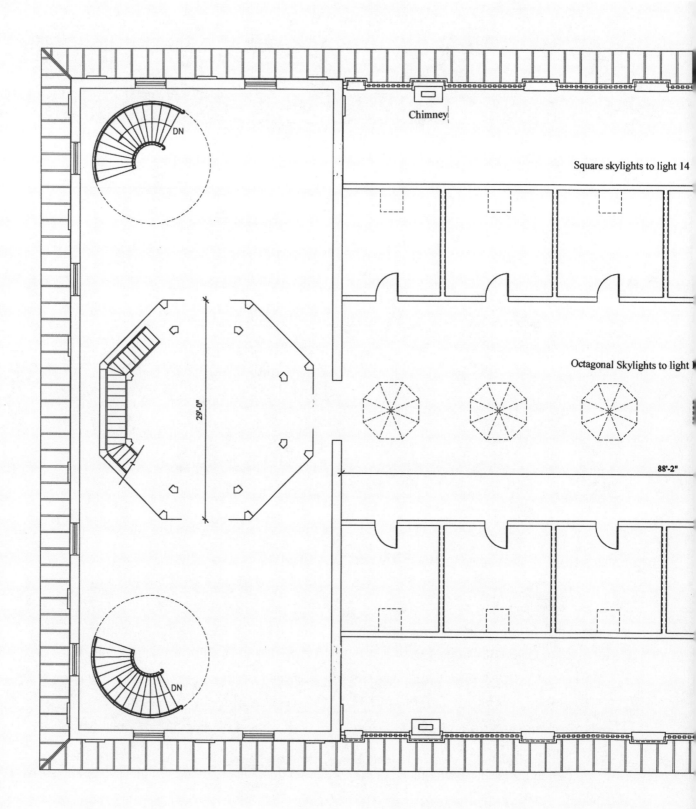

Chimney

Square skylights to light 14

Octagonal Skylights to light

29'-0"

88'-2"

DN

DN

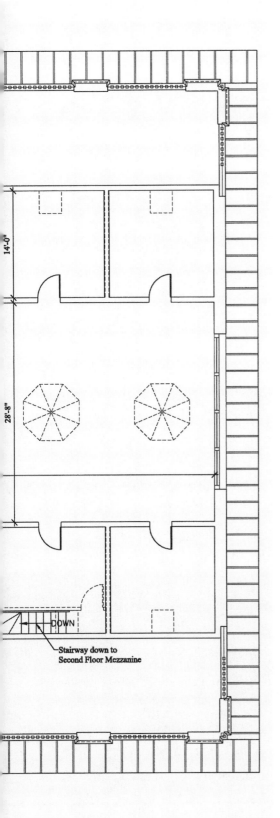

The

main room of

the attic story is

eighty-eight feet

two inches long and

twenty-eight feet

eight inches wide.

—BRIGHAM YOUNG

Figure 8.16 Attic Story of Temple, drawing, 2000, FFKR Architecture. This drawing was modified and adapted from historic reproduction drawings by Steve Goodwin, an architect working on the Nauvoo Temple reconstruction project, at the request of the author. The east attic section was partitioned, plastered, painted, furnished, and considered finished. The west attic may have been finished at the same time. The framed area inside the tower support structure was apparently given only a rough finish. The entire attic, both east and west sections, received extensive use by Church members and leaders.

fits well with a report indicating that the ceilings of these rooms were "not sufficiently high near the eaves, for a person of six feet, to stand erect."[169]

Finish and Furnishings

Billing records indicate that this east attic area (and possibly the west attic as well) "was finished by a running baseboard 11½ inches wide and 1¼ inches thick for the main room and was to be six inches by one inch for the small rooms."[170]

Heating the attic was accomplished by wood-burning stoves. While the attic was being painted, two of these stoves were put up in the large council room.[171] Additional stoves were added just prior to the commencement of the endowment ordinances. Heber C. Kimball reported: "John D. Lee and others have been fitting up stoves in the two west rooms, as they will be devoted to washing and Anointing and to heat water."[172] Wood was pulled up to the attic level by a windlass, and men were assigned to keep the fires going.[173]

Floors were finished by early November 1845. On Saturday, 22 November, "the plasterers [had] finished the attic story of the Temple."[174] Paint was then applied to columns, base boards, door frames, window frames, other woodwork, and possibly the walls. On 26 November "the painters finished painting the attic."[175] Elder Kimball noted that "the painters had got three co[a]ts on. We concluded that would do."[176] Next came borrowed carpets contributed by several Church members for use in the temple. On Saturday, 29 November, they "laid the carpet on the main floor of the attic story and also on several of the small rooms."[177] Elder Kimball related that "we had carpit in plenty to lay down in all the rooms."[178] The large half-round complex of gothic windows was also finished and decorated. Brigham Young explained, "I fitted up the curtains on the east windows."[179]

After the rooms had been painted and carpeted, Church leaders set about preparing the attic story for administering the temple ordinances. The large central main room was divided by canvas partitions. Heber C. Kimball explained: "We are now putting up petitions [partitions] in the big Hall."[180] "The big Hall is converted into six sepret [separate] rooms for the conven-

Borrowed carpets were contributed by several Church members for use in the temple.

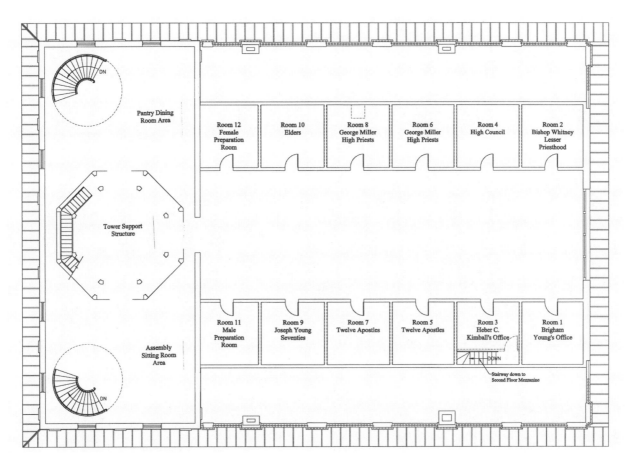

Figure 8.17   *East Attic Room Assignments, drawing, 2000, FFKR Architecture. This drawing was modified and adapted from historic reproduction drawings by Steve Goodwin, an architect working on the Nauvoo Temple reconstruction project, at the request of the author.*

ience of the Holy Priesthood, two Large ones and fore small and a Hall pacing through between the small ones, pacing from the west done [down] through the Center, and doers in to each room."[181] These hallways are described by William Clayton: "Beginning from the door at the West end is an all[e]y about 5 feet wide extending to about 3 feet beyond the first Beam of the arch."[182]

Patrons entering the temple to receive their endowment ordinances met at the outside porch or vestibule of the temple. Leaving the vestibule, they entered into a circular stairway located in the southwest corner of the building.

They then passed up through a series of winding stairs to the attic story. Here was a sitting, reception, or assembly room where they took off their coats, hats, bonnets, etc. After being seated for a time they were called out and asked to stand before a closed door. This door opened onto the main east attic section of the building. As they passed through this door, they entered a narrow hallway formed by canvas partitions. Walking to the end of this hallway, they met a man who asked the women to enter through a door on the left and the men to pass through one on the right in an opposite direction. Husbands and wives were later brought back

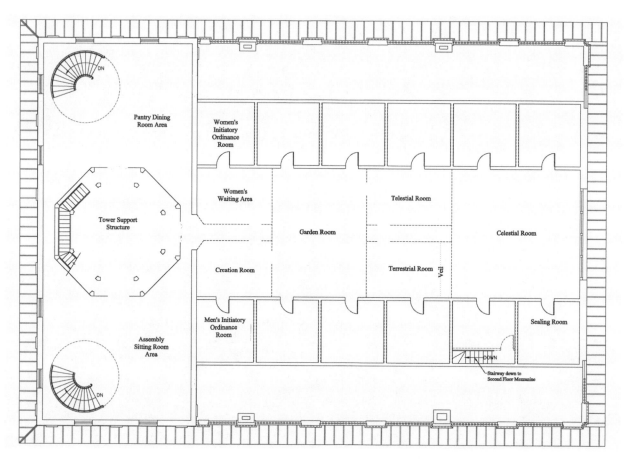

Figure 8.18   East Story Ordinance Room Arrangements, drawing, 2000, FFKR Architecture. This drawing was modified and adapted from historic reproduction drawings by Steve Goodwin, an architect working on the Nauvoo Temple reconstruction project, at the request of the author.

together. At the completion of their endowment ordinances they were welcomed into a large, beautifully furnished and decorated room known as the celestial room of the temple.[183]

A possible organization of these rooms can be seen by viewing Figure 8.18. Two of these rooms were extensively furnished. One of these was the garden room. Heber C. Kimball, along with his son William, had picked up "about 25 or thirty Flower Pots with Ever greens in them to adorn our garden."[184] These evergreens, later referred to as cedar trees, had been kept indoors during the cold weather in various houses throughout the city. They had been col-

lected by Hiram Kimball at his home and were now available for use in decorating the temple.

The eastern one-third of the large central main room (as it was partitioned off) became known as the celestial room of the temple. Dimensions of this area were about 27 by 28 feet. It was described as a "very large and spacious room, perfectly light, all nicely furnished" with "splendid tables and four splendid sofas." Also placed around the room were chairs and a marble clock. Hung on the walls were mirrors, maps, painted portraits and landscapes.[185] This celestial room area was described by a visitor as "handsomely and even elegantly furnished."[186]

Another significant furnishing was added in early January 1846. This was the new altar located in Brigham Young's office (Room 1). It was put into use for the first time on 7 January. On this occasion four couples, each in their turn, knelt at this sacred altar. Husbands and wives were sealed to each other for time and for all eternity. "The altar is about two and one-half feet high and two and one-half feet long and about one foot wide, rising from a platform about 8 or 9 inches high and extending out on all sides about a foot, forming a convenient place to kneel upon. The top of the altar and the platform for kneeling upon are covered with cushions of scarlet damask cloth; the sides of the upright part or body of the altar are covered with white linen."[187]

Services in the Attic Story

The large central room as divided by canvas partitions was utilized in providing endowment ordinances to thousands of faithful Church members. The altar in Room 1 was used for numerous sealing ordinances and eternal marriages. There is indication that Rooms 2 and 4 were also used for some sealing ordinances.[188] Side Rooms 11 and 12 were used for thousands of washing and anointing ordinances. Rooms 1 and 3 were also extensively used as offices. The remaining side rooms were used for offices, prayer meetings, and leadership meetings. This attic area was also used for recreational purposes and even as a temporary residence for some leaders and patrons, as explained in chapter 4.

Beginning in December 1845, those previously endowed, known as "the quorum," met in the attic story of the temple. "Elder B. Young Said this quorum should meet heare evry Sabath and take of the Sacrament."[189] This announcement was greeted with feelings of great joy. Those attending noted: "Great solemnity rested upon the brethren and sisters; great union in our meeting."[190] As endowment ordinances were given to others over the next few weeks, this group was greatly enlarged. By 4 January over fourteen hundred individuals had been endowed.[191] One such meeting was held on Sunday, 28 December. "About two hundred of the brethren and sisters met at ten-thirty a.m. in the attic story of the Temple, some of the side rooms were filled, and the curtains withdrawn."[192] These curtains were undoubtedly the canvas partitions that had been placed in the central main hall.

Large crowds of people resulted in problems for the structure. John D. Lee reported that "the floor in the attic story or more properly speaking—the trams and joists that support the floor was not sufficiently strong to bear up such an immense weight as would necessarily be upon it—when filled with people. The ceiling has already cracked in many places, the door frames were also cracked by the weight—in so much that it actually became necessary for the preservation of the building to stop holding anymore public meetings."[193] Heber C. Kimball reported that as Brigham Young addressed those present on Sunday, 28 December, he declared: "Weight on the floor . . . has already caused the walls to crack, prevents the doors from shutting and will injure the roof."[194]

Brigham Young reported that on Sunday, 4 January: "No public meeting was held in the Temple this day, on account of the floor being insufficient to support a large congregation."[195] Smaller leadership and prayer meetings were still conducted in the offices, but large meetings were curtailed. The problem of where to meet was resolved as other parts of the building were completed. Within two weeks even larger public meetings were being held on the new floor of the second story.

furnished by the bretheren and Sisters for the occasion." On 29 April "in the afternoon met in the attic story of the temple with the members who formed the prayer circle in No. 1 and a part of No. 2 with our wives and had a feast of cakes, pies, wine, &c. where we enjoyed ourselves with prayer preaching, administering for healing, blessing children, and music and Dancing untill near Midnight."[196]

Following the temple's dedication, all furnishings were removed from the building.

The builders were satisfied fulfilled their obligation to Go cated the building, left Nauvo

After temple ordinance work ceased, most members joined in the western exodus. The crew left behind to finish the building concluded their work in late April. They then gathered in the attic story with their families to celebrate the completion of the temple.

On 28 April "about noon they ceased and all hands with their wives repaired to the temple for the feast, a large company were gathered, a plenty of cakes with cheese, and Raisens was

Thomas L. Kane described this interesting event: "The sacred rights of consecration ended, the work of removing the sacrosanct proceeded with the rapidity of magic. It went on through the night; and when the morning of the next day dawned, all the ornaments and furniture, everything that could provoke a sneer, had been carried off; and except some fixtures that would not bear removal, the building was dismantled to the bare walls."[197]

CONCLUSION

Lighting for the interior of the building was provided by chandeliers, lanterns, lamps, and candles. This imposed some limitations on the building, making it more desirable to use during daylight hours, when it was well illuminated by its many windows.

Thick walls kept the building cool in summer and helped subdue extreme cold in winter. The building could be heated by stoves utilizing the four chimneys (two on each side of the day Saints remained in Nauvoo, they would have further embellished interior sections of the structure and given it a more perfect finish. All portions of the building were, however, both accessible and usable. Extensive use had been made of each floor level. From a functional point of the view, the temple was completed. Every section of the structure had been given a rough finish and many areas a final finish as well. President Joseph Fielding Smith observed:

> the structure was acceptable; they had
>
> ...eling content with their efforts, they dedi-
>
> ...d joined their companions on the plains.

building), which ran up from the basement. The east attic had four stoves with chimneys coming out of the roof.

Water used in the building had to be carried to the various floor levels from the well in the east end of the basement or from sources outside. There were no inside toilet facilities, so workers and patrons must have used outhouses somewhere near the temple.

There can be no doubt that had the Latter-

It made no difference whether the Temple was finished or not. The revelation of January 19, 1841, provided, "That when I (the Lord) give a commandment to any of the sons of men, to do a work unto my name, and those sons of men go with all their might, and with all they have, to perform that work, and cease not their diligence, and their enemies come upon them, and hinder them from performing that work; behold, it behooveth me to require that work no

more at the hands of those sons of men, but to accept of their offerings" [D&C 124:49].[198]

The Saints were diligent in their labors, and they were also hindered by their enemies. . . . It made no difference, so far as the Church and its authority is concerned, even if the Temple had not been completed, or finished, in the technical sense of that word. Some of the embellishments, the ornamentations and fixtures, may not have been placed in the building according to the original intention, and in that technical sense the building may not have been "finished completely." But if so, what difference would it make? The Lord, thank heaven, is not as technical and peevish as men are, or woe be unto all of us. The revelation does not say that the Church would be rejected with its dead if every identical board and plank or fixture was not in the building according to the original design. The thing the revelation does require is that a place be prepared, or built, where the Lord could reveal the Priesthood and its ordinances which had been taken away or that had not been restored.[199]

The builders were satisfied that the structure was acceptable; they had fulfilled their obligation to God. Feeling content with their efforts, they dedicated the building, left Nauvoo, and joined their companions on the plains of Iowa.

NOTES

1. Virginia S. Harrington and J. C. Harrington, *Rediscovery of the Nauvoo Temple* (Salt Lake City: Nauvoo Restoration, 1971), 13.

2. B. H. Roberts, ed., *History of the Church of Jesus Christ of Latter-day Saints, Period 2: Apostolic Interregnum* (Salt Lake City: Deseret Book, 1932), 7:358.

3. *New-York Messenger* 2 (30 August 1845): 67.

4. Harrington and Harrington, *Rediscovery of the Nauvoo Temple,* 20.

5. Ibid., 17.

6. Ibid.

7. Ibid., 20–21.

8. Ibid., 22.

9. Ibid., 23.

10. Ibid., 17.

11. Ibid., 16.

12. Ibid.

13. Ibid., 17; also, William A. Gallup Journal Entry, 1848, LDS Church Archives; also, a writer for the *Peoria Democratic Press* of 29 May 1844, "who claimed to have seen a 'diagram model' of the temple which was shown to him by Joseph Smith gives the dimensions as 130 by 90," as cited in Stanley B. Kimball, "The Nauvoo Temple," *Improvement Era,* November 1963, 982.

14. A report in the *Liberty Hall and Cincinnati Gazette* 40 (19 October 1843): 1, as cited in J. Earl Arrington, "Story of the Nauvoo Temple," 10, LDS Church Archives, describes the temple basement as "about 12 feet in the clear, half of which is underground." Harrington and Harrington, *Rediscovery of the Nauvoo Temple,* 16, confirms that the foundation walls of the excavated basement were about 5 feet below the ground level. The floor of the first story was 6 feet 4 inches above ground level.

From study of architectural sketches and documented descriptions, it is evident that the original basement level was either 5 feet 8 inches or 6 feet 8 inches below ground level. This all depends on whether the 12-foot depth was measured at the top or at the bottom of the 1-foot-thick beam and floor joists supporting the first floor. Drawings of the stairs indicate that the rise of the stairs from the basement floor to the level of the first floor was 11 feet 8 inches. This would tend to support the view that the 12-foot height of the basement was to the top of the first floor beams and floor joists. If this was the case, then there would only be a total of 11 feet of clearance between floor and ceiling. This would result in restricted headroom at the top of the baptismal font.

With the first story at 6 feet 4 inches above ground level, the original basement floor at the outside walls would be at 5 feet 8 inches below ground level. This height of the basement area would also be more consistent with the excavation reports indicating ground level at about 5 feet above the basement floor, as reported by Harrington and Harrington, *Rediscovery of the Nauvoo Temple*, 16.

15. Harrington and Harrington, *Rediscovery of the Nauvoo Temple*, 20. They note that there is clear evidence to show "that the bottoms of the [stone] partitions as originally built were higher than the final brick floor. . . . Apparently when it came time to lay the brick paving in 1845, the earth had worn down or it was arbitrarily decided to lay the floor at a lower level. . . . It appears that the earth was channeled out and a brick course inserted under the stone walls, and the brick floor laid up to this brick filler."

16. Joseph Smith, *History of the Church of Jesus Christ of Latter-day Saints*, ed. B. H. Roberts, 2d ed., rev. (Salt Lake City: Deseret Book, 1957), 4:446; also, Journal History, 8 November 1841, LDS Church Archives.

17. See explanation on possible heights of the basement story in note 14. If the basement had only 11 feet of clearance, then head room at the top of the wooden font would have been just 4 feet.

18. Thomas Gregg, *History of Hancock County, Illinois* (Chicago: C. C. Chapman, 1880), 2:373. William Weeks's drawings show the height at 7 feet 6 inches. See also Harrington and Harrington, *Rediscovery of the Nauvoo Temple*, 32. If the basement had only 11 feet of clearance, then head room at the top of the stone font would have been just 3 feet. The architect's drawings of the stairs show a rise from the basement floor to the level of the first floor as only 11 feet 8 inches.

19. Truman O. Angell to John Taylor, 11 March 1885, as cited in Laurel Andrew, "Nineteenth-Century Temple Architecture of the Latter-day Saints" (Ph.D. diss., University of Michigan, 1973), 88.

20. Smith, *History of the Church*, 4:446; also, Journal History, 8 November 1841.

21. *Nauvoo Neighbor*, 1 May 1844.

22. *New York Herald*, 6 September 1846.

23. John Reynolds, *My Own Times* (Belleville, Ill.: B. H. Perryman and H. L. Davison, 1855), 580.

24. John C. Bennett, *History of the Saints* (Boston: Leland and Whiting, 1842), 190.

25. *Times and Seasons* 6 (15 January 1845): 779.

26. Roberts, *History of the Church*, 7:430.

27. *Times and Seasons* 6 (1 July 1845): 956.

28. *New York Herald*, 6 September 1846.

29. *Illinois Journal*, 9 December 1853, as reprinted in Journal of the Illinois State Historical Society 38 (1945): 482.

30. *New-York Messenger* 2 (30 August 1845): 67.

31. Harrington and Harrington, *Rediscovery of the Nauvoo Temple*, 32.

32. *New-York Messenger* 2 (30 August 1845): 67. This report states the dimensions as 15 feet by 11 feet 6 inches. This is confirmed by evidence on the ground during archaeological excavation. "A substantial part of the font base was found. . . . From their location, shape, and position in reference to the adjacent sand floor, these stones appear to be spalled slabs from the bottom of the font base, left in place when the fire cracked base stones were removed. . . . If it is assumed that the font was centered in the basement, by projection a width of 11 to 11½ feet is arrived at for the font base . . . and the assumed south curve gives an east west length of about 15 feet." Harrington and Harrington, *Rediscovery of the Nauvoo Temple*, 34, 39.

33. *Times and Seasons* 6 (15 January 1845): 779.

34. *New-York Messenger* 2 (30 August 1845): 67.

35. *Illinois Journal*, 9 December 1853, as reprinted in *Journal of the Illinois State Historical Society* 38 (1945): 482; *New-York Messenger* 2 (30 August 1845): 67.

36. *New-York Messenger* 2 (30 August 1845): 67.

37. Harrington and Harrington, *Rediscovery of the Nauvoo Temple*, 28, 34.

38. Archaeological excavation reports found in Nauvoo Restoration files describing and showing measurements of stone fragments found during excavation, LDS Church Archives.

39. Harrington and Harrington, *Rediscovery of the Nauvoo Temple*, 38.

40. Ibid., 28.

41. *New-York Messenger* 2 (30 August 1845): 67.

42. *Missouri Reporter* 5 (2 May 1846): 2, as cited in Arrington, "Story of the Nauvoo Temple," 377.

43. Charles Lanman, *A Summer in the Wilderness* (New York: D. Appleton, 1847), 31.

44. Emily M. Austin, *Mormonism; or, Life among the Mormons* (New York: AMS, 1971), 202.

45. The Lewis sketch clearly shows that the arrangement of the oxen around the stone font was the same as that of the temporary font. See Joseph Smith, *History of the Church*, 4:446; also, Journal History, 8 November 1841; Thomas Gregg, *History of Hancock County, Illinois*, 373.

46. *Illinois Journal*, 9 December 1853, as reprinted in *Journal of the Illinois State Historical Society* 38 (1945): 482; also, *Journal of History* 3 (April 1910): 143.

47. J. H. Buckingham, "A Visit to Nauvoo in 1847," *Saints' Herald*, 15 March 1954, 11.

48. *Journal of History* 3 (April 1910): 143.

49. Roberts, *History of the Church*, 7:383.

50. Harrington and Harrington, *Rediscovery of the Nauvoo Temple*, 41.

51. Smith, *History of the Church*, 4:446.

52. Phoebe Swain and Lizzie Anderson, "History of Hiram Oaks," LDS Church Archives, as quoted in Harrington and Harrington, *Rediscovery of the Nauvoo Temple*, 29.

53. Reynolds, *My Own Times*, 580. There is evidence in the "Nauvoo Temple Building Committee Records," July 1845, LDS Church Archives, of five days of labor for taking the boiler out of the basement. Also a purchase of stove coal for the temple as early as July 1842.

54. Roberts, *History of the Church*, 7:535.

55. *St. Louis Morning Missouri Republican*, 24 September 1846, as quoted in Harrington and Harrington, *Rediscovery of the Nauvoo Temple*, 30.

56. Harrington and Harrington, *Rediscovery of the Nauvoo Temple*, 31.

57. Ibid., 32.

58. *New York Herald*, 6 September 1846.

59. *Messenger and Advocate* 2 (March 1846): 463.

60. Diary of William Mendenhall, 1842–1896, 20

March through 4 April 1846, LDS Church Archives, as cited in Harrington and Harrington, *Rediscovery of the Nauvoo Temple,* 23.

61. *The Missouri Whig* 7 (21 May 1846): 3, as cited in Arrington, "Story of the Nauvoo Temple," 378.

62. Lanman, *A Summer in the Wilderness,* 31.

63. Hiram G. Ferris, "A Description of the Mormon Temple," *Carthage Republican,* 19 March 1890, as quoted in Harrington and Harrington, *Rediscovery of the Nauvoo Temple,* 28.

64. Harrington and Harrington, *Rediscovery of the Nauvoo Temple,* 25.

65. Ibid., 45.

66. *New-York Messenger* 2 (30 August 1845): 68. This report lists twenty-two windows, including six on the east end of the building. It is more accurate to conclude that only five windows were on the east end. This would fit the pattern on the front or west end and also match the number of five spaces or panels between the six pilasters of the east end.

67. *Liberty Hall and Cincinnati Gazette* 40 (19 October 1843): 1, as cited in Arrington, "Story of the Nauvoo Temple," 30.

68. Ferris, "A Description of the Mormon Temple," as quoted in Harrington and Harrington, *Rediscovery of the Nauvoo Temple,* 30.

69. Maxwell, personal communication, after careful study of an enlarged copy of the Chaffin daguerreotype.

70. *Nauvoo Neighbor,* 1 May 1844.

71. Ferris, "A Description of the Mormon Temple," as quoted in Harrington and Harrington, *Rediscovery of the Nauvoo Temple,* 30.

72. Joseph Smith, *History of the Church,* 4:454.

73. Certificate dated 16 December 1845 giving permission to Theodore Rogers for the "privilege of the Baptismal Font," LDS Church Archives, as quoted in Harrington and Harrington, *Rediscovery of the Nauvoo Temple,* 33.

74. *Deseret News,* 26 November 1932.

75. Hosea Stout, *On the Mormon Frontier, the Diary of Hosea Stout 1844–1861,* ed. Juanita Brooks (Salt Lake City: University of Utah Press, 1964), 1:110.

76. *New-York Messenger* 2 (30 August 1845): 67.

77. Harrington and Harrington, *Rediscovery of the Nauvoo Temple,* 14.

78. Tim Maxwell, personal communication, after careful study of Temple Billing Records and Account Books.

79. J. H. Buckingham, "A Visit to Nauvoo in 1847," *Saints' Herald,* 15 March 1954, 11.

80. Harrington and Harrington, *Rediscovery of the Nauvoo Temple,* 25.

81. *Millennial Star* 8 (1 August 1846): 31.

82. *New-York Messenger* 2 (30 August 1845): 67; also, *Liberty Hall and Cincinnati Gazette* 40 (19 October 1843): 1, as cited in Arrington, "Story of the Nauvoo Temple," 18–19.

83. "Nauvoo Temple Building Committee Records," LDS Church Archives. Seven entries for flagging stones are recorded between 27 May and 16 June 1842. The type of stone and the dates when ordered corroborate the probability that this phase of construction included a flagstone-covered floor in the portico or front vestibule area.

84. Aurelia S. Rogers, as quoted in Arrington, "Story of the Nauvoo Temple," 23.

85. Maxwell, personal communication.

86. George Washington Bean, *Autobiography of George Washington Bean,* comp. Flora Diana Bean Horne (Salt Lake City: Utah, 1945), 23.

87. Joseph Smith III, *Joseph Smith III and the*

Restoration, ed. Mary Audentia Smith Anderson (Independence, Mo.: Herald House, 1952), 105; also, *True Latter-day Saints Herald*, 1 January 1872, 224–25, as cited in Arrington, "Story of the Nauvoo Temple," 22.

88. "Nauvoo Temple Building Committee" 9 August 1842 and 31 July 1845.

89. Ibid., 9 August 1842.

90. Harrington and Harrington, *Rediscovery of the Nauvoo Temple*, 16.

91. *New-York Messenger* 2 (30 August 1845): 67.

92. *Niles' Register* 69 (22 November 1845): 187, quoting an article from the New York Post.

93. Brigham Young, *The Journal of Brigham*, comp. Leland R. Nelson (Provo, Utah: Council, 1980), 121; also, Roberts, *History of the Church*, 7:560.

94. Buckingham, "A Visit to Nauvoo in 1847," 11.

95. *New York Tribune* 7 (13 May 1848), as cited in Arrington, "Story of the Nauvoo Temple," 13.

96. Director, Lyceum of Philadelphia, Lecture, 10 April 1847, 11, as cited in Arrington, "Story of the Nauvoo Temple," 13.

97. Buckingham reported that in the grand hall "seats are provided in this hall for the accommodation at one time of thirty-five hundred people." Buckingham, "A Visit to Nauvoo in 1847," 11. A report published in the *New-York Messenger* estimated that each floor of the temple could accommodate four thousand people. *New-York Messenger* 2 (20 September 1845): 93. Hosea Stout claimed that four thousand individuals were present at the October conference of 1845. *On the Mormon Frontier,* 80. Brigham Young's record of the same meeting indicates that five thousand individuals crowded into the building to attend this conference. Roberts, *History of the Church,* 7:456. These attendance figures must have been cumulative or included reports of individuals in other rooms of the temple. Since the total inside floor space of the first floor was only 8,000 square feet, it could not have accommodated these large numbers of people on one floor, especially with seats and pulpits taking up some of the space. Temporary galleries may have been utilized in the open, rough-finished first-story mezzanine to hold some of the crowd.

98. Director, Lyceum of Philadelphia, Lecture, 10 April 1847, 11, as cited in Arrington, "Story of the Nauvoo Temple," 13.

99. Maxwell, personal communication.

100. *New York Evening Express,* 7 November 1844, as cited in Arrington, "Story of the Nauvoo Temple," 12.

101. Young, *The Journal of Brigham*, 114.

102. Ibid., 121.

103. *Times and Seasons* 5 (1 January 1845): 759.

104. Buckingham, *Papers in Illinois History and Transactions*, 1937; "Illinois as Lincoln Knew It," Illinois State Historical Society, Springfield, Illinois, 172. Some confusion has arisen from Buckingham being quoted in three different versions of the same observation. In this article from "Illinois Historical Society," he describes the next to the highest pulpit as being inscribed with gilded letters of PSZ. A second version from the same report is quoted in *Saint's Herald*, 15 March 1954, 11, designating these letters as PSQ. In a third version he is quoted in "The Palmyra Courier Journal," 22 September 1847, as cited in E. Cecil McGavin, *Nauvoo the Beautiful* (Salt Lake City: Stevens and Wallis, 1946), 38, describing the letters PSR. The most accurate version seems to be that of PSZ as found in the Illinois Historical Society report. It is confirmed by the observation of James Scott (see note 106) and is also confirmed by the exact same lettering PSZ being used on pulpits in the St. George Utah Temple, as confirmed by examination of photographs in LDS Church

Archives.

105. James A. Scott, Journal of James A. Scott, 4, LDS Church Archives.

106. Director, Lyceum of Philadelphia, Lecture, 10 April 1847, 11, as cited in Arrington, "Story of the Nauvoo Temple," 13; also *Times and Seasons* 5 (1 January 1845): 759.

107. Director, Zane St. Public School, Philadelphia, Lecture, "A Journey on the Mississippi River," 10 April 1847, 11, as cited in Arrington, "Story of the Nauvoo Temple," 551.

108. *Burlington Hawk-Eye*, 24 September 1846.

109. Lanman, *A Summer in the Wilderness*, 32; also, Journal of James A. Scott, 4, LDS Church Archives.

110. *Chillicothe Advertiser* 16 (25 July 1846): 1, as cited in Arrington, "Story of the Nauvoo Temple," 69.

111. *New-York Messenger* 2 (8 November 1845): 150.

112. Ibid.

113. *Niles' Register* 69 (22 November 1845): 187. It is not known if there was an actual plan to build additional galleries or if this just referred to the area of a gallery for the choir. A gallery was in place for a large choir and also the band, but no galleries beyond this have been reported unless they were possibly temporary galleries in the unfinished first mezzanine in October 1845.

114. *Hancock Eagle*, 24 April 1846.

115. *Lee County Democrat* 5 (4 October 1845): 2.

116. J. M. Davidson, editor of the *Carthage Republican*, 25 February 1864, as cited in E. Cecil McGavin, *The Nauvoo Temple* (Salt Lake City: Deseret Book, 1962), 95.

117. *Iowa Territorial Gazette and Advertiser* 9 (18 April 1846): 1, as cited in Arrington, "Story of the Nauvoo Temple," 54, 516.

118. *Illinois Journal*, 9 December 1853, as reprinted in Journal of the Illinois State Historical Society 38 (1945): 484.

119. "Nauvoo Temple Building Committee Records," Daybook K.

120. Ibid.

121. Ibid.

122. Ibid.

123. *Deseret Evening News*, 7 March 1876, reprinted from the Cincinnati Times.

124. Lanman, *A Summer in the Wilderness*, 32; also, *New-York Messenger* 2 (30 August 1845): 68.

125. *Times and Seasons* 6 (15 January 1845): 779; also, John Taylor, "The John Taylor Nauvoo Journal," ed. Dean C. Jesse, *BYU Studies* 23, no. 3 (summer 1983): 19.

126. *New-York Messenger* 2 (8 November 1845): 150.

127. *New York Herald*, 6 September 1846.

128. Richard W. Jackson, "Meeting Places of the Latter-day Saints," copy of preliminary manuscript in possession of author, 64–66.

129. Maxwell, personal communication.

130. Lanman, *A Summer in the Wilderness*, 32.

131. *Times and Seasons* 6 (15 January 1846): 1096. The notice was dated 20 January 1846.

132. Stout, *On the Mormon Frontier*, 1:104.

133. Roberts, *History of the Church*, 7:573. This meeting was held on Saturday 24 January 1846.

134. Ibid., 578.

135. *Saints' Herald*, 29 May 1943.

136. "Nauvoo Temple Building Committee Records," Daybook K.

137. *Illinois Journal*, 9 December 1853, as reprinted in *Journal of the Illinois State Historical Society* 38 (1945): 484.

138. Stanley B. Kimball, *Heber C. Kimball: Mormon Patriarch and Pioneer* (Urbana, Ill.: University of Illinois Press, 1981), 117.

139. *Illinois Journal*, 9 December 1853, as reprinted in

Journal of the Illinois State Historical Society 38 (1945): 483; also, *New-York Messenger* 2 (30 August 1845): 68; Austin, *Mormonism; or, Life among the Mormons,* 201.

140. Austin, *Mormonism; or, Life among the Mormons,* 201.

141. *Nauvoo Independent* 17 (3 January 1890): 32–33.

142. Roberts, *History of the Church,* 7:565; also, Elden J. Watson, *Manuscript History of Brigham Young,* 7; also, *The Journal of Brigham Young,* comp. Leland R. Nelson, 123; and Marie and Increase Van Dusen, *A Dialogue between Adam and Eve, the Lord and the Devil, Called the Endowment* (Albany: C. Killmer, 1847), 4–5. Van Dusen refers to this area as a "sitting room" and Brigham Young described it as the "reception room," indicating that "an immense crowd was assembled and waiting there for admission" on Wednesday 7 January 1846. On that day a total of 121 persons received their endowments.

A careful study of available resources leads to the conclusion that the most likely point of assembly by patrons waiting to receive endowment ordinances was in this southwest corner room of the west front attic section of the temple. Assembly of such groups could not have been held on the first floor level because that portion of the building was under construction from 9 November 1845, when they started removing the temporary floor and its supports, until 22 February 1846, when for the first time a congregation met on the newly finished floor of this story. The second story was also under construction and the first reference to any meetings or assembly in this area was from journal entries of a meeting held on Sunday, 11 January 1846. See Hosea Stout, Diary of Hosea Stout, 1845, 2, 121, typescript, Brigham Young University Special Collections; Thomas Bullock, Journal of Thomas Bullock, *BYU Studies* 31, no. 1 (winter 1991): 43.

143. *New-York Messenger* 2 (30 August 1845): 68.

144. Buckingham, "A Visit to Nauvoo in 1847," 11; also, *Palmyra Courier-Journal,* 22 September 1847, as cited in McGavin, *Nauvoo the Beautiful,* 38.

145. *Illinois Journal,* 9 December 1853, as reprinted in *Journal of the Illinois State Historical Society* 38 (1945): 483.

146. *Chillicothe Advertiser* 16 (25 July 1846): 1, as cited in Arrington, "Story of the Nauvoo Temple," 24.

147. Judith Brown, as quoted in Arrington, "Story of the Nauvoo Temple," 24; also, *Journal of History* 3 (10 April 1910): 225–26.

148. Journal History, 9 October 1848, citing an article in the *Nauvoo Patriot* of the same date.

149. *Warsaw Signal,* 19 October 1848, quoting the *Monmouth Atlas.*

150. "Nauvoo Temple Building Committee Records," Daybook I.

151. *Illinois Journal,* 9 December 1853, as reprinted in *Journal of the Illinois State Historical Society* 38 (1945): 483.

152. Roberts, *History of the Church,* 7:542. The offices on the sides had earlier been assigned somewhat differently: "The first, in the southeast corner as a private office. The second by Heber C. Kimball, W. Richards and myself. The third and fourth by others of the Twelve; Fifth, by Joseph Young and Presidency of the Seventies; Sixth, for washing and anointing the elders. On the north side: first, bishops and lesser priesthood. Second, president of the stake and high council; third and fourth, high priests quorum; fifth elders quorum; sixth, washing and anointing room occupied by the sisters." Roberts, *History of the Church,* 7:535.

153. Lisle G. Brown, "The Sacred Departments for Temple Work in Nauvoo: The Assembly Room and the Council Chamber," *BYU Studies* 19, no. 3 (spring 1979): 368–69.

154. Van Deusen, *A Dialogue,* 4.

155. Catherine Lewis, *Narrative of Some of the Proceedings of the Mormons* (Lynn, Mass.: Catherine Lewis, 1848), 10.

156. Journal of Heber C. Kimball, 21 December 1845, LDS Church Archives, as extracted by Historical Department staff; also, as cited in David R. Crockett, *Saints in Exile*, 96.

157. Journal of Heber C. Kimball, 23 December 1845; Crockett, *Saints in Exile*, 99.

158. Journal of Heber C. Kimball, 26 December 1845; Crockett, *Saints in Exile*, 103.

159. Buckingham, "A Visit to Nauvoo in 1847," 11; also, as quoted in *Palmyra Courier-Journal*, 22 September 1847; Buckingham, *Papers in Illinois History of Transactions*, 171.

160. William Clayton, *An Intimate Chronicle: The Journals of William Clayton* (Salt Lake City: Signature, 1991), ed. George D. Smith, 205; Roberts, *History of the Church*, 7:542; *The Journal of Brigham Young*, 112

161. Heber C. Kimball, *On the Potter's Wheel: The Diaries of Heber C. Kimball* (Salt Lake City: Signature and Smith Research Associates, 1987), ed. Stanley R. Kimball, 204.

162. Roberts, *History of the Church*, 7:542; also, The Journal of Brigham Young, 112.

163. *New-York Messenger* 2 (30 August 1845): 68.

164. *Times and Seasons* 6 (1 April 1845); also, *New-York Messenger* 2 (30 August 1845): 68. "At the east end of this room, is already constructed the frame of a window twenty and a half feet in the span, which forms four gothic windows, and three irregular triangles which partake of the eliptic and gothic." Buckingham, "A Visit to Nauvoo in 1847," 11; also, as quoted in Palmyra Courier-Journal, 22 September 1847.

165. Roberts, *History of the Church*, 7:542; also, The

166. Elwin C. Robinson, *The First Mormon Temple* (Provo, Utah: Brigham Young University Press, 1997), 131. "The Nauvoo Temple roof was framed with a queen post truss, which leaves the central portion of the attic undivided." The temple billing records show a bill for "18 queen posts, 14 ft long, 12 by 12" some of which could have been used in this attic area. Newell K. Whitney, Whitney Collection, Box 3, Folder 5, Harold B. Lee Library, Brigham Young University.

167. *Illinois Journal*, 9 December 1853, as reprinted in *Journal of the Illinois State Historical Society* 38 (1945): 484.

168. Lanman, *A Summer in the Wilderness*, 32. Doors for use somewhere in the temple were constructed and "ready to be put together" as early as August 1845; *New-York Messenger* 2 (30 August 1845), 68. Locks and keys for several doors as well as dozens of hinges had been purchased. "Nauvoo Temple Building Committee Records," Daybook H. This attic area was heavily utilized. It is therefore logical to conclude that the offices of these side rooms had doors. This is also born out by John D. Lee, who indicated that the weight of large crowds in this attic area had cracked the door frames. John D. Lee, "Diary Selections, February 5, 1844–January 25, 1846," 10, LDS Church Archives.

169. Lyman O. Littlefield, *New-York Messenger* 2 (30 August 1845): 68.

170. "Nauvoo Temple Building Committee Records," as cited in Arrington, "Story of the Nauvoo Temple," 55.

171. Kimball, *On the Potter's Wheel*, 150.

172. Ibid., 166; also, John D. Lee, *Mormonism Unveiled* (St. Louis: Byron, Brand, and Co., 1877), 168–69.

173. *Autobiography of George Washington Bean*, 23; also, Kimball, *On the Potter's Wheel*, 157.

174. Roberts, *History of the Church*, 7:531.

175. Ibid., 532.

176. Kimball, *On the Potter's Wheel*, 151.

177. Roberts, *History of the Church*, 7:533.

178. Kimball, *On the Potter's Wheel*, 153.

179. Roberts, *History of the Church*, 7:539.

180. Kimball, *On the Potter's Wheel*, 157.

181. Ibid., 161.

182. Clayton, *An Intimate Chronicle*, 205.

183. Based on the descriptions provided by Van Deusen, *A Dialogue*, 3–5, 15. See note 142 for a more detailed explanation justifying the conclusion that this was the area where patrons assembled prior to receiving their endowments.

184. Kimball, *On the Potter's Wheel*, 156.

185. Ibid., 162–67; also, Andrew Jenson, *LDS Biographical Encyclopedia* (Salt Lake City: Western Epics, 1901), 2:380–81; also, *Journal of Heber C. Kimball, 1801–1848*, 11 December 1845, Kimball Collection, LDS Church Archives, as quoted in Richard Neitzel Holzapfel and Jeni Broberg Holzapfel, *Women of Nauvoo* (Salt Lake City: Bookcraft, 1992), 150–51.

186. *Iowa Territorial Gazette and Advertiser* 9 (18 April 1846): 1.

187. Roberts, *History of the Church*, 7:566; also, *The Journal of Brigham Young*, 123.

188. Lee, "Diary Selections, February 5, 1844–January 25, 1846," 10; also, C. Edward Jacob, *The Record of Norton Jacob* (Salt Lake City: Norton Jacob Family Association, 1949), 18.

189. Kimball, *On the Potter's Wheel*, 164–65.

190. *Journal of Heber C. Kimball*, 1801–1848, 10 December 1845.

191. Roberts, *History of the Church*, 7:542–62.

192. Ibid., 555–56; also, *The Journal of Brigham Young*, 118.

193. Lee, "Diary Selections, February 5, 1844–January 25, 1846," 10.

194. Helen Mar Whitney, "Scenes in Nauvoo, and Incidents from H. C. Kimball's Journal," *Woman's Exponent* 12 (15 August 1883): 42.

195. Roberts, *History of the Church* 7:562; also, *The Journal of Brigham Young*, 122.

196. Diary of Samuel Whitney Richards, 1:17–18, Harold B. Lee Library, Brigham Young University.

197. Thomas L. Kane, *The Mormons: A Discourse* (Philadelphia: King and Baird, 1850), 21.

198. Joseph Fielding Smith, *Origin of the "Reorganized" Church and the Question of Succession* (Salt Lake City: Deseret News, 1909), 36. It was D&C 124:25–40 that gave divine authorization and commandment to build the Nauvoo Temple. Verse 51 explains: "Therefore, for this cause have I accepted the offerings of those whom I commanded to build up a city and a house unto my name, in Jackson county, Missouri, and were hindered by their enemies, saith the Lord your God." If such an exception was granted in Missouri, then this would also logically apply to Nauvoo. This is especially true when considering the sacrifice, effort, and opposition encountered while building the Nauvoo Temple.

199. Joseph Fielding Smith, *Origin of the "Reorganized" Church and Question of Succession* (Salt Lake City: Deseret News, 1913), 47.

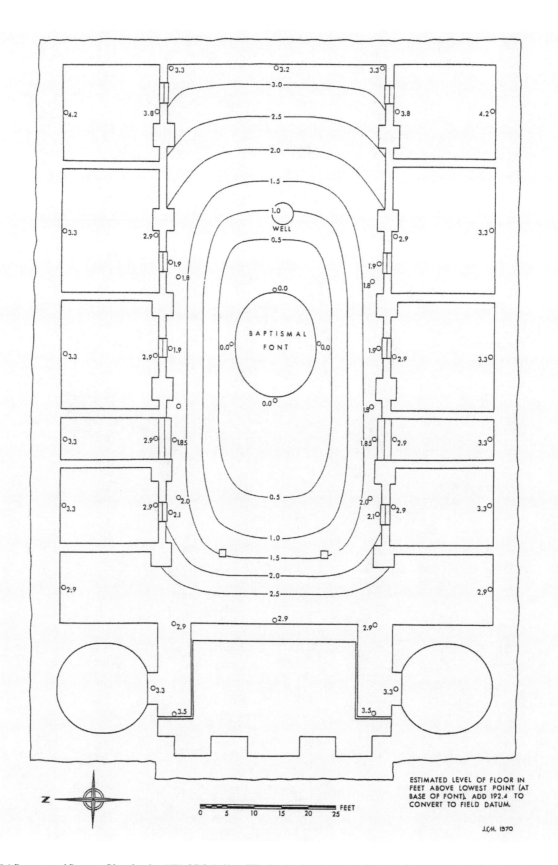

Figure 9.1 Reconstructed Basement Plan, drawing, 1970, LDS Archives. This drawing, based on archaeological findings, was produced by Nauvoo Restoration and was published in 1971 in J. C. and Virginia Harrington's Rediscovery of the Nauvoo Temple. *This drawing shows the contour of the finished brick floor and clearly illustrates how the basement had been scooped out and lowered as much as 4 feet 2 inches on the east end and 3 feet 3 inches on each side to allow for the increased depth needed for the baptismal font.*

9

In June 1962 the First Presidency announced the formation of Nauvoo Restoration Incorporated. A board of directors was established, and Dr.

CHAPTER NINE

NAUVOO RESTORATION

DRAWINGS & PHOTOGRAPHS

J. LeRoy Kimball was appointed to serve as president. Church president David O. McKay explained that the corporation was formed for the purpose of restoring much of historic Nauvoo to the way it appeared before the Saints left it in 1846.

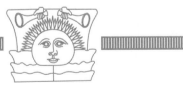

Figure 9.2 Well, photograph, 1960s, LDS Church Archives. This is traditionally known as the temple well. It was located toward the east end of the basement and used to supply water needs in the temple.

One of the major contributions of Nauvoo Restoration was the archaeological excavation of the Nauvoo Temple site. This work was conducted with great care under the direction of professional, well-respected archaeologists. Preliminary trenching undertaken in an attempt to locate the remains of the temple was conducted under the direction of Dr. Melvin L. Fowler, curator of North American Archaeology from Southern Illinois University. He was assisted by Dee Green, a Salt Lake archaeologist who served as crew chief of the excavation work. The direction of all archaeological research for Nauvoo Restoration was later turned over to Dr. J. C. Harrington, formerly chief archaeologist for the U.S. National Parks Service. Over a three-year period J. C. Harrington and his wife, Dr. Virginia S. Harrington, directed the examination of the entire basement area.

Upon completion of the project, an excellent book was published illustrating and describing the excavation work as well as outlining the understandings they gained from the work. This book, *Rediscovery of the Nauvoo Temple*, was written by Virginia and J. C. Harrington. Many of the photographs and drawings they produced provide valuable

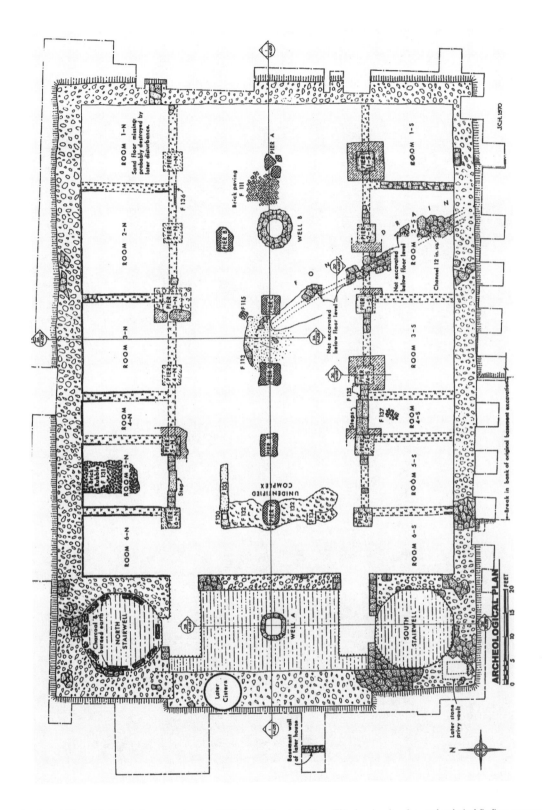

Figure 9.3 Archaeological Plan of the Temple Basement, drawing, 1970, LDS Church Archives. This drawing, based on archaeological findings, was produced by Nauvoo Restoration and was published in 1971 in J. C. and Virginia Harrington's Rediscovery of the Nauvoo Temple. *This drawing shows archaeological remains of the original temple, along with remains of the French Icarion piers, which were put into the basement in 1848 just prior to the destruction of the walls. Note the 30-foot section at the lower right where the original bank had been sloped down to facilitate the removal of soil from the basement area during construction.*

One

of the major contri-

butions of Nauvoo

Restoration was

the archaeological

excavation of the

Nauvoo Temple site.

Figure 9.4 Portion of Stone Font Base (inverted), photograph, 1960s, Nauvoo Restoration, LDS Church Archives. This stone font base is upside down. The stone arcs were cut to fit under the bellies of two of the stone oxen.

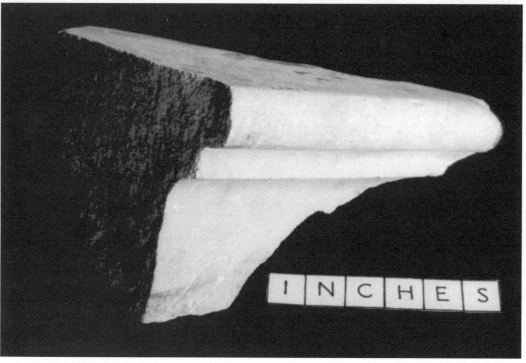

Figure 9.5 (Top) Remnant of Stone Baptismal Font Rim, photograph, 1960s, LDS Church Archives.

Figure 9.6 (Bottom) Remnant of Baptismal Font Stone Step, photograph, 1960s, LDS Church Archives.

Figure 9.7   Font Drain, photograph, 1960s, LDS Church Archives. This photograph was taken facing southeast; the font drain has an opening of 12 inches square.

insights concerning the Nauvoo Temple. By permission of Nauvoo Restoration and The Church of Jesus Christ of Latter-day Saints, many of these illustrations have been reproduced in this book. A number of the photographs and drawings are included in the text of chapters 5 (Figure 5.2), 6 (Figure 6.9), and 8 (Figures 8.2–8.5). Several additional illustrations are included in this chapter.

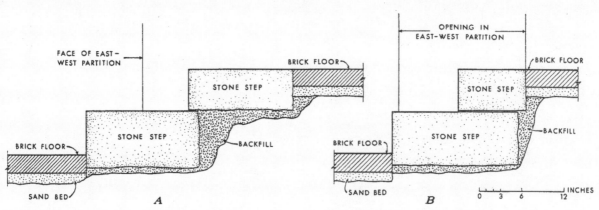

Figure 9.8 (Top) North Stairwell, photograph, 1960s, LDS Church Archives. This is a photograph of the northwest corner stairwell after removal of debris and burned wood. There was an open area 6 feet in diameter in the middle of each spiral stair. George Washington Bean was a young teenager living in Nauvoo who worked in the temple running a windlass in the north stairwell, carrying up to the attic story the wood and water needed to carry on the endowments.

Figure 9.9 (Bottom) Steps to Side Rooms in Basement, drawing, 1970, LDS Church Archives.

Figure 9.10 South Stairwell, photograph, 1960s, LDS Church Archives. This is a photograph of the southwest corner stairwell and remains of masonry at the time of excavation.

Mormon Temple at Nauvoo, sketch or painting, 1847, William Murphy, Museum of Church History and Art, The Church of Jesus Christ of Latter-day Saints; hereafter cited as Museum of Church History and Art. This detailed drawing by William Murphy, a former resident of Nauvoo, was completed in 1847.

10

As each section of the building was completed, it became the practice of Church leaders to dedicate that portion of the temple to God and then to press it into

CHAPTER TEN

THE DEDICATION OF THE TEMPLE

service. Such a procedure was justified under the peculiar circumstances of the time. The Saints in Nauvoo felt a great need for the facilities offered by the temple. No chapels existed in Nauvoo for worship services, and office space for

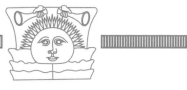

administrative needs was either limited or nonexistent. The Saints were also anxious to perform their temple ordinance work at the earliest opportunity. Added to these conditions was the relentless and ever-growing pressure by enemies to drive the Latter-day Saints out of Illinois. Had they waited until the building was completed before dedicating and using any portion, it is very doubtful that the structure would have ever served its builders.

cial general conference of the Church ever held in the enclosed building took place. By this time the building was nearing completion with all the outside work finished. President Brigham Young "opened the services of the day by a dedicatory prayer, presenting the Temple, thus far completed, as a monument of the saints' liberality, fidelity, and faith, concluding: 'Lord, we dedicate this house and ourselves, to thee.'"[2] Following this dedication, Sunday worship services, prayer meet-

We . . . asked him to enable him, and we would leave it Lord to accept the labors of I

THE DEDICATION OF SEPARATE SECTIONS
The Wooden Baptismal Font

Pushed to completion during the first year of construction, the temporary wooden baptismal font was the first portion of the building to be used. Brigham Young dedicated it in appropriate ceremonies at 5 P.M. on 8 November 1841.[1]

The Enclosed Building

On 5 October 1845 the first and only offi-

ings, and administrative meetings were conducted regularly in the temple.

The Attic Story

On Sunday, 30 November 1845, the newly completed attic story was dedicated. The meeting was called to order at noon, and William Clayton was requested to keep minutes of the proceedings. After an opening song Brigham Young offered the prayer of dedication. He

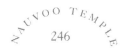

prayed that God would sustain and deliver his servants from their enemies until they could accomplish his will in the temple. Additional prayers and songs were also part of the meeting.[3] This portion of the building was then used for council meetings, quorum leadership meetings, and more importantly for endowment ordinances, eternal marriages, and sealings.

A Sealing Altar

A new altar, located in the southeast corner

met with the Council of the Twelve in the southeast corner room of the attic of the Temple. We knelt around the altar, and dedicated the building to the Most High. We asked his blessing upon our intended move to the west; also asked him to enable us someday to finish the Temple, and dedicate it to him, and we would leave it in his hands to do as he pleased; and to preserve the building as a monument to Joseph Smith. We asked the Lord to accept the labors of his servants in this land. We then left the temple."[5]

meday to finish the Temple, and dedicate it to

s hands to do as he pleased. . . . We asked the

rvants in this land. We then left the temple.

room of the main attic, was dedicated on 7 January 1846. It was used for the sealing of marriages and family groups. The dedication took place in the afternoon, attended by the Twelve, the Presiding Bishops, and their wives.[4]

Dedication Prior to Exodus

On the occasion of the exodus from Nauvoo, another dedication of the then incomplete structure took place, recorded by Brigham Young: "I

THE FORMAL DEDICATION OF THE ENTIRE BUILDING

The final formal dedication of the temple took place after most members of the Church had left the city. Under the direction of Truman Angell, a special crew of workmen remained behind to complete the first story and some other parts of the structure. Orson Hyde, a member of the Quorum of the Twelve Apostles, was assigned to stay in Nauvoo to

Figure 10.1 Nauvoo Temple Key, photograph, 1960, LDS Church Archives. The principal and possibly only entrance into the temple was through one of two main doors on the west end of the building. It has been claimed that this key was made and used to open these doors. Lorin Whiting Babbitt served during 1846 as a custodian for the Nauvoo Temple. According to his family, he kept this key when he was driven from his home in Nauvoo. It was then passed down through the family for many years. One of his descendants, Loretta Rice Child of Clearfield, Utah, turned this key over to The Church of Jesus Christ of Latter-day Saints on 27 July 1960. This key and other keys with similar claims (all located in the LDS Museum of History and Art) have never been fully authenticated. Another set of sixteen smaller keys, reported to have been used to open various doors of the Nauvoo Temple, is located in the Quincy Historical Museum at Quincy, Illinois.

represent Church leaders. He was to oversee the successful conclusion of the project and dedicate the edifice if the Twelve were unable to return.[6] It had been hoped that the dedication could take place on 6 April, the sixteenth anniversary of the Church's origin. Though work continued at a steady pace, the building simply could not be completed by that date, so Elder Hyde reported to Brigham Young: "The Temple will not be finished to dedicate on the sixth of April."[7] A new date was set for the completion, and the committee issued an announcement of the intended dedication. This announcement, published in three successive issues of the *Hancock Eagle* (10, 17, and 24 April 1846), reads as follows:

DEDICATION OF THE TEMPLE OF GOD IN THE CITY OF NAUVOO

This splendid edifice is now completed, and will be dedicated to the Most High God on Friday, the 1st. day of May, 1846. The services of the dedication will continue for three days in succession, commencing on each day at 11:00 o'clock a.m. Tickets may be had at the watch house near the door of the Temple, and also at the office of the Trustees in Trust at $1.00 each.

One object of the above is, to raise funds to enable the workmen who have built the Temple to remove to the west with their families, and all who are disposed to see the Mormons remove in peace and in quietness so soon as circumstances will allow, and [which is the earnest wish of every Latter-day Saint] are respectfully invited to attend. We expect some able speakers from abroad to favor us.

Done by order of the Trustees in Trust.

James Whitehead, clerk[8]

As the long-awaited day approached, the temple was a scene of feverish activity. Information on the preparations and an eyewitness account of the private dedication of 30 April 1846 were furnished by Samuel W. Richards:

This splendid edifice is now completed, and will be dedicated to the Most High God.

Thursday 30th spent most of the day at the temple, sweeping out the rooms and making preparation for the Dedication of the House, which had been published to take place on the 1st, 2nd, 3rd days of May. The 1st day being set apart for those who would pay one dollar for admitance which Money should go on payment to the T. hands This day finished my work on the temple and took a cirtificate of the same. . . . Met at sundown in the temple for prayers as usual, after which (with our clothing) we repaired to the lower room for the purpose of Dedicating the same. 30 men selected for that purpose were present. Orson Hyde, W. Woodruff, Joseph Young, & W. W. Phelps were in the company. After some conversation and singing a prayer circle was formed immediately in front of the Melchisedeck stand, O. Hyde was President, and Joseph Young, Mouth after which those present were seated in the stands to represent the order of the priest hood, myself being seated in the Teachers stand, and a Dedication prayer was offered by O. Hyde, to which all responded "amen." After the prayer was ended all shouted with loud voices: "Hosanna, Hosanna, Hosanna to God and the Lamb, Amen Amen, and Amen," which was three times repeated.[9]

This official dedication was held privately as a sacred and reverent occasion by selected Church leaders. It may also have been private because of fear that the public dedication might be disturbed by enemies of the Church. Wilford Woodruff recorded his impressions of this important occasion:

At the edge of the evening I repaired to the Temple And dressed in our Priestly robes in company with Elder Orson Hyde And about 20 others of the Elders of Israel. We dedicated the Temple of the Lord built by the

Church of Jesus Christ of Latter-day Saints, unto His Most Holy name. We had An interesting time. Notwithstanding the many false Prophesies . . . that the roof should not go on nor the House be finished And the threats of the mob that we should not dedicate it yet we have done both.

At the Close of the dedication we raised our voices in the united Shout of Hosanna to God And the Lamb which entered the Heavens to the joy And consolation of our hearts. We prayed for the Camp of Israel, for good weather, that we might not be disturbed by any mob untill the dedication was over. I returned home thankful for the privilege of Assisting in the dedication of the Temple of Lord.[10]

President Brigham Young, though not present in person, made this observation:

Elder Joseph Young offered up the dedicatory prayer, dedicating the Temple and all that pertained thereto to the Lord, as an offering to Him as an evidence of the willingness of his people to fulfill his commandments and build His holy house, even at the risk of their lives, and the sacrifice of all their labor and earthly goods. He prayed for the Twelve and all the authorities of the church, for the workmen that had wrought upon the Temple in the midst of persecution, want and suffering, and for the deliverance of the poor; that the Lord would direct the brethren of the camp of Israel, open the way before them and lead them to a place of his own appointment for the gathering of all the Saints.[11]

Following the dedicatory prayers, Elder Hyde made some remarks. After the services were concluded, the entire party assembled in the attic story at the invitation of Elder Hyde and partook of some refreshments. The public dedication began in the morning on the following day, 1 May 1846. Samuel W. Richards recorded an interesting account of this event: "Friday, May 1st. The Temple was dedicated in the presence of strangers and all who would pay one dollar for admittance, attended with my wife. I was one of three who was appointed to seat the congregation, in the house, and stood part of the time at the door to receive tickets. The cervises closed between one and two."[12]

The prayer of dedication was offered by Elder Hyde, who presided over the meeting.

Holy and Everlasting Father, before Thee this morning we present ourselves and acknowledge Thy mercy that has been extended to us since we have been on Thy footstool, and for this opportunity of dedicating this house. . . . We thank Thee that Thou hast given us strength to accomplish the charges delivered by Thee. Thou hast seen our labors and exertions to accomplish this purpose. By the authority of the Holy Priesthood now we offer this building as a sanctuary to Thy Worthy Name. We ask Thee to take the guardianship into Thy hands and grant that Thy Spirit shall dwell here and may all feel a sacred influence on their hearts that His Hand has helped this work. Accept of our offering this morning. . . . Let Thy Spirit rest upon those who have contributed to the building of this temple, the laborers on it that they may come forth to receive kingdoms and dominions and glory and immortal power. Accept of us we pray Thee, inspire every bosom to do Thy will, cause that truth may lead them for the glorious coming of the Son of God when you come in the name of the King, the Lord of Hosts shall be the King. Gather us in Thy kingdom through Jesus Christ, our Lord, Amen.[13]

No report is available on the number of people attending the dedication services of 1 May or 2 May, but it is quite likely that many were in attendance. On the final day of dedication, meetings were mainly attended by Latter-day Saints. During the services a resolution was passed that called for the sale of the temple, with the funds to be used for removing the poor to the main body of the Saints in the West. The resolution was adopted by a unanimous vote.[14] With the temple dedicated, the remaining Church members were now free to join their companions in the trek westward. Less than five months after the temples dedication, its builders had departed Nauvoo, leaving their beloved building behind as a symbol of their faith and sacrifice.

NOTES

1. Joseph Smith, *History of the Church of Jesus Christ of Latter-day Saints*, ed. B. H. Roberts, 2d ed., rev. (Salt Lake City: Deseret Book, 1957), 4:446.

2. B. H. Roberts, ed., *History of the Church of Jesus Christ of Latter-day Saints, Period 2: Apostolic Interregnum* (Salt Lake City: Deseret Book, 1957), 7:456–57.

3. Roberts, *History of the Church*, 7:534–35.

4. Ibid., 566.

5. Ibid., 580.

6. Journal History, 9 March 1846, LDS Church Archives.

7. Ibid., 27 March 1846.

8. *Hancock Eagle*, 10 April 1846.

9. Diary of Samuel Whitney Richards, 1824–1919, 18, Harold B. Lee Library, Brigham Young University.

10. Wilford Woodruff, *Wilford Woodruff's Journal*, ed. Scott G. Kenney (Midvale, Utah: Signature Books, 1983), 3:41–42.

11. Brigham Young, *Manuscript History of Brigham Young*, ed. Elden J. Watson (Salt Lake City: E. J. Watson, 1971), 1 May 1846.

12. Diary of Samuel Whitney Richards, 19.

13. David R. Crockett, *Saints in Exile* (Tucson: LDS Gems, 1996), 295; *Deseret News 1999–2000 Church Almanac* (Salt Lake City: Deseret News, 1998), 463.

14. *Hancock Eagle*, 8 May 1846.

View of Temple Ruins, drawing, date unknown, Joseph Kirschbaum, LDS Church Archives.

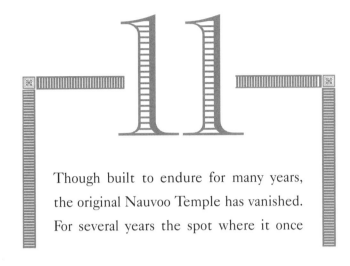

11

Though built to endure for many years,
the original Nauvoo Temple has vanished.
For several years the spot where it once

CHAPTER ELEVEN

THE FATE OF

THE TEMPLE

stood was an open plot of earth, excavated
to the level of the temple footings and
covered with grass. The story of its
destruction and the events relating to its
fate combine to make an interesting story.

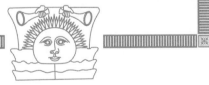

ABANDONED TO THE MOBS

Following the temple dedication of May 1846, most Latter-day Saints still in Nauvoo departed to join their friends and families on the prairies of Iowa. They left behind only a small portion of the original population, around 640 persons consisting mainly of the poor, the sick, the aged, and single mothers with their children.[1] Having no means to purchase equipment for transportation across the plains, they had remained in the city attempting to sell would be safe for a season from further provocation. This hope proved to be unfounded. Instead of relenting, mob elements became increasingly bolder in threats and persecution. Major Warren, an officer in the state militia who had been in charge of the governor's troops in Hancock County, had been an effective deterrent to the mobs. When he was released from command, the soldiers left to protect Nauvoo were reduced in number, and the citizens of Nauvoo were at the mercy of their enemies. As

The ferry boats were crowded fugitives, sadly awaiting the march to the wilderness.

their property, awaiting the arrival of relief wagons from the West. Church leaders had promised to send help to the poor and sick as soon as circumstances would permit. In fact, prior to the exodus, Church members entered into a solemn covenant, pledging to use every exertion and means possible to remove every person who wished to go.[2]

Since the vast majority of the Saints had left the state, many felt that the remaining few summer progressed the situation grew worse. Remaining Church members were warned to leave the state or face extermination.[3]

In early September 1846, a mob estimated at around fifteen hundred men, armed with rifle and cannon, approached the city. The Saints, aided by the new citizens who had recently purchased property in the city, marshaled themselves in defense. An armed battle ensued with weapons being fired by both

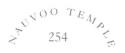

forces. Battles raged off and on for three days with casualties on both sides.[4] During this conflict the temple was used as a point of observation, with a lookout posted in the tower to watch the approach of enemy forces. When mob forces were spotted, the lookout would alert defenders by beating on a bass drum and ringing the temple bell.[5]

A truce was arranged on 16 September, and both sides agreed to sign a treaty. Mob forces were to enter the city and take possession the

veyance, without tents, money, or a day's provision, with as much of their household stuff as they could carry in their hands. Sick men and women were carried upon their beds, weary mothers with helpless babes dying in their arms hurried away—all fleeing, they scarcely knew or cared whither, so it was from their enemies, whom they feared more than the waves of the Mississippi, or the heat and hunger . . . and dreaded death of the prairies on which they were about to be cast. The ferry boats were

d the river bank was lined with anxious

rn to pass over and take up their solitary

next day. Throughout the night and during the next morning, Church members could be seen fleeing across the river, hoping to escape before the mob took possession of the city. Mason Brayman, designated by Governor Thomas Ford to be an official observer of these events, reported: "In every part of the city scenes of destitution, misery and woe met the eye. Families were hurrying away from their homes, without a shelter, without means of con-

crowded, and the river bank was lined with anxious fugitives, sadly awaiting their turn to pass over and take up their solitary march to the wilderness."[6]

Mob forces numbering between fifteen hundred to two thousand marched into the city during the afternoon of 17 September. Most of the Saints fled prior to the occupation. Others, defenseless women and children, the sick and the aged, were literally driven by the mob down to the water's edge and across the river into Iowa. Many were actually pushed into the water. Charles Lambert, a faithful worker in the construction of the temple, was seized and led to the river. "In the midst of cursing and swearing, one man said—By the Holy Saints I baptize you, by order of the commanders of the temple, (plunged him backward) and then said—the commandments must be fulfilled and God ___ you, you must have another dip; (then threw him in on his face), then sent him on the flatboat across the river, with the promise that, if he returned to Nauvoo, they would shoot him."[7]

Lambert added this observation: "He held me until my breath was gone but he held onto me I staggered and gasped and wanted to go out but he damned me and said you must have another dip and threw me on my face. It was pretty hard on me but I got over it."[8]

The exiles established themselves some two miles north of Montrose, Iowa, on the banks of the Mississippi. Their camp came to be known as the Camp of the Poor. The people suffered considerably as they camped out in the open, exposed to the elements. Many died as a result of exposure and lack of provisions. On 9 October they were rescued by a relief party traveling two hundred fifty to three hundred miles from Winter Quarters, where the main body of the Saints was encamped.[9]

Keys to the temple were given up by Henry I. Young, caretaker of the building, to the chairman of the Quincy committee, and mob forces took possession of the temple and made it their headquarters. The temple remained in their hands until 20 October 1846, when the keys were returned to the trustees.[10] An agreement in the form of a pledge had been entered into in June 1846 by a unanimous vote of five hundred men in the camp of the anti-Mormons. They pledged that they would not injure the temple and would use their influence to protect it, looking upon it as a work of art that should be preserved.[11]

Prior to and during the exodus, the Saints removed most of the furnishings and some ornamentation from the temple. This was especially true of those items considered to be of a sacred nature.[12] It was also true of those items that could be sold to pay the wages of workers and to assist the poor. This being the case, only the permanent fixtures and the bare walls remained in the rooms of the building.

As anti-Mormon forces occupied the temple, it is reported that some of their number ran to the top of the tower, beat on the drum, rang the bell, and shouted. A preacher in their number proclaimed in a loud voice from the tower: "Peace! Peace! Peace! to the inhabitants of the Earth, now the Mormons are driven."[13] An interesting account regarding the occupation of the temple by mob forces was published the day after the building had been evacuated by the Saints. "On entering the vestibule of this renowned edifice, a singular spectacle presented itself.—The seats of the High Priests of the 'Twelve' and of the Seventy were occupied by a grim visaged soldiery. Some lay sleeping on their 'arms,' and others lay rolled up in their blankets.

On every hand lay scattered about in beautiful confusion, muskets, swords, cannon balls and terrible missiles of death. Verily, thought I, how are the *holy places* desecrated! . . . I am penning this scrawl to you in the upper seat of the Sanctuary. Over my head there is an inscription in large gold letters, The Lord is our Sacrifice—on my right lie three soldiers asleep, resting on their arms—my feet are resting on a pile of chain shot—and a keg of powder, just discovered, lies at my elbow."[14]

Additional information was also recorded: "In front of the building, in battle array, with their mouths pointed towards the setting sun, had been placed several cannon, heavily charged."[15] The temple also became the scene of a mock court, or as Bancroft calls it, an "Inquisition," where numerous Latter-day Saints and new citizens were intimidated and abused, being given various sentences and threats.[16] This sacred edifice was further defiled by the mobs indulgence in a drunken show of boisterous behavior, vulgar song, and loud oaths.[17]

Though it is plain that from a spiritual sense the temple was defiled by the behavior of its new tenants, it is difficult to ascertain just how much physical abuse and damage the building suffered. Rumors were circulated among the Saints encamped on the plains, telling that the building had been defaced to a great extent, both inside and out. These reports, however, were apparently inaccurate.

An interesting eyewitness account of the physical desecration was provided by Christiana D. Pyper. As a young lady she had been driven out of Nauvoo in the fall of 1846. After a short period of exile, she and her family returned to the city. Christiana described her visit to the temple, following its occupation by the anti-Mormons: "We went up to the temple. From basement to tower, that sacred edifice was defaced with the most vile and wicked writing that could be imagined.[18] With great sadness Joseph Fielding wrote about the mobs and desecration of his beloved temple: They rendivouzed in the Temple, we had guarded it by Night and Day, a long time feeling unwilling to leave it in their Hands, but they now had it to themselves, they even Preached in it and cursed the Saints but did no great damage to it thinking it would add to the Value of their Property.[19]

Mob forces took possession of the temple and made it their headquarters.

Though some physical damage and abuse was sustained by the structure, it was not extensive. This conclusion is upheld by the report of President Wilford Woodruff, who visited the building in 1848. "I went over it, however, and found it in a much better state of preservation than I expected. Two horns, one ear off the oxen was all the damage I saw."[20] From this account it would appear that the mob forces, though severe in their treatment of the Saints, and abusive by their actions in the temple, had nevertheless kept their earlier pledge to each other. They had inflicted only limited physical damage to the building (see note 20, which includes a more detailed report on this subject). Following the occupation by anti-Mormons, another act of defacing the temple became common with visitors who toured the famed structure. Quoting from the record of some visitors who went through the building: "We found ourselves standing upon the highest accessible point, where thousands stood before us. . . . We placed our name within the uppermost dome, along with hundreds of others from all parts of the habitable globe.[21]

ATTEMPTS TO SELL THE TEMPLE

While preparing to leave Nauvoo, Church leaders deemed it advisable to sell all Church property as best they could. Included with other property put up for sale was the temple. As early as 16 September 1845, agents conferred with leading Catholic priests, offering to

Figure 11.1 Old Nauvoo, drawing, 1859, Johann Schroeder, Museum of Church History and Art.

sell them the property.[22] Almon W. Babbitt left on a mission to St. Louis, Cincinnati, and Chicago with the purpose of arranging a sale. On 1 December 1845 he reported on his mission, stating that the Catholics were making considerable exertions to have their members purchase the property but found reluctance to do so. They were anxious to lease the temple but not willing at that time to buy.[23]

On 18 January 1846, during a meeting in the temple for the captains of the emigrating companies, trustees were selected to remain in Nauvoo and sell Church property. Those selected were Almon W. Babbitt, Joseph L. Heywood, John S. Fullmer, Henry W. Miller, and John M. Bernhisel, and they were given power of attorney by letters authorizing them to act legally in behalf of the Church.[24] Though their lives were in constant danger, they were well suited for this difficult assignment. Brigham Young noted: "I appointed the Trustees myself, Babbitt for lawyer, Fullmer for bulldog and growl, and Heywood to settle debts."[25]

In April 1846 a letter from Elder Orson Hyde to President Brigham Young reported that a bid of two hundred thousand dollars had been made by a Catholic official for the purchase of the temple. The letter also declared that there was likely to be a judgment against the temple, and if it was not sold quickly the Church might lose it.[26] This offer fell through, but other efforts continued with attempts to lease the building on a long-term lease or to sell it if buyers could be found. Trustees placed the following ad in newspapers over a period of several months:

Temple For Sale.

The undersigned trustees of the Latter-day Saints propose to sell the Temple on very low terms, if an early application is made. The Temple is admirably designed for Literary and Religious Purposes.

Address the Undersigned Trustees

Almon W. Babbitt

Joseph L. Heywood

John S. Fullmer[27]

Following the forced exodus in the fall of 1846, the trustees were advised to sell as opportunities presented themselves and to use their own best judgment on the price of the property. They were told to use the money so derived to pay for labor on the temple and to relieve the suffering of the poor.[28] Due to the uncertain situation existing in Nauvoo, with mobs in possession of the temple during part of the fall of 1846, no sale could be effected. As a new year began, further complications arose as Dr. Isaac Galland swore out an attachment on all Church property in Nauvoo for the sum of twenty-five thousand dollars.[29] Almon Babbitt reported this action to Brigham Young: "Galland has commenced a suit in Chancery, as well as at common law. All these are impediments against a sale of the property."[30]

Additional legal entanglements complicated conditions in 1848. Emma Smith, widow of the Prophet, married a man named Lewis Bidamon. Shortly after this marriage, they threatened action to acquire all Church property in Nauvoo. John Fullmer commented on this action: "Now they . . . concocted a grand scheme by which they could effectually block our wheels and enrich themselves. They hit upon the idea that the Church could hold only ten acres of land, according to a limited construction of one of our State laws, and that consequently, the deed from Emma & Joseph Smith, to Joseph as 'Trustee' was illegal. They have therefore, now jointly conveyed all the lots that were ever in her name which she had not previously conveyed to others. This, you will see at a glance, places the Trustees in the extremest difficulty, as to title, while it destroys the confidence of every one, and prevents those who would have purchased, from doing so. . . . It requires a judicial decision to restore confidence."[31]

Though these actions clouded the title for a time, arrangements were finally made on 2 October 1848 for rental of the temple property. The building was rented to the Home Mission Society of New York for a period of fifteen years. No terms were mentioned in the report of this transaction.[32] Before final arrangements became official, the temple was destroyed by fire. Joseph Smith III commented on the matter: "A company from New York had just leased the property for the purpose of establishing a school there, thinking—rightly, no doubt—that such an enterprise would receive considerable support and patronage in the community. On the very day of its destruction word had been received that a committee would start next day for Nauvoo, to perfect the arrangements. This school would have been a benefit and a blessing to a great many people; but destiny seemed to

have decreed matters otherwise, and it was necessary to send a message back to the committee in New York telling them of the sad disaster."[33]

Although the trustees had been faithful in trying to arrange for the sale or rental of the temple, they were prevented from being successful when potential buyers were frightened away by threatened destruction of the building and by various legal entanglements that threw the title of the property into question.

DESTRUCTION BY FIRE

Earlier, on two separate occasions the building had narrowly escaped destruction from natural causes. The first such event took place in February 1846, when the first groups of Church members were exiting the city. Stoves in the attic story had become overheated while drying clothing, resulting in a fire that burned a large hole in the roof before it was extinguished. "Willard Richards called on the brethren to bring out all their buckets, to fill them with water, and pass them on. Lines inside were formed, and the buckets passed in quick succession. The fire raged nearly half an hour. . . . It burned from the west stovepipe from the ridge to the railing, about sixteen feet north and south, and about ten feet east and west on the north side. The shingles on the north were broken in several places."[34] Then in September 1846 the temple tower was reportedly struck by lightning. Though the building did not catch fire, a large scar was left to mark the event.

During its brief history, the temple had been the target of numerous threats and dangers. Prior to the Mormon exodus and even during nearly two years of the construction period, an armed guard kept constant watch over the temple to ensure its protection. As well as threats being made to burn the building, there were threats to blow it up. A report of such a plan was published in June 1846: "A gentleman from Fort Madison informs us that numbers had crossed the river to augment the force

apparently as an act to forever discourage the Latter-day Saints from returning to the city. A description of this fire, which resulted in the destruction of the temple, was published in the *Nauvoo Patriot*:

> Destruction of the Mormon Temple. On Monday (October 9th) our citizens were awakened by the alarm of fire, which, when first discovered, was bursting out through the spire of the temple, near the small door that opened from the East side to

opposite that place, and they make no hesitation in saying the Temple *must be destroyed*. One of them boasted that he could put his hand upon the powder that was intended to be used for this purpose. If foiled in that, they threaten to burn the town."[35]

Finally, on Monday, 9 October 1848, at 3 A.M. the citizens of Nauvoo were awakened to witness the great Mormon temple enveloped in flames. It had been set on fire deliberately,

the roof, on the main building. The fire was seen first about three oclock in the morning, and not until it had taken such hold of the timbers and roof as to make useless any effort to extinguish it. The materials of the inside were so dry, and the fire spread so rapidly, that a few minutes were sufficient to wrap this famed edifice in a sheet of flame.

It was a sight too full of mournful sublimity. The mass of material which

had been gathered there by the labor of many years afforded a rare opportunity for this element to play off some of its wildest sports. Although the morning was tolerably dark, still when the flames shot upwards, the spire, the streets and the houses for nearly a mile distant were lighted up, so as to render even the smallest object discernible. The glare of the vast torch, pointing skyward, indescribably contrasted with the universal gloom and darkness around it.[36]

throughout and cracked by the intense heat. The melted zinc and lead was dropping from its huge block during the day. On Tuesday morning the walls were too hot to be touched. The naked walls still stand, and if not demolished by the hand of man, for centuries may stand."[37]

The structure was entirely consumed by the flames, and only bare walls were left standing. These were reported to have been "calcined and rendered useless." The oxen and font in the basement also shared the same fate. The reac-

dry, and the fire spread so rapidly, that a

ap this famed edifice in a sheet of flame.

l sublimity.

To this account is added another descriptive report: "The fire presented a most sublime spectacle. It commenced in the cupola, and as the flames shot up to the sky, they threw a lurid glare into the surrounding darkness. Great volumes of smoke and flame burst from the windows, and the crash of falling timbers was distinctly heard on the opposite side of the river. The interior of the building was like a furnace; the walls of solid masonry were heated

tion by citizens of Nauvoo and the surrounding country was one of shock and dismay. Even the *Warsaw Signal,* a publication that voiced opposition to the Latter-day Saints, spoke out in disapproval: "No doubt the work of some nefarious incendiary. This edifice was the wonder of Illinois. . . . As a work of art and a memorial of Mormon delusion, it should have stood for ages. None but the most depraved heart could have applied the torch to effect its destruction."[38]

The *Nauvoo Patriot* announced that the act of burning the temple was evidently the work of an arsonist. A writer was puzzled as to who it was and what could have been his motives "to destroy a work of art, at once the most elegant and most renowned in its celebrity of any in the whole west, would, we should think, require a mind of more than ordinary depravity; and we feel assured that no one in this community could have been so lost to every sense of justice, and every consideration of interest, as to become the author of the deed."[39]

Lewis A. Bidamon, who had married the widow of Joseph Smith, was a witness to the destruction. He reported in 1856 that the burning of the temple had the effect of diminishing the importance of Nauvoo. Bidamon was proprietor of the Mansion House and was using it as a hotel. He declared that after the fire, his business was only one-fourth of what it had been previously.[40]

The act of burning the temple was evidently the work of an arsonist.

Rumors and speculation spread as people tried to determine who had done the fateful deed. It was announced in the *Warsaw Signal* that the citizens of Nauvoo were offering a reward for the capture of the arsonist.[41] There were several suspects considered as possible perpetrators of the deed. One mentioned with some prominence was John W. Palmer, a former major in the anti-Mormon forces that expelled the last of the Saints from Nauvoo. His name was later cleared of the charge.[42]

The most frequently mentioned suspect was Joseph B. Agnew. Bidamon is reported to have heard a deathbed confession of a Mrs. Walker, who boarded at the Agnew home when the temple was burned. He reported that she strongly implicated Agnew in the act.[43] Bidamon reported the following to Elders George A. Smith and Erastus Snow in November 1856: "The inhabitants of Warsaw, Carthage, Pontusuc and surrounding settlements, in consequence of jealousy that Nauvoo would still retain its superior importance as a town and might induce the Mormons to return, contributed a purse of Five hundred dollars which they gave to Joseph Agnew in consideration of his burning the temple and that said Agnew was the person who set the building on fire."[44]

Joseph Smith III, who lived in the Bidamon household, was also convinced that Joseph Agnew was the guilty party. He claimed that Agnew was "a 'river rat,' a drunken lout who confessed to the deed quite some time

Figure 11.2 Front of Nauvoo Temple Ruins, tintype (daguerreotype), ca. 1850, T. W. Cox, LDS Church Archives.

after, and stated he had been hired to do it."[45] This conclusion was reinforced in 1885 as B. H. Roberts was informed by M. N. Morrill, the mayor of Nauvoo at that date, "that one Joseph Agnew confessed to being the incendiary." Morrill had assisted in repelling the mobs during the battle of Nauvoo.[46]

In addition to the reports just cited, what purports to be a reliable statement came to light many years after the temples destruction. It was a lengthy account of the reported confession of Joseph Agnew. The statement was issued by George H. Rudisill of Bowling Green, Florida, who as a boy had lived in Fort Madison, Iowa, a short distance from Nauvoo. He reported that Agnew, who died in the fall of 1870 at the age of fifty-eight, came to him just prior to his death. In the course of their conversation Agnew told Rudisill the complete story of the temples burning. He then pledged Rudisill to secrecy, asking that the story not be told until after the death of all parties concerned in the deed, since those who had been in on the act had pledged themselves to secrecy.[47] Following Agnew's death, the story was released and published in many newspapers. The earliest date found on the printing of this confession is April 1872, when it appeared in the *Peoria Transcript*.[48] This article was then quoted by other newspapers.

There is a discrepancy, however, between the reported confession of Agnew and the report of the *Nauvoo Patriot* regarding the time the fire took place. The Agnew account places the beginning of the event in the evening easi-ly before midnight. In contrast to this, the newspaper account gives the time when the fire was first noticed as 3 A.M. This latter account is corroborated by the report of Christiana D. Pyper, who witnessed the conflagration. She remembered the event taking place between two and three o'clock in the morning.[49] This places some suspicion on the Rudisill narrative. However, since the story was told to Rudisill some twenty years after the event occurred, a lapse of accuracy in memory could account for the discrepancy in time. Silas McKaig, a close friend of Joseph Agnew, wrote a detailed article published in the *Fort Madison Democrat* refuting several points of the Rudisill narrative. He declared that Agnew "told me that several men had repeatedly quizzed him in regard to his burning the temple and in order to silence them he had 'stuffed' them as he expressed it to me but had made each one solemnly promise not to breathe a word of what he had told them until all parties concerned were dead. He further stated that he had told no two of them the same story, considering it a huge joke as he knew it would almost kill these persons to keep a secret." He felt that Rudisill was one of those individuals who had only honestly repeated what Agnew had told him, that the real person who burned the temple was a citizen of Nauvoo who now lies buried in the Nauvoo cemetery.[50] Rudisill then wrote a reply (also published in the *Fort Madison Democrat*) contesting McKaig's article and clearly reasserting his certainty of both Agnew's guilt and the reliability of his confession.[51]

It would appear from the evidence available that although Joseph Agnew is the chief suspect in the burning of the temple, sufficient conflicts exist to cast doubt or questions about his guilt or innocence. So the question of who really set the temple on fire still remains an unsolved mystery.

To many Latter-day Saints, the loss of their sacred structure was a crushing, demoralizing blow. The experience of Mary Field Garner is an example. Her mother was a widow with six children. They were driven out of Nauvoo in September 1846 and were among those who were too poor to cross the plains and join the main body of the Church. After crossing the river into Iowa, they had gone somewhat down-river and so had not been rescued by the rescue party from Winter Quarters. Months later they made their way back to Nauvoo and were there when the temple burned. "One night mother heard a terrible crackling of timber, she went outside, looking up she saw the beautiful Nauvoo Temple in flames. She ran back into the house waking us . . . to watch it burn to the ground. It is impossible to describe the feelings of the saints to see their sacred temple . . . being destroyed."[52] In spite of this, however, the strong feelings of most Church members were summarized by Brigham Young when he stated, "I would rather it should thus be destroyed, than remain in the hands of the wicked."[53]

DESTRUCTION OF THE WALLS

Following the great fire of 1848, the bare walls of the temple stood as a silent witness to the former grandeur of the building. It was in this condition when Nauvoo was inhabited by a new group of colonizers in the spring of 1849. The new settlers who occupied Nauvoo in March of that year were French Icarians. They were a communal society who had left France under the leadership of Etienne Cabet. First organized in 1847, the group had located in northeastern Texas prior to living in Nauvoo. In Texas their attempt at colonization and the realization of their ideal society had met with failure.[54] Upon arriving in Nauvoo, they purchased the temple ruins. One report indicates that they paid one thousand dollars for the site,[55] and the American Guide Series puts the amount at five hundred dollars.[56] No information exists regarding who sold them the property. Though the Icarians purchased the property, no immediate attempt was made to renovate the burned-out structure. This is evidenced by a report of Dr. John M. Bernhisel, who wrote to Brigham Young on 10 September 1849 concerning his recent visit to Nauvoo: "Though the walls of the Temple are standing, yet they are much cracked, especially the east one; and not a vestige of the once beautiful font remains. There has been nothing done to rebuild it, except clearing away some rubbish, and it is highly probable there will never be anything more done. The Temple is enclosed with a rude fence, and is used as a sheepfold and cow-pen."[57]

Sometime between September 1849 and May 1850, the Icarians started working in the gutted ruins of the temple, hoping to reclaim it for their own use. In the midst of these preparations the building was struck by the full force

I would rather it should thus be destroyed, than remain in the hands of the wicked.

—BRIGHAM YOUNG

Figure 11.3 Nauvoo Temple Ruins, drawing, date unknown, Charles Piercy, LDS Church Archives. This was drawn by Frederick Piercy and published in his Route from Liverpool to the Great Salt Lake Valley, *1853.*

of a tornado on 27 May 1850, making any future attempts at renovation impractical. An account of the Icarian preparations and damage inflicted by the storm was reported by the *Missouri Republican:*

> On arriving at Nauvoo, in March 1849, the Icarian Community bought the walls of the Temple with a view to refit it for schools, etc. Much preparation had been made for re-establishing the roof and floors; a steam mill was purchased to fit up a saw mill; the saw mill was nearly finished; a vast shed was raising near the Temple, to shelter the carpenters, the masons were laying in the interior the bases of the pillars, when this frightful hurricane, the most terrible experienced in the country in many years, burst suddenly on the hill of Nauvoo, where lightnings, thunder, wind, hail and rain, seemed united to assail the building.
>
> The storm burst forth so quickly and with such violence that the masons, overtaken unawares in the Temple, had not time to flee before the northern wall, sixty feet high, bent down over their heads, threatening to crush and bury them up.[58]

Eight men were working in the temple. The rocks landed at their feet but did not strike them.

Fearing that the east and south walls would also fall, they fled from the structure. Another account of the destruction was preserved by the *Nauvoo Patriot:*

> The dreadful tornado on May 27th, which invaded the city of Nauvoo and neighboring places, has been for us, *Icarians* . . . a spectacle of frightful sublimity, and also a source of mortal anguish, on account of the disasters and catastrophes which have resulted from it, to the inhabitants of this county, and to us. . . .
>
> Here are some particulars of what has happened to us during that storm; in its first blow which has been the most fatal to us, and everyone will certainly think so when they know, that part of the Temple walls was immediately blown to the ground. The Temple, which we were preparing so actively and resolutely to rebuild; the temple which we hoped to cover this year; and in which we were to settle our refectories, our halls of reunion, and our schools; that it is the temple; that gigantic monument, which has become the first victim of the tornado.[59]

The next morning a general assembly of the Icarian community decided to tear down the east and south walls of the temple. They were so badly damaged that they were a hazard to safety. This was accomplished, and all that remained of the famous edifice was the west face of the temple, "united by its sides to another wall in the interior part, and surmounted by an arch."[60] An excellent view of these ruins is furnished by an examination of a daguerreotype (Figure 11.2), along with an artist's sketch of the ruins (Figure 11.3). The ruins of the west end of the temple were still standing in December 1856.[61] Joseph Smith III recorded that "the walls kept falling from time to time, bit by bit, until only the southwest corner remained. It was then deemed advisable by

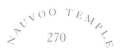

the City Council of Nauvoo to raze the remaining portion, and the temple destruction became complete."[62]

The building site was described in 1870 as not having one stone upon another. Where the Saints once practiced their sacred temple ordinances there was now a vineyard.[63] An interesting account of the fate of the temple stones is furnished by Joseph Smith III: "During the years which followed there was a gradual spoliation of the ruins of the Temple, to which I was a witness. The place became a veritable quarry and provided the materials with which many homes, wine cellars, and saloons in the town were built. At last the time came when the last stone was upturned from its resting place and taken away, and little remained to indicate the spot where once the magnificent and stately edifice had reared its proud head. Of all the stones placed in position by human hands during its erection the only ones left are those lining the well which was dug in the basement to supply water for the baptismal font and other needs of occupation."[64]

The stones used in the temple were later used in many buildings in Nauvoo, and some were carried off to other parts of the country. In 1883 nothing remained that would give evidence to the casual observer that a magnificent temple had once stood in Nauvoo.[65] All that remained were broken, scattered stones and memories.

FATE OF THE NAUVOO TEMPLE BELL

September 1845 had been a time of tension and anxiety in Nauvoo. Armed mobs were pil-

laging farms of Church members living outside the city, burning crops, hay stacks, houses, and barns. Men were being whipped and beaten and families driven from their property.[66] Refugees from these depredations fled to Nauvoo. During this time of crisis and alarm, Church leaders at the request of sheriff Jacob Backenstos organized themselves for the purposes of defense. Guards were placed around the temple and at various strategic places in the city. On 18 September 1845 Hosea Stout reported that all companies of the Nauvoo Legion were "to be in readiness for actual service at a moments warning & that they immediately repair to the ground they now occupied. At firing of the artillery it shall be the signal of alarm."[67]

Zina Diantha Huntington Jacobs cited an event taking place the next day. "This morning at about 7 o'clock 2 cannons ware fired near the Temple which signified for all to be on the ground."[68] While the troops were assembled, Brigham Young explained: "As signals—we will have the flag hoisted and then let all men be on the ground as a flag with strips is hoisted it is a signal for all commissioned officers to meet in council. . . . We intend shortly to have a light at night on the top of the temple which can be seen for miles—the white flag is for the mustering of men."[69] On 19 September 1845 Hosea Stout reported: "At about six o'clock the white flag was for the first time hoisted as a signal for mustering."[70] This signal was also observed by Zina Jacobs: "The first thing I saw as I looked toward the Temple just as the sun was risen, a white flag, a signature to gather."[71] This flag, apparently hoisted on top of the steeple, was visible from a long distance.

An additional means of sounding an alert is noted by the report of Hosea Stout: "At the tolling of the Temple Bell every man know it as an alarm & repair forthwith armed & equipd to the parade ground."[72] There is also a report that on 21 September 1845 "the flag was raised and the Temple bell rang to collect a posse to go to Carthage."[73] These reports of a temple bell in September 1845 raise many questions. How large was this bell? Was it hanging in the temple or just in position on the temple grounds? The record of any purchase or installation is absent. No additional reports of its use, its description, or any comments about it surface again until June 1846, nine full months after Stout's observation.[74] Is this what came to be the accepted temple bell? What about the bell that was to be purchased in England?

Did the temple bell come from England?

In an effort to let British members contribute something tangible toward the construction of the temple, it was concluded during the summer of 1845 that they could provide its bell. Brigham Young wrote: "We have thought it might be very agreeable to the feelings of the English Saints to furnish a bell for the temple, if this is their pleasure, you can forward it [at] the first conveyance, and we will have it hung as the building is going up. We are but little acquainted with the weight of bells: we have thought of 2000 lbs. weight, but we leave this to your judgment. We want one that can be heard night or day."[75]

In August 1845 an editorial in the *Millennial Star* stated that all further donations of the British Saints would be used to obtain the bell and also a clock for the temple. The members were urged by Wilford Woodruff, president of the mission, to respond to this call for funds.[76] In late January when Wilford Woodruff was about to leave England and return to Nauvoo, he reported that 535 British pounds had been contributed.[77] There are reports that the bell was cast in a foundry in England, brought across the ocean on a sailing vessel, then moved up the Mississippi to Nauvoo on a riverboat.[78] These same sources indicate that the bell had come to Nauvoo from England under the care of Wilford Woodruff.[79] If this is accurate, then such a bell probably would not have arrived prior to 13 April 1846, since that was when Wilford Woodruff arrived back in Nauvoo from England. His family had arrived just a few days earlier, having gone on ahead of him by way of New Orleans and then up the Mississippi. He had taken a later ship to New York and traveled overland to Nauvoo.[80]

George Washington Bean worked on the temple as a young man. He was present at the temple's dedication and traveled back to Nauvoo from the plains of Iowa in early June 1846. Bean's son Willard, who was with his father during his last illness, reported the following: "Among other things he spoke of a large bell some of the brethren (missionaries) had sent from England by ship to New Orleans, thence by river steamer up the Mississippi River to Nauvoo, where it was hung, with some difficulty, in the steeple of the Temple."[81] If this report is correct, then the British Mission presidency would have purchased a bell and shipped it to Nauvoo with Wilford Woodruff's family or on another ship after their departure. No records have been found regarding purchase or shipment of a bell from England.

Was the bell purchased in America?

Increasing persecution during the fall of 1845 resulted in a decision to leave Nauvoo the following spring. This action apparently prompted another decision— that the bell for the temple would be purchased in the United States. A letter from Brigham Young to Wilford Woodruff on 19 December 1845 comments on this decision: "I wrote you in my last letter that we intended to purchase the bell in this country and desired you to transmit the money collected for that purpose by the first safe opportunity. I feel as ever anxious this should be done."[82]

Figure 11.4 The Traditionally Accepted Nauvoo Temple Bell, photograph, date unknown, Utah State Historical Society. This is how the bell was displayed in the Church Museum on Temple Square in Salt Lake City. It is now housed in the campanile on Temple Square.

Since this was an official action by the leader of the Church, it seems likely that the bell was purchased in the United States. There are, however, no clear reports of its purchase in America, its shipment or its installation in the building. Records are seemingly not available regarding this event in the temple's construction, though we do have an observation made in late November 1845 that the Saints "are finishing the Temple, putting in the carpets, &c., and intend to hang a bell."[83] This report, if accurate, along with the above cited letter of Brigham Young, strongly indicates that no bell had been purchased or installed in the steeple by mid-December 1845. It is also possible that the bell used as a signal in September 1845 actually became the temple bell. Evidence may in time surface providing answers on the subject.

Was a bell ever installed in the steeple?

Thomas Bullock, a secretary to Brigham Young and a reliable record keeper, reported that on 14 June 1846 men had been called together "at the ringing of the Temple Bell."[84] They had been assembled to defend the temple and other property in the city from threatened mob attack. Over the next several weeks, this bell was regularly used to sound an alarm. This establishes solid evidence that a bell was very likely hanging in the belfry of the temple during the summer and fall of 1846. A bell and bass drum are reported to have been in the belfry when armed mobs attacked the city during mid-September 1846. Placed in the

Temple night after night upon the hard wooden benches with my rifle by my side expecting an attack every minute, I have laid in my bed with my clothes on and my gun leaning against my pillow where I could lay my hand upon it at any hour of the night and jumped from my bed at all hours of the night at the sound of the big drum and the ringing of the Temple bell which was a signal for us to gather and I have been armed and equipped and at the place of rendevous inside of 5 minutes."[85]

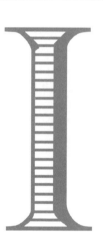

I have been on guard night after

between Nauvoo and Carthage

and setting fire to the city and m

temple tower, these were utilized by lookouts to warn of mob forces approaching the city. George Morris, who remained behind to assist in the completion of the temple, vividly described this use of the bell prior to his departure from the city in mid-July: "I have been on guard night after night with my brethren on the prairies between Nauvoo and Carthage to prevent the mob from coming in unaware and setting fire to the city and murdering more of our friends. I have lain in the

Thomas Bullock recorded another use of the bell following the surrender of Nauvoo to mob forces. He wrote, "The mob went through the temple and up to the dome of the tower, ringing the bell, shouting and hallowing."[86] Colonel Thomas L. Kane, who visited Nauvoo just a few days after the final exodus of the Saints, found the temple in the possession of mob forces. Permitted to view the interior of the building, he climbed to the observation

section of the tower and viewed the city. In the steeple he found "fragments of food, cruises of liquor and broken drinking vessels, with a bass drum and a steam-boat signal bell." He described the bell as being in the high belfry of the temple.

> In and around the splendid Temple, which had been the chief object of my admiration, armed men were barracked, surrounded by their stacks of musketry and pieces of heavy ordnance. These challenged me to

They particularly pointed out to me certain features of the building, which, having been the peculiar objects of a former superstitious regard, they had as a matter of duty sedulously defiled and defaced. . . .

A cruel spirit of insulting frolic carried some of them up into the high belfry of the Temple steeple, and there, with the wicked childishness of inebriates, they whooped, and shrieked, and beat the drum that I had seen, and rang in charivaric unison their loud-tongued steam-boat bell.[87]

ight with my brethren on the prairies

event the mob from coming in unaware

ering more of our friends.

render an account of myself, and why I had had the temerity to cross the water without a written permit from a leader of their band.

Though these men were generally more or less under the influence of ardent spirits; after I had explained myself as a passing stranger, they seemed anxious to gain my good opinion. . . .

They also conducted me inside the massive sculptured walls of the curious Temple. . . .

Kane's description of the bell as a "steam-boat bell" may have been accurate, or he may have been using descriptive language adding color to his lectures. He did at least witness that some kind of bell was hanging in the belfry of the temple. If this is what is now accepted as the Nauvoo Temple bell, then it did not long remain in the temple. The bell was reported to have been taken out of Nauvoo and brought across the plains to Utah in the early days of the

Mormon migration. That there was a bell recognized and accepted as the temple bell and that it was to be brought out of Nauvoo in the fall of 1846 is shown by a letter of Brigham Young dated 27 September. Having just recently been informed of the forced exodus of the poor and sick Latter-day Saints from Nauvoo, he wrote to the trustees of the remaining Church property in the city: "Since you will have no further use of the Temple Bell, we wish you to forward it to us by the first possible chance, we have much need of it at this place."[88] Joshua Hawkes reported that "he and James Houton took the Nauvoo Temple bell over the Mississippi river in 1846 and that it was in [the] charge of Joseph P. Heywood."[89] Heywood, a member of the committee left behind to look after the temple and other Church property, apparently was the one who carried out the request of President Brigham Young, removing the bell from Nauvoo and sending it to Winter Quarters.

We do have accurate information that the bell arrived in Winter Quarters by December 1846, that it was placed in the public square, and that it was used for calling people to church and other meetings.[90] When the advance company of pioneers were starting their historic trek across the plains and mountains to Utah in the spring of 1847, the Twelve, instructing the groups that would follow, issued this order: "The first company will carry the Temple bell, with fixtures for hanging at a moment's notice, which will be rung at daylight or at a proper time and call all who are able to arise to pray, after which ringing

of bell and breakfast, or ringing of bell and departure in 15 minutes, to secure the cool of the day. . . . The bell may be needed, particularly in the night, if Indians are hovering around, to let them know that you are at your duty."[91]

One of the lead pioneer companies to cross the plains following Brigham Young's vanguard group departed Winter Quarters on 14 June 1847. This group, led by Charles C. Rich, took with them the Nauvoo bell. "Thare was allso a skift or a boat fitted up on wheels, and the cannon placed on that. . . . So the boat and one cannon and the big bell was in our company. Mr. Rich had charge of the company. . . . The bell was so arainged over the boat and cannon, that it could be rung by pulling a roap." The weight of the bell, cannon, and boat required two yoke of oxen to pull the wagon on which they were carried. The bell arrived in the Salt Lake Valley with this group of pioneers on 2 October 1847.[92]

Following its arrival in Salt Lake City, the bell was used at the old bowery to call the Saints to religious services and in various other community functions.[93] The bell was cracked as a result of a hard frost during the severe winter of 1849–50. Following this the *Deseret News* reported: "It is about being re-cast, and enlarged, and we hope to hear its cheerful tones again in a few days. It is a heavy undertaking for our present means, but it is confidently believed, that the iron furnace left by the gold diggers last season, when attached to the flue of the mint, can accomplish the object."[94] In 1860 a bell that came to be accepted as the Nauvoo Temple bell was placed in the

belfry of the Brigham Young schoolhouse, where it remained until 1902. It was later presented to the Utah Historical Society. They turned it over to the LDS Church museum, where it was displayed for many years in the museum on Temple Square.[95]

No records are available on the size and weight of the original bell. It certainly could not have weighed more than a few hundred pounds. Otherwise it would have been too difficult to hang in the temple or to remove without the use of cranes.

The bell long accepted as the Nauvoo Temple bell can be seen today near the Tabernacle on Temple Square in Salt Lake City, Utah, where it is permanently housed and on display in a thirty-five-foot campanile, or bell tower, erected to commemorate the one-hundred-year anniversary of the Relief Society. The bell rings every hour and is "controlled by an electronic system in the basement of the Tabernacle. The system is set according to Greenwich time, the standard time throughout most of the world."[96] Its melodic tones have been recorded and are broadcast each day, on the hour, over radio station KSL in Salt Lake City. The bell housed on Temple Square measures 23½ inches tall, 33 inches wide at the bottom, and is about 2½ inches thick.[97]

The bell arrived in Winter Quarters by December 1846.

What about the bell supposedly rescued from a Protestant chapel?

A story has been widely circulated in the LDS Church connecting David Lamoreaux with the rescue of the Nauvoo bell from the tower of a Protestant church. According to the accounts, the bell reportedly had been stolen from the tower of the Nauvoo Temple and installed in a Protestant church steeple during the period when the temple was being occupied by mob forces. Lamoreaux and others reportedly took the bell down from this church steeple and buried it for a time in a river.[98]

This account, which is accepted by many and printed as reliable, raises many questions. The most accurate information available on this bell (more properly referred to as the "Hummer's Bell") is that it was purchased by a Reverend Michael Hummer for a Presbyterian church in Iowa City, Iowa. Hummer had disagreements with the Iowa City presbytery, and they

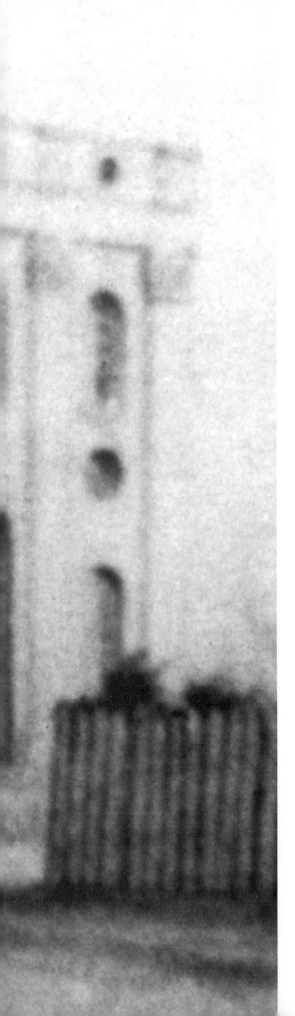

expelled him from their ministry. Feeling that the bell was due him as compensation, he with the help of Dr. J. W. Margrave let the bell down from the church tower where it had been installed. While it rested in a wagon, David Lamoreaux (a member of the LDS Church), James Miller, A. B. Newcomb, and others took the bell and sank it in the Iowa River, hiding it from Hummer and Margrave. In 1850 some in this group left for California, taking the bell with them. It arrived in the Salt Lake Valley in September 1850. Undoubtedly in an effort to accrue additional funds, those of this group going on to California offered the bell for sale to the LDS Church. It was eventually purchased by the Church for six hundred dollars.

Years later, Presbyterian Church leaders in Iowa were informed by Brigham Young of this bell's existence in Utah, and negotiations were conducted to return the bell to Iowa. The Church wanted to see it returned to its rightful owners but desired proof of ownership and some reimbursement for the funds expended in its purchase. Disputes over rightful ownership then arose between Reverend Hummer and the Presbyterian congregation, resulting in a breakdown of communication with the LDS Church. Later the Church even offered the bell without compensation if the rightful owner would just pick it up. Nothing was ever consummated, and this bell, still in its box and lacking its clapper, slipped from history. No one seems to know what happened

Figure 11.5 View of Temple Ruins, drawing, date unknown, Joseph Kirschbaum, LDS Church Archives.

to it.[99] This information throws serious doubt that this bell ever had any direct association with the Nauvoo Temple.

Summary and Conclusions

Although the original intent was to purchase a bell in England for the Nauvoo Temple, this apparently was never done, and stories of a bell traveling to America from England most likely belong to the realm of folklore. The most reliable evidence available indicates that the bell was obtained in the United States, but when and where it was purchased remains a mystery. When it arrived in Nauvoo and when it was installed in the temple also remains unanswered. It may have been purchased in the eastern states, transported down the Ohio River, and then up the Mississippi to Nauvoo. If it did come partway up the river by boat, then this could help to clarify some reports of such an arrival. The best evidence now available leads to the well-established conclusion that what has officially been acknowledged as the Nauvoo Temple bell came across the plains with the pioneers in 1847 and was later recast and enlarged.

A careful examination of the bell now hanging on Temple Square reveals six bead markings around the bell, each measuring 3/16 of an inch. In addition to these markings, there is a filed-off area on the side of the bell some 2½ inches high by 13 inches long, strongly hinting of a former inscription on the bell. It has been common practice to file off inscriptions on used bells when sold to a new owner. These markings and the filed-off area strongly indicate that the bell on Temple Square has never been recast. It is evident that some questions still remain unanswered concerning the Nauvoo Temple bell, and hopefully additional information will yet be found to provide the correct answers.

FATE OF THE ANGELIC WEATHER VANE

Clear and sufficient evidence (as reviewed in chapter 6) establishes that an angelic weather vane was placed at the top of the temple steeple in January 1846. How long it remained in place and what eventually happened to it remains a mystery. Thomas Bullock, who was driven from Nauvoo with the sick and poor members of the Church on 20 September 1846, provided this interesting report. For several days following his forced exodus from the city, he had camped near the bank of the Mississippi river opposite Nauvoo in "the camp of the poor." Bullock recorded in his journal entry of Sunday, 4 October 1846, that Benjamin Baker had informed him that "the mob had taken away the angel and ball from the top of the temple last Friday." This would have been on either 25 September or 2 October 1846. At the side of this journal entry, Bullock apparently later wrote, "I saw the angel on [the] 8th. all safe."[100] What he meant by this added note is open to conjecture. This report seems to be corroborated by a reminiscence regarding two young men who reportedly climbed to the top of the steeple in the fall of 1846. Their report indicates that one of them comfortably seated

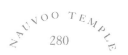

himself "on the dome with his legs around the flag staff." This observer then describes "a naked flag-staff [no angel on it—she was in the dome]."[101] If these reports are accurate, then it is possible that the angelic weather vane had been removed from the steeple by mob forces in late September or early October 1846. How long it remained off the steeple is not known. There seems to be clear evidence, however, that if indeed it had been removed, then it also had soon been reinstated in its proper place at the top of the tower. This conclusion is borne out by later witnesses. Notable among these observers is Thomas L. Kane, who visited the temple in early October 1846. He provided a detailed description of his visit to the temple and told of an angel being in place on the steeple at that time.[102]

If we knew the sequence of visits by these observers, it would possibly clear up the matter. The conclusion that an angel was in place on the steeple after the fall of 1846 is also upheld by the observations of a reporter from the *Illinois Journal* who, as best as can be determined, visited Nauvoo in the summer of 1848 shortly before the temple was burned. His reminiscence of the visit portraying an extensive tour of the building from the basement to the top of the tower was published in December 1853. Describing many features of the temple in some detail, he wrote that there was an angel affixed on top of the dome "holding in one hand a trumpet, and in the other a book," which angel was "composed of tin gilded."[103] Several artists between 1846 and 1848 also sketched an angel on the steeple.

It has generally been concluded that the angelic weather vane was most likely destroyed in the fire of 1848. Some, however, have claimed that the angel found its way to Cincinnati, Ohio, where it was placed on the steeple of a Protestant church.[104] This claim was summarized by Marie Dickore, a noted local historian and member of the Salem Evangelical Reformed Church. She related the story that over one hundred years ago, a committee of this church had an angelic weather vane built to place upon the top of their church steeple. When the finished product arrived, the congregation was upset to discover that it was an angel in a standing position. The committee and congregation had wanted the figure of an angel to be placed in a horizontal position, serving as a weather vane. The one they received could not be modified or used as desired. In frustration the project was set aside and years later taken up by another committee. They at that time reportedly heard of a horizontally designed angel weather vane for sale at Nauvoo, Illinois. This angelic weather vane had supposedly flown over the Mormon Temple at Nauvoo. The story goes on to claim that the figure was purchased and placed on the steeple of the Salem Evangelical Reformed Church at Sycamore and Orchard Streets in 1867. The congregation looked upon it as the angel Gabriel blowing his horn. Miss Dickore claimed that there was a strong tradition among ministers and members of the congregation that they were possessors of the angel that once flew over the Latter-day Saint temple at Nauvoo. She also claimed to have read the purchase records from the old German script records of the church located on bookshelves in the minister's office.

The possibility of this being the Nauvoo weather vane was called to the attention of local Cincinnati LDS Church officials and the Church Historians office as early as 1961. On 20 July 1961 Robert D. Craig, a member of the LDS Church, interviewed Miss Dickore and listened to her story. By this time her own personal records or notes from the old German script had been lost. In 1962 Marie Dickore, accompanied by Robert Craig and Mrs. H. Frersing, conducted a search looking for the old books that outlined the purchase from the Mormons. The books could not be found; they had supposedly been destroyed. In 1966 a violent wind storm nearly tore this Cincinnati angelic weather vane from the church steeple. It was then taken down, and a decision was made to construct a duplicate of the original. This new duplicate angel was placed on the steeple in the late summer of 1968. The former Cincinnati angelic weather vane was stored in the basement and later offered to the LDS Church.[105]

In November 1968, the old Cincinnati weather vane was transferred to Nauvoo Restoration Inc. It was hauled in an open pickup truck to Nauvoo, Illinois, by J. Byron Ravsten, resident manager of Nauvoo Restoration at the time. He was accompanied on the trip by his wife Elva.[106] At first glance there was some consideration that the Cincinnati weather vane might have come from the Nauvoo Temple.[107] However, after further examination, officials of Nauvoo Restoration concluded that claims of this being the original Nauvoo Temple weather vane were subject to serious question. There was a general feeling and agreement that it was not a work of quality in line with the excellence of other temple artwork. Dr. J. Leroy Kimball, president of Nauvoo Restoration, and his son James Kimball Jr., an associate researcher, were confident that this Cincinnati vane was never part of the temple.[108] Dr. T. Edgar Lyon, research historian for Nauvoo Restoration, seriously questioned its authenticity, as did the Harringtons, who were in charge of the temple site excavation.[109] Donald L. Enders, who is a materials culture specialist and a senior curator of historic sites for the LDS Church, worked for Nauvoo Restoration. He personally examined the Cincinnati vane on at least six separate occasions. He concluded:

1. The Cincinnati weather vane was not a religious icon of the 1840s era. Angel weather vanes of that period came in various formats, but they were all clearly angels. The cherublike figure such as the Cincinnati vane is an icon for other than that of a religious structure, possibly a theater.

2. The construction of the Cincinnati tin figure is unlike the work competent tinsmiths of the 1840s produced.

a. It was not constructed of hand-dipped tin but of a later, less-quality tin.

b. Its three-dimensional shape was crude, its edges not "joined" nor

soldered by competent hand crafts-men—which the Nauvoo Temple Tinners Association was comprised of—but was the work of a machine-aided maker.

c. Rather than a finely produced three-dimensional shape appearing almost humanlike, the Cincinnati "angel," was simply two mirrored images joined by a strip of tin between, curving to accommodate the shape of the creature.

d. The Cincinnati angel was painted to give body and clothing colors, very unlike the gold-leaf vane purported for the Nauvoo Temple.

Altogether, the style, materials used, construction method, and finish in no way represented what is described in the sources about the weather vane of the Nauvoo Temple.[110]

Other problems are raised by the Cincinnati weather vane. It did not look the same nor clearly resemble drawings of the original angelic weather vane intended for the Nauvoo Temple. Photographs of the Cincinnati angel show no book in its left hand, as was clearly shown in drawings and descriptions of the Nauvoo angel. Concluding that this Cincinnati production was not authentic, it was stored away and has since disappeared.

NOTES

1. Thomas L. Kane, *The Mormons: A Discourse* (Philadelphia: King and Baird, 1850), 8–11.

2. B. H. Roberts, ed., *History of the Church of Jesus Christ of Latter-day Saints, Period 2: Apostolic Interregnum* (Salt Lake City: Deseret Book, 1957), 7:465.

3. B. H. Roberts, *The Rise and Fall of Nauvoo* (Salt Lake City: Bookcraft, 1965), 357–58.

4. Ibid., 363–64; and John S. Fullmer, *Expulsion of the Saints from Nauvoo* (Liverpool: F. D. Richards, 1855), 38–39.

5. E. Cecil McGavin, *Nauvoo the Beautiful* (Salt Lake City: Bookcraft, 1946), 241.

6. Mason Bryman, as quoted by David R. Crockett, *Saints in the Wilderness* (Tucson: LDS Gems, 1997), 173. This is not documented but is likely taken from Ford's History of Illinois or Gregg's History of Hancock County.

7. *Millennial Star* 10 (15 January 1848): 29.

8. Charles C. Lambert, "Reminiscences and Diaries, 1844–1881," 20, LDS Church Archives.

9. *Millennial Star* 10 (15 January 1848): 29; and Hubert H. Bancroft, *History of Utah* (Salt Lake City: Bookcraft, 1964), 232–34.

10. Journal History, 4 November 1846, LDS Church Archives.

11. *Quincy Whig*, 24 June 1846, taken from news clippings, Mormons in Ohio, Illinois, Missouri and Iowa, Collection 8:135, Harold B. Lee Library, Brigham Young University.

12. Kane, *The Mormons*, 21; also, Deseret Evening News, 7 March 1876; "James Ferguson's First View of the City of Nauvoo," *Liahona, the Elders' Journal* 11 (20 January 1914): 502.

13. Andrew Jenson, *Historical Record* 8 (June 1889): 856; and Journal History, 18 September 1846.

14. *Burlington Hawk-Eye*, 24 September 1846.

15. *Warsaw Signal*, 19 October 1848, quoting the Manmouth Atlas.

16. Bancroft, *History of Utah*, 230.

17. Kane, *The Mormons*, 11.

18. Christiana D. Pyper, "True Pioneer Stories," *Juvenile Instructor* 57, no. 5 (May 1922): 246.

19. Andrew F. Ehat, "'They Might Have Known That He Was Not a Fallen Prophet'—The Nauvoo Journal of Joseph Fielding," *BYU Studies* 19, no. 2 (winter 1979): 165.

20. Journal History, 22 August 1848. This report by Wilford Woodruff differs with three other accounts that each describe more extensive physical damage to the building.

The *Hancock Eagle* of 5 October 1846, written during the time that the mob was in possession of the temple, provides the following description: "The damage done to the temple is considerable. Some who have examined it say that $1,000 will not cover the damage. Holes have been cut through the floors; the stone oxen in the basement have been considerable disfigured, horns and ears dislodged and nearly all torn from their standing. Names have been chiseled in the wood engraving in the upward passage, in a very careless manner." As cited by E. Cecil McGavin, *The Nauvoo Temple*, 128. If holes had indeed been cut into the floor and the oxen dislodged from their standing as here reported, then it is possible or likely that this damage had been repaired prior to the visit of Wilford Woodruff, who came two years after this account.

John Scott in a journal entry for 28 February 1848 describes his visit to the temple as part of his "Journey from Winter Quarters to St. Louice [sic]." "I then obtained the key of the temple of the Lord, and went in and locked myself in, there to view the destruction of the hard labor of the Saints for many years. The temple is very much [sic] disfigured the walls and doors are all written over the names of the Governors mob and other who have visited the temple and city. All the rooms both above and below are damaged very mutch and the carved work and molding cut and destroyed, there are all kinds of writing and disgraceful figures drawn on the walls, the oxen and

that the font rests upon is very mutch defaced, some of the horns broken off, thee [sic] ears, and other parts mutch injured." John Scott, Journal of John Scott, 3, LDS Church Archives.

An article written by an unknown author who most likely visited the building in 1848 and whose observations were published in the *Illinois Journal* of 9 December 1853, reported the following damage to the building: "Many names were scratched on the dome and cut in the balustrade. . . . The woodwork of the doors and windows was composed of beautifully carved work. The top of the doorjams being ornamented with Corinthian capitals of the most exquisite workmanship. But these, alas! shewed the marks of sacrilegious hands of the visitors who wished to preserve some relic of the wonderful edifice. The beautiful vine-work had been deprived of many delicately executed leaf and bud, and a smiling cherub of its nose—then, another of the feathered tip of its wing." As republished in *Journal of the Illinois State Historical Society* 38 [1945]: 484–85.

It appears that some of the damage listed in these reports was the result of mob actions during the fall of 1846 and that other damage was the result of visitors who toured through the building over the next two years.

21. *Warsaw Signal*, 19 October 1848, quoting the Manmouth Atlas.

22. Journal History, 16 September 1845.

23. Roberts, *History of the Church*, 7:537.

24. Journal History, 18 January 1846.

25. Minutes of Trustees Meeting, 22 January 1847, Brigham Young Papers, LDS Church Archives, as cited in Richard E. Bennett, *We'll Find the Place* (Salt Lake City: Deseret Book, 1997), 317.

26. John D. Lee, Diaries and Official Records, 117–18, Harold B. Lee Library, Brigham Young University.

27. *Hancock Eagle*, 15 May 1846 and 12 December 1846.

28. Roberts, *History of the Church*, 7:346.

29. Journal History, 20 January 1847.

30. Ibid., 5 April 1847.

31. Ibid., 27 January 1848.

32. Ibid., 2 October 1848.

33. Ibid., also Joseph Smith III, *Joseph Smith III and the Restoration*, ed. Mary Audentia Smith Anderson (Independence, Mo.: Herald House, 1952), 101.

34. Roberts, *History of the Church*, 7:581; also Norton Jacob, "The Life of Norton Jacob," 27, Harold B. Lee Library, Brigham Young University, states: "He said they would start to-morrow, and that some of the brethren had already crossed over three or four days ago, and that they are crossing all the time. . . . Mon. About four o'clock p.m. a fire broke out in the temple by a stove pipe in the main deck roof, and for some time it looked rather fearful but by cutting up a portion of the deck and roof it was subdued after doing about $100.00 damage." Norton Jacob was foreman of all the framing of the roof, the tower structure, and the dome. Also, Thomas Bullock, as quoted in Gregory R. Knight, "Journal of Thomas Bullock," *BYU Studies* 31, no. 1 (winter 1991): 49, states: "The clothing in the Temple was being washed and dried in the upper room. The stove got over heated. The wood work caught fire and burned from the railing to the ridge about 16 feet North and South and about 10 feet East and West. The shingles on the north side were broken through in many places. The damage to that part is about 100 dollars but other damage was also done in the anxiety to put out the fire. When it was completely extinguished the Saints gave glory to God and shouted Hallelujah which made the air rejoice." And additionally Brigham Young, as quoted in Roberts, *History of the Church*, 7:581: "I went to the Temple as soon as I could, after the fire had been extinguished, the brethren gave a loud shout of Hosanna, while standing on the deck roof."

35. McGavin, *Nauvoo the Beautiful*, 279, citing an article in the *Daily Missouri Republican*, 15 June 1846.

36. Journal History, 9 October 1848, citing an article in the Nauvoo Patriot, of the same date.

37. *Keokuk Register*, 21 September 1848, taken from *News Clippings* 2, no. 18, 2; also *Iowa Sentinel*, 20 October 1846.

38. *Warsaw Signal*, 19 October 1848, quoting the *Burlington Hawk-Eye*.

39. Journal History, 9 October 1848, quoting an article in the *Nauvoo Patriot*, of the same date.

40. Journal History, 9 October 1848.

41. *Warsaw Signal*, 30 December 1848.

42. J. Earl Arrington, "Story of the Nauvoo Temple," 10, LDS Church Archives.

43. Ibid., 9.

44. Journal History, 9 October 1848.

45. *Joseph Smith III and the Restoration*, 101.

46. Roberts, *The Rise and Fall of Nauvoo*, 369.

47. The Rudisill narrative is found in its complete form in identical wording in the following sources: Robert Aveson, "Burning of the Nauvoo Temple," *Newspaper Clipping*, no date, on file in the Utah Historical Society Library. He produced the article from his scrapbook, the original appearing in the *Fort Madison Iowa Democrat*, no date given; McGavin, *Nauvoo the Beautiful*, 284–87, quoting a newspaper account, but not documented; a condensed version appeared in *Salt Lake Tribune*, 18 April 1872, citing the *Peoria Transcript*; also, *Chicago Post*, 30 April 1872.

48. *Salt Lake Daily Tribune*, 18 April 1872, quoting the *Peoria Transcript*, no date given.

49. Pyper, "True Pioneer Stories," 247.

50. *Fort Madison Democrat*, 14 January 1895, republished in the Nauvoo Independent, 25 January 1895.

51. *Fort Madison Democrat*, 28 January 1895, republished in the *Nauvoo Independent*, 12 February 1895.

52. Annie Gardner Barton, "Life of Mary Field Gardner," 7, LDS Church Archives.

53. *Deseret News*, 14 October 1863; also, Barton, "Life of Mary Field Gardner," 7.

54. Will Griffith and Katherine Griffith, ed., *Historic Nauvoo* (Peoria, Ill.: Quest, 1941), 30–32.

55. Ibid., 32.

56. Federal Writers' Project of Illinois, Nauvoo Guide (Chicago: A. C. McClurg, 1939), 38.

57. Journal History, 10 September 1849.

58. Ibid., 27 May 1850, quoting the *Daily Missouri Republican*.

59. Ibid., 27 May 1850, quoting the *Nauvoo Patriot*.

60. Ibid.

61. Ibid., 8 December 1856.

62. *Joseph Smith III and the Restoration*, 101–2.

63. Journal History, 7 December 1870.

64. *Joseph Smith III and the Restoration*, 102.

65. Richard W. Young, "In the Wake of the Church," *Contributor* 4 (January 1883): 150–51.

66. Roberts, *History of the Church*, 7:439–45.

67. Hosea Stout, *On the Mormon Frontier, the Diary of Hosea Stout 1844–1861*, ed. Juanita Brooks (Salt Lake City: University of Utah Press, 1964), 1:66.

68. Maureen Ursenbach Beecher, "All Things Move in Order in the City': The Nauvoo Diary of Zina Diantha Huntington Jacobs," *BYU Studies* 19, no. 3 (spring 1979): 320.

69. Stout, *Diary of Hosea Stout*, 1:67.

70. Ibid., 1:68–69.

71. Beecher, "All Things,'" 320.

72. Stout, *Diary of Hosea Stout*, 1:66.

73. Journal History, 21 September 1845.

74. Bullock, as quoted in Gregory R. Knight, "Journal of Thomas Bullock," 68.

75. *Millennial Star* 6 (15 July 1845): 43.

76. Ibid., 6 (15 August 1845): 77.

77. Ibid., 7 (1 January 1846): 5; 7 (1 February 1846): 44.

78. Mary Grant Judd, "A Monument with a Message," *Relief Society Magazine*, January 1942, 11.

79. Lois Leetham Tanner, "I've Heard There Is a Story behind the Bell on Temple Square. Can You Relay It?" *Ensign*, February 1981, 16.

80. Matthias Cowley, *Wilford Woodruff—His Life and Labors* (Salt Lake City: Bookcraft, 1964), 245.

81. Willard Bean, as quoted by Joseph J. Cannon, "President Joseph J. Cannon's Message," *Temple Square Topics, Official Organ of Temple Square Mission*, August 1939, no. 3.

82. Brigham Young to Wilford Woodruff, 19 December 1845; LDS Church Archives.

83. *Burlington Hawk-Eye*, 20 November 1845.

84. Bullock, as quoted in Gregory R. Knight, "Journal of Thomas Bullock," 68.

85. George Morris, "Autobiography," 26, typescript 1953, Harold B. Lee Library, Brigham Young University.

86. *Deseret News*, 17 June 1939; also Benjamin Ashby, Autobiography of Benjamin Ashby, 16, LDS Church Archives.

87. Kane, *The Mormons*, 6–8, 11.

88. Journal History, 27 September 1846; and Preston Nibley, *Exodus to Greatness* (Salt Lake City: Deseret News, 1947), 245.

89. Andrew Jenson, Andrew Jenson Papers, Nauvoo Bell Folder, LDS Church Archives.

90. *Manuscript History of the Church*, 20 December 1846; also John D. Lee, *Journals of John D. Lee*, ed. Charles Kelley (Salt Lake City: Western Printing, 1938), 127.

91. Journal History, 16 April 1847; and Nibley, *Exodus to Greatness*, 368.

92. Sara De Armon Pea Rich, as cited in Carol Cornwall Madsen, *Journey to Zion* (Salt Lake City: Deseret Book, 1997), 376–77.

93. Judd, "A Monument with a Message," 12.

94. *Deseret News*, 14 September 1850.

95. Ibid., 4 August 1902; also Ronald G. Watt, "A Tale of Two Bells: Nauvoo Bell and Hummer's Bell," *Nauvoo Journal* 11, no. 2 (fall 1999): 33. This article clears up the confusion and inaccurate reports regarding the Nauvoo Temple bell having been stolen, etc.

96. "Nauvoo Bell Rings Out on Day of Thanksgiving," *Church News*, 13 April 1991, 5.

97. On 15 March 2000 the bell housed in the Camponile on Temple Square was carefully measured by Robert Dewey (a Church temple architect who worked on the Nauvoo Temple reconstruction project) along with Roger Jackson and Steve Goodwin, architects from the FFKR architectural firm in Salt Lake City, Utah, that was engaged by the Church to draw plans for and supervise construction of the rebuilding of the Nauvoo Temple.

98. Tanner, "Story behind the Bell on Temple Square," 16.

99. Watt, "A Tale of Two Bells," 33–40; also, note 18 of this article citing the Shadrach Roundy Diary, which indicates that the purchase was made by Asa Calkin of the Church while President Brigham Young was in southern Utah.

100. Thomas Bullock, *The 1846 and 1847 Mormon Trail Journals of Thomas Bullock*, ed. Will Bagley (Spokane, Wash.: Arthur H. Clark, 1997), 71.

101. J. M. Davidson, editor of the *Carthage Republican*, 25 February 1864, as cited in E. Cecil McGavin, *The Nauvoo Temple* (Salt Lake City: Deseret Book, 1962),

93–95; also, "The Old Temple," Nauvoo Independent 7, no. 9 (20 December 1889): 7.

102. Kane, *The Mormons*, 20; also, *Illinois Journal*, 9 December 1853.

103. *Illinois Journal*, 9 December 1853, as republished in the Journal of the Illinois State Historical Society 38 (1945): 484.

104. Robert D. Craig, "Mormon Angel in Cincinnati," LDS Church Archives; also, collected material concerning a weather vane in Cincinnati, Ohio, LDS Church Archives, including articles and letters by Marie Dickore, Robert D. Craig, and John A. Taylor.

105. Ibid.

106. Elva Ravsten, interview by author, Ogden, Utah, 3 January 2000.

107. Ibid.

108. James R. Kimball Jr., interview by author, Ogden, Utah, 3 January 2000.

109. Ibid., also Donald L. Enders, interview by author, Ogden, Utah, 3 January 2000.

110. Donald L. Enders, interview by author, Ogden, Utah, 3 January and 10 January 2000; also Donald L. Enders, personal communication, 25 January 2000.

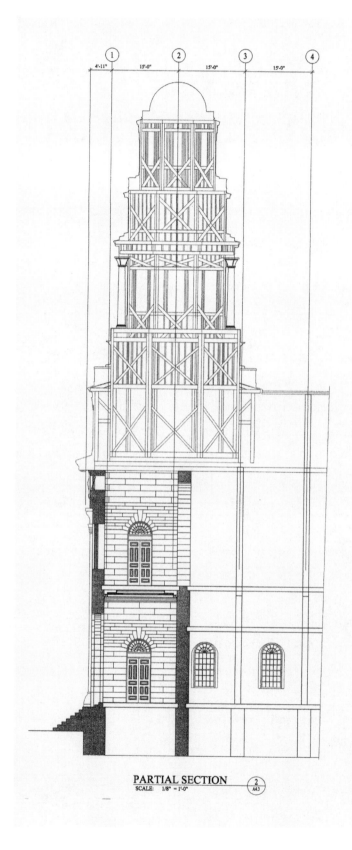

Figure 12.1 Partial Section Showing Tower Framework, drawing, 2000, FFKR Architecture.

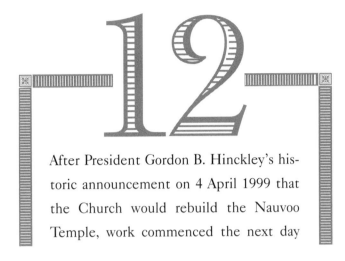

After President Gordon B. Hinckley's historic announcement on 4 April 1999 that the Church would rebuild the Nauvoo Temple, work commenced the next day

CHAPTER TWELVE

HISTORIC RECON-

STRUCTION DRAWINGS

toward drafting architectural plans. Private architectural firms were engaged under the direction of the Temple Construction Department to draw plans in close consultation with Church temple architects. The firm of FFKR Architecture

Planning/Interior Design of Salt Lake City moved ahead on the exterior of the new building, as Richardson Design of Salt Lake City worked on the interior features. After completion of preliminary sketches, the work was largely turned over to FFKR and their team of fourteen staff members, who worked under the direction of Roger P. Jackson, a partner of the firm. They were contracted to work in close consultation with Robert T. Dewey and later Vern G. Hancock, the Nauvoo Temple construction managers, to draft final plans for reconstructing the temple and to supervise its construction.

As plans were drafted, every effort was made to collect all possible sources of information regarding the original building. Architects then produced modern historic reconstruction drawings of the original Nauvoo Temple based on this collected information. These drawings were produced to serve as the basis for designing the reconstruction of the temple. At various stages during development, these architectural drawings were carefully evaluated and critiqued by the Historical Review Committee, a group of selected historians and architects called to assist in this appraisal. Further information regarding these procedures is provided in chapter 13. This evaluation was conducted with an effort to ensure accuracy insofar as possible in replicating the exterior of the original structure. While every effort was made to collect and evaluate all known sources of information, it was well understood by those who worked on the project that future research and discovery of information could alter the currently accepted conclusions. By permission of the Temple Sites and Construction Committee of the Church, several of these reconstruction drawings have been included within the text of chapters 6 (Figures 6.11–6.12, 6.14–6.17) and 8 (Figures 8.1, 8.6, 8.7, 8.11, and 8.14–8.18) and on the pages that follow.

These architectural drawings were carefully evaluated and critiqued by the Historical Review Committee.

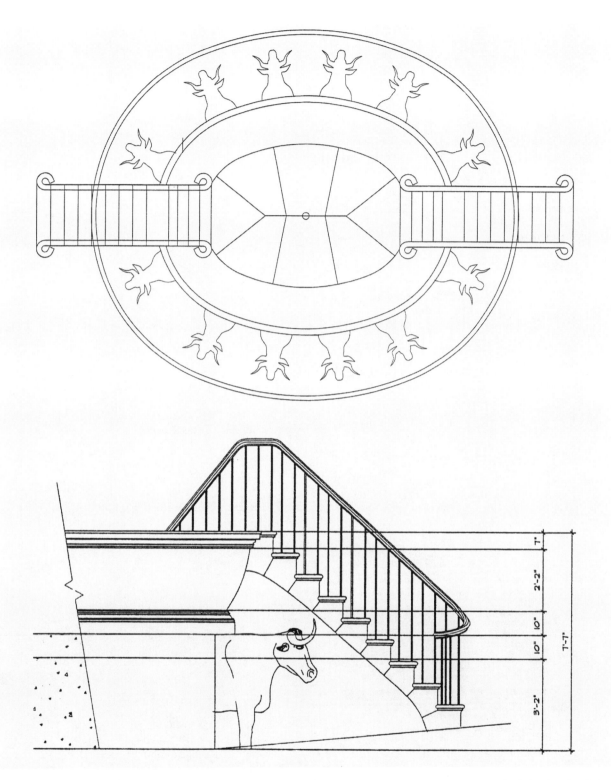

Figure 12.2 (Top) Baptismal Font Plan, drawing, 2000, Richardson Design Partnership Inc., The Church of Jesus Christ of Latter-day Saints; hereafter cited as Richardson Design Partnership Inc. This is a preliminary reconstruction drawing of the original stone baptismal font based on original drawings, descriptions, and archaeological findings.

Figure 12.3 (Bottom) Font Section Elevations, drawing, 2000, Richardson Design Partnership Inc. This is a preliminary reconstruction drawing of the original stone baptismal font elevations based on original drawings, descriptions, and archaeological findings.

FONT DIMENSIONS	BASIN	BASE	TOT. HEIGHT
	SEE HARRINGTON PAGE 32		
WILLIAM WEEKS	15'-3" X 11'-3" 4'-6" DEEP	12' X 8' 5'-2" HIGH	7'-7"
JOSEPH SMITH	16' X 12' 4'-0" DEEP	NONE	7'-0" (FROM FONDATION TO TOP)
BRIGHAM YOUNG	NONE	12' X 8'	NONE
LITTLEFIELD	NONE	15'-0" X 11'-6"	NONE
JOHN REYNOLDS	NONE	16' X 12' 4'-0" DEEP	6'-8" ESTIMATE
BUCKINGHAM	NONE	16'X12' (4'-6" TO 5'-0" DEEP)	NONE
HISTORY OF HANCOCK COUNTY	18'X 8' 4' DEEP	NONE	ABOUT 8'
ARCHEOLSICAL REPORT	NONE	15'-0" X 11'6"	NONE

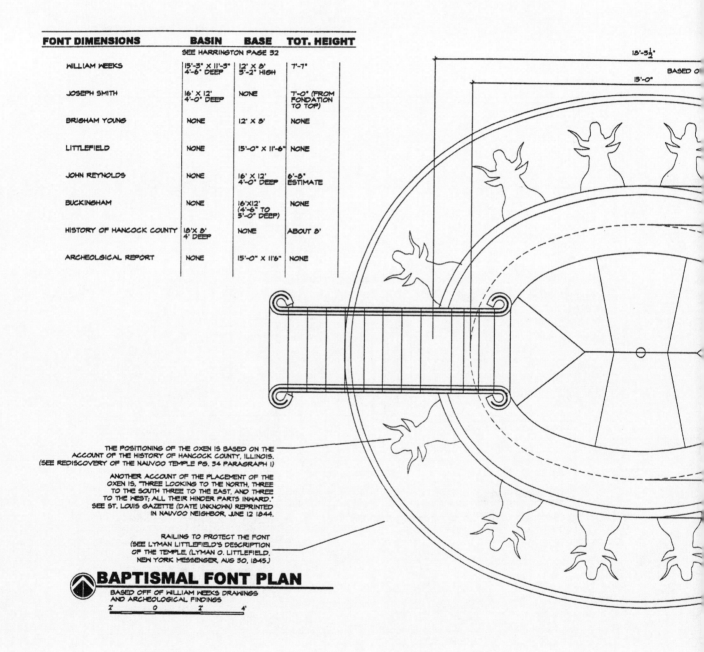

18'-3½"

BASED O

15'-0"

THE POSITIONING OF THE OXEN IS BASED ON THE
ACCOUNT OF THE HISTORY OF HANCOCK COUNTY, ILLINOIS.
(SEE REDISCOVERY OF THE NAUVOO TEMPLE PG. 34 PARAGRAPH 1)

ANOTHER ACCOUNT OF THE PLACEMENT OF THE
OXEN IS, "THREE LOOKING TO THE NORTH, THREE
TO THE SOUTH THREE TO THE EAST, AND THREE
TO THE WEST; ALL THEIR HINDER PARTS INWARD."
SEE ST. LOUIS GAZETTE (DATE UNKNOWN) REPRINTED
IN NAUVOO NEIGHBOR, JUNE 12 1844.

RAILING TO PROTECT THE FONT
(SEE LYMAN LITTLEFIELD'S DESCRIPTION
OF THE TEMPLE. (LYMAN O. LITTLEFIELD,
NEW YORK MESSENGER, AUG 30, 1845)

BAPTISMAL FONT PLAN

BASED OFF OF WILLIAM WEEKS DRAWINGS
AND ARCHEOLSICAL FINDINGS

2'   0   2'   4'

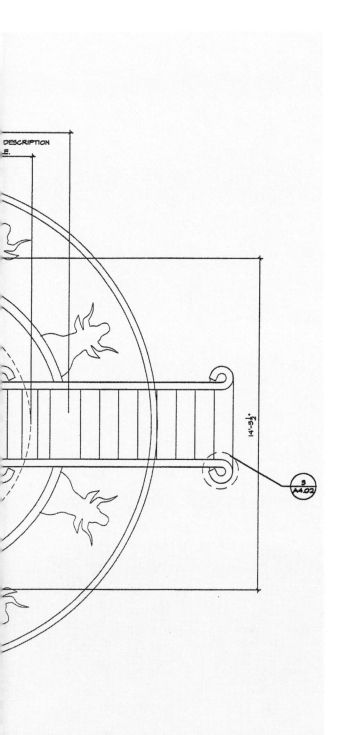

DESCRIPTION
E.

14'-3½'

As plans were drafted, every effort was made to collect all possible sources of information regarding the original building.

Figure 12.4 Baptismal Font Plan, drawing, 2000, Richardson Design Partnership Inc. This is a preliminary reconstruction drawing of the original stone baptismal font based on original drawings, descriptions, and archaeological findings.

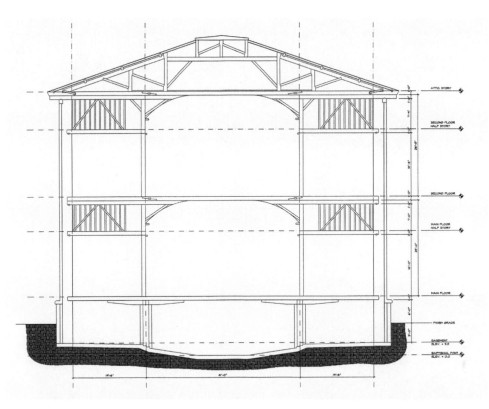

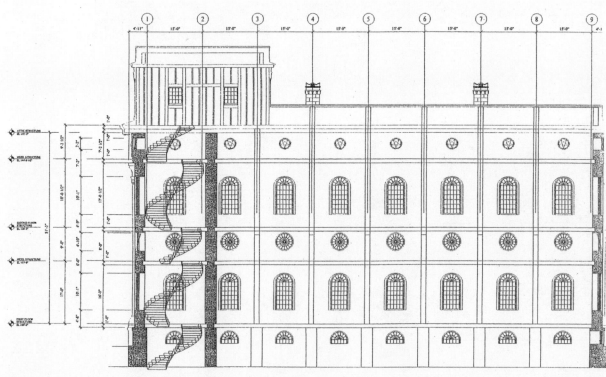

Figure 12.5 (Top) Temple Cross-Section North/South, drawing, 2000, Richardson Design Partnership Inc. This is a drawing by modern architects of the cross-sectional view of the temple framework based on the earlier drawing of William Weeks (see Figure 7.1). This new drawing was prepared to assist in the design of the new Nauvoo Temple.

Figure 12.6 (Bottom) Longitudinal Section, drawing, 2000, FFKR Architecture.

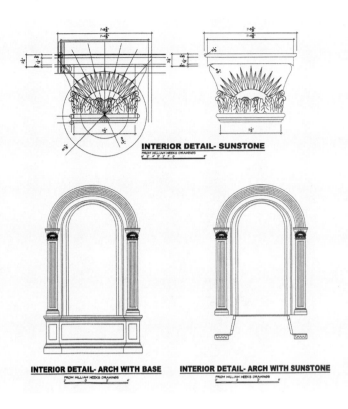

INTERIOR DETAIL- SUNSTONE
FROM WILLIAM WEEKS DRAWINGS

INTERIOR DETAIL- ARCH WITH BASE
FROM WILLIAM WEEKS DRAWINGS

INTERIOR DETAIL- ARCH WITH SUNSTONE
FROM WILLIAM WEEKS DRAWINGS

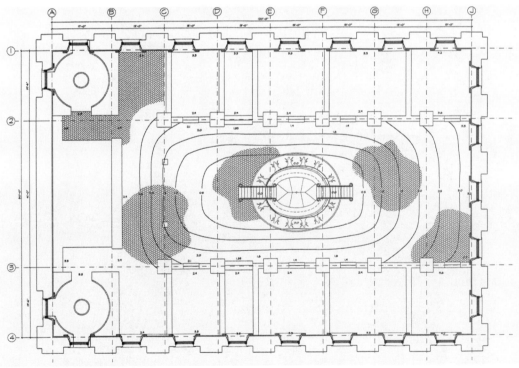

Figure 12.7 (Top) Interior Wood Trim and Moldings around Large Main Windows, drawing, 2000, Richardson Design Partnership Inc. These drawings show details of the arch, base, and sun stone used in trim and moldings around the interior of each of the large main windows. This new drawing was prepared to assist in the design of the new Nauvoo Temple.

Figure 12.8 (Bottom) Basement Floor Plan, drawing, 2000, Richardson Design Partnership Inc. This is a drawing by modern architects of the basement floor plan showing measurements, elevations, brick paving, and the location and design of the baptismal font. This new drawing was prepared to assist in the design of the new Nauvoo Temple.

West Elevation of the Nauvoo Temple, drawing, 2000, FFKR Architecture.

13

Near the end of the general conference session, "there was a moment of shock . . . then . . . some applause. . . . Then everyone caught themselves quickly, and for

CHAPTER THIRTEEN

THE TEMPLE
IS REBUILT

most of the rest of the meeting there was crying."[1] Such was the response as Nauvoo Illinois Stake members listened by satellite to President Gordon B. Hinckley's closing remarks during the Church's April 1999 general conference.

He had just stated:

> I feel impressed to announce that among all the temples we are constructing, we plan to rebuild the Nauvoo Temple. A member of the Church and his family have provided a very substantial contribution to make this possible. We are grateful to him. It will be a while before it happens, but the architects have begun their work. This temple will not be busy much of the time; it will be somewhat isolated. But during the summer months, we anticipate it will be very busy. And the new building will stand as a memorial to those who built the first such structure there on the banks of the Mississippi.[2]

I n 1962 the Church once again had ownership of the entire temple block.

He added, "The new edifice will be named the Nauvoo Illinois Temple."[3]

No announcement in the long history of the Church has created more universal excitement, interest, and positive support. This rebuilding project brings to realization the vision of many who long ago dreamed of and labored for such a day.

REPURCHASE OF THE TEMPLE BLOCK

It was on 20 February 1937 that Wilford C. Wood purchased the first piece of the original Nauvoo Temple property. Acting on behalf of the Church, he acquired the land at a sale of some of C. W. Reimbold's estate for the price of nine hundred dollars.[4] The *Deseret News* reported this purchase to Church members: "The First Presidency today announced that the Church had purchased the Nauvoo Temple lot at Nauvoo, Ill. Together with the lot, the purchase brought to the Church possession of the old well which fed the font to the Temple when that building was used before the departure of the Saints for the West. . . . The purchase was effected at a public sale held in Nauvoo this morning. Wilford C. Wood represented the Church in the negotiations."[5]

Just two months later Wood, acting on his own volition, purchased a large piece of land on the northeast corner for $1,100.[6] This second parcel amounted to nearly one quarter of the temple block. It became Church property just six months later when it was purchased from Mr. Wood.[7] Following these initial acquisitions, a crew from the Chicago Stake of the Church spent a full day's labor (in July 1937) in an effort to beautify the property. Numbering twenty-two persons, they were led by Dr. Ariel L. Williams and Wilford Wood. While clearing the property, they succeeded in salvaging forty-six tons of cut face stones that had originally been part of the temple. These stones reportedly weighed from two hundred to three thousand pounds each. The work was accomplished with the assistance of a bulldozer and tractors. All of the stones were piled together as the land was leveled for planting and beautification.[8]

Over the next several years, while acting as agent for the Church, Wood's persistent and determined efforts resulted in various other parcels of the temple block coming back into Church possession. These purchases included four pieces of property comprising the southeast quarter.[9] In June 1951 he negotiated the purchase of property on the northwest corner. This piece of land contained a large spacious home that was immediately converted into a bureau of information for the Church.[10] Altogether, Wood was instrumental in seven separate purchases of the temple block equaling over two-thirds of the total property. He also pushed for and acquired many other historic sites for the Church and dreamed of old Nauvoo being restored as a historical treasure.

Richard C. Stratford, acting as agent for the Church, purchased the narrow strip of telephone company property on 22 February 1959.[11] In 1961 the Church purchased and acquired title to the southwest quarter of the property, formally owned by the Catholic Church.[12] The final parcel of property was acquired in 1962 through an exchange of properties between the LDS Church and the Reorganized Church. The piece of property formerly owned by the RLDS Church was acquired in exchange for three parcels of land in Independence, Missouri.[13] With this last purchase the Church once again had ownership of the entire temple block (see summary after figure 13.1).

Lane K. Newberry, an artist and descendant of Nauvoo pioneers, spent considerable time over several years enlisting the aid of Church leaders, civic officials, and others in an effort to build monuments and restore portions of old Nauvoo. He wrote: "I feel that the World should honor men and women who accomplished what the Mormons accomplished in Nauvoo—the building of a substantial city in the short period of six years. . . . There was a spirit back of the building of this city that the World needs today, and it only can be attained by honoring those who had it yesterday."[14]

Newberry, a resident of Chicago, enlisted the aid of Bryant S. Hinckley, then serving as president of the Northern States Mission, which included the state of Illinois. President Bryant S. Hinckley became a powerful force in the restoration effort, making many visits to Nauvoo and holding numerous meetings promoting the restoration of Nauvoo. In a 1938 article printed in the *Improvement Era*, he wrote:

> If the project outlined by the citizens of Illinois is completed, . . . this extraordinary project will be a matter of far reaching significance. It will bring into relief one of the most heroic, dramatic, and fascinating pioneer

achievements ever enacted upon American soil. It will reveal a record of fortitude and self-reliance; of patriotic and courageous endeavor, that should stimulate faith in the hearts of all men. . . . Annually thousands . . . will visit it. . . . Nauvoo is destined to become one of the most beautiful shrines of America."[15]

Bryant S. Hinckley's restoration efforts resulted in a centennial celebration commemorating the founding of Nauvoo in 1839. Over seven hundred Church members assembled for two days of pageants, tours, and meetings. On Sunday, 25 June 1939, hundreds gathered on the temple lot at Nauvoo. Following a speech by Bryant S. Hinckley, Brother Newberry spoke regarding his dream of seeing Nauvoo restored and "the Temple rebuilt in full-size on this spot where it once stood."[16]

NAUVOO RESTORATION INCORPORATED

Next to carry on the dream of rebuilding Nauvoo was Dr. James LeRoy Kimball, a physician from Salt Lake City. He had visited and become interested in Nauvoo while attending the Northwestern University School of Medicine.[17] In 1954 he purchased and restored the home of his great-grandfather Heber C. Kimball. Then, after taking up residence in Nauvoo, he initiated projects toward realizing his dream of the restoration of Nauvoo. He later said: "The Mormon migration west from Nauvoo to the Rocky Mountains is the only migration in history in which an entire community moved itself and its industries, institutions,

professions, crafts, religion, schools and political and cultural concepts to the far west. . . . [Nauvoo's] place in American history and its great contribution to the settlement of a western United States has never been told adequately."[18]

Dr. Kimball saw the need to acquire more old Nauvoo properties. Through determination and the aid of influential friends, he succeeded. Under his direction, archaeological exploration of the temple site began in December 1961, when Dr. Melvin L. Fowler, curator of North American archaeology from Southern Illinois University, started preliminary trenching in an attempt to locate remains of the temple.[19] Members of the First Presidency of the Church visited the site in May 1962.[20] Shortly following this visit, the Church formed a nonprofit corporation to direct the restoration of Nauvoo.

The *Deseret News* reported this historic event:

> Heading the new unit, Nauvoo Restoration Incorporated as president is Dr. J. LeRoy Kimball, Salt Lake physician who has taken an active leadership in purchasing property in Nauvoo during the past several years. Harold P. Fabian, recently elected chairman of the Citizens Advisory Board of National Parks Historic Sites Buildings and Monuments of the U.S. Department of Interior is vice president and trustee. A. Hamer Reiser, chairman of the Utah Park and Recreation Commission and who is Secretary of the First Presidency, is Secretary Treasurer and trustee. J. Willard Marriott . . . and David M.

Kennedy . . . are trustees. President McKay explained . . . that the new corporation is formed for the purpose of restoring . . . historic Nauvoo as . . . when the Mormons evacuated the city in 1846. The purpose of restoring Nauvoo, is to "perpetuate in history the part played by the Mormon pioneers in the building of the West."[21]

Beginning in June 1962, Dee Green, an archaeologist from Salt Lake City, served as crew chief of excavation work under the direction of Dr. Fowler. Working for about five months, the archaeologists were successful in uncovering the entire area of the temple. The dimensions of the original building were established, and the basement area was excavated to a depth of five feet. Beginning in August 1966, Dr. J. C. Harrington, who had served as chief archaeologist for the U.S. National Parks Service, took charge of archaeological research for Nauvoo Restoration. Over the next three years and under the joint direction of J. C. Harrington and his wife, Dr. Virginia S. Harrington, the temple site was carefully examined as the entire basement area was excavated to the original floor level.[22] The excellent work completed under their direction has made a significant contribution toward understanding the temple.

Over a century and a half after the fateful exodus from Nauvoo and amid favorable reactions, the Latter-day Saints officially returned to Nauvoo. Though the temple had been destroyed, it still remained a shrine in the hearts of Church members. As old Nauvoo was restored, the temple site became an integral art of the nearby Nauvoo Visitors' Center and has annually been visited by thousands.

REBUILDING THE NAUVOO TEMPLE

The historic announcement to rebuild the temple came in the April general conference of 1999. During the spring and throughout the summer, several architects worked diligently on the project. Every possible source that could shed light and provide information on the original building was collected, carefully examined, and evaluated for accuracy and authenticity. This included the partial set of original architectural drawings, historical accounts, daguerreotypes (early photographs), sketches, paintings, eyewitness descriptions of the building, personal journals, building and billing records, archaeological excavation reports, and any other resources that could be found. In addition to this, any existing stones that could be found from the old structure were measured and carefully examined. On the basis of these efforts, the architects designed new sets of plans, historically reproducing the original plans of the temple. These historic reproductions would essentially form plans for the exterior of the new building. They would also serve as the basis for modified plans on interior sections of the building.

Under the direction of F. Keith Stepan, managing director of the Temple Construction Department, and Robert T. Dewey, the construction manager, a Historical Review Committee was formed.[23] Committee members composed of historians and architects having in-depth knowledge of the subject or extensive experience with Nauvoo Restoration were asked to submit any pertinent information they possessed regarding the original Nauvoo Temple. As plans were drafted, these committee members (in varying degrees of involvement) were asked to carefully review and critique the historical reproduction drawings for accuracy and authenticity.[24] Every effort was made to construct as accurately as possible an

FFKR Architecture Planning/Interior Design of Salt Lake City (see chapter 12), which drafted plans and oversaw construction under the direction of Roger P. Jackson, a principal member of the firm.

On 24 October 1999 more than five thousand people crowded onto the old temple site as President Gordon B. Hinckley presided over the groundbreaking ceremonies. Among those in attendance were the mayor of Nauvoo and members of the city council, along with other

There will grace this site that which existed here an great epic period of the hi

authentic replication of the original structure. Some areas, such as the west front portico and the east end of the building, were planned using only fragmentary evidence. Plans for those sections of the structure were completed with careful attention to features common in other buildings of the 1840s and were faithful to the fragments of known information. After the completion of preliminary sketches, the work was largely turned over to the firm of

government officials and Church and business leaders. President Hinckley explained: "There will grace this site a magnificent structure, a recreation of that which existed here and served our people so briefly during that great epic period of the history of the Church."[25] He went on to explain that the building's exterior would look the same as the original. Though made of reinforced concrete, it would be faced with the same kind of stone as the original. "It will be stronger and will last a very long time."[26] He further said that in the interior some changes would be made to accommodate current building codes and ordinance work. The first floor of the temple will include an assembly room, but the second floor will be occupied by ordinance rooms.[27]

President Hinckley declared that the idea of rebuilding the temple is not a new one. He explained that his father, Bryant S. Hinckley, while serving as president of the Northern

for sacred purposes. "This will be the House of the Lord. It will be dedicated as His Holy House. It will be reserved and set aside for the accomplishment of His divine and eternal purposes. It will occupy a special place in the belief and testimony and the conviction of this people. It will have great historical significance. It will be a thing of beauty and, I hope, a joy forever."[29]

At the conclusion of his address, President Hinckley offered a dedicatory prayer upon the site. Assisted by other Church leaders and city

agnificent structure, a re-creation of

erved our people so briefly during that

y of the Church.

States Mission in 1939, suggested to the First Presidency that the Nauvoo Temple be rebuilt. "I count it something of a strange and wonderful coincidence that I've had a part in the determination of rebuilding this temple."[28]

Those in attendance were informed that when reconstruction of the temple was finished, the building would be open to the public "to look over . . . carefully and thoroughly," following which it then would be dedicated

officials, he then led in the ceremonial groundbreaking. It was then announced that anyone in attendance who so desired could participate by taking a shovel and turning some of the soil. "Hundreds accepted the offer and lingered in line for as long as an hour to have a chance to be part of that history."[30]

Following the groundbreaking ceremonies, work on the rebuilding of the temple proceeded at a rapid pace. The new temple is con-

structed to replicate the original temple built on the same site in the early 1840s. The limestone exterior is a near duplicate of the original.

The reconstructed Nauvoo Illinois Temple is scheduled for completion during the spring of 2002 and for dedication on 27 June 2002, the 158th anniversary of the martyrdom of Joseph and Hyrum Smith. The work of the reconstruction, like that of the original building, has been attended by answers to prayers, spiritual blessings, and divine guidance. The saga of this magnificent structure is a "story of faith" that continues to be written.

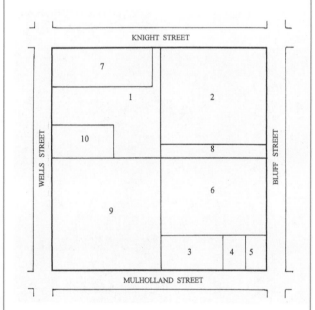

Figure 13.1 Repurchase of the Nauvoo Temple Block, drawing, 2000, Don Colvin. This is a catalog of the different purchases of the temple block.

LDS CHURCH PURCHASES:

Parcel 1. Purchased 20 February 1937 at a land sale for $900, Wilford Wood acting as agent for the Church.

Parcel 2. Purchased by Wilford Wood on his own voli-

tion 19 April 1937. Known as the "Opera House" property, it sold for $1,100. Six months later it was purchased from Mr. Wood by the Church.

Parcels 3, 4, 5, and 6. All purchased by Wilford Wood acting as agent for the Church. The small lot on the southeast corner was purchased for $350.

Parcel 7. Purchased in June 1951 by Wilford Wood acting as an agent for the Church. The property contained a large old house that was turned into a Bureau of Information and Visitors Center.

Parcel 8. A small 25-foot-wide lot purchased from the telephone company on 22 February 1959. Richard Stratford made the purchase acting as agent for the Church.

Parcel 9. Purchased by the LDS Church from the Catholic Church in 1961.

Parcel 10. This last piece of the temple block was purchased from the RLDS Church in 1962. The property came in trade for properties in Independence, Missouri.

NOTES

1. Durrell N. Nelson, as quoted by R. Scott Lloyd, "Historic Nauvoo Temple to be Rebuilt," *Church News,* 10 April 1999, 3.

2. *Ensign,* May 1999, 89.

3. Greg Hill, "Rebuilding of Magnificent Temple," *Church News,* 30 October 1999, 6.

4. *Carthage Gazette,* 26 February 1937.

5. *Deseret News,* 20 February 1937.

6. Richard L. Evans, "Nauvoo Opera House Acquired," *Improvement Era,* April 1937, 356; *Carthage Gazette,* 7 May 1937.

7. Wilford C. Wood, "Exhibits of Mormonism," *BYU*

Leadership Week Lectures (Provo, Utah: Brigham Young University, 1953), Special Lecture Series J, 15 June 1953, 5.

8. *Deseret News,* 2 July 1937.

9. Wood, "Exhibits of Mormonism," 6.

10. Ibid., 7.

11. *Ogden Standard-Examiner,* 22 February 1959.

12. A. Hamer Reiser, interview by the author, Ogden, Utah, 1962. Mr. Reiser was the secretary-treasurer of Nauvoo Restoration Inc. and secretary to the First Presidency of The Church of Jesus Christ of Latter-day Saints.

13. Ibid., also Janath R. Cannon, *Nauvoo Panorama* (Nauvoo, Ill.: Nauvoo Restoration, 1991), 82.

14. Bryant S. Hinckley, "The Nauvoo Memorial," *Improvement Era,* August 1938, 460.

15. Ibid., 460, 511.

16. *Nauvoo Independent,* 29 June 1939, as cited in Cannon, *Nauvoo Panorama,* 75.

17. Cannon, *Nauvoo Panorama,* 78.

18. Luacine C. Fox, "The Nauvoo Dream," presentation at a Nauvoo Mission Reunion, September 1983; Nauvoo Restoration Inc., files, Nauvoo Visitors' Center, 7–8, as cited in Cannon, *Nauvoo Panorama,* 78–79.

19. Virginia S. Harrington and J. C. Harrington, *Rediscovery of the Nauvoo Temple* (Salt Lake City: Nauvoo Restoration, 1971), 6; also, Dee F. Green, "Archaeologists 'Digging' into History of Nauvoo," *Church News,* 14 July 1962, 7. Excavation work at the temple site was conducted under the direction of Dr. Melvin Fowler of Southern Illinois University. The Church of Jesus Christ of Latter-day Saints supplied a financial grant to the university to cover the expense of the project. Dee F. Green, a member of the Church, served as field director of the work.

20. *Deseret News,* 5 May 1962.

21. Ibid., 24 June 1962.

22. Harrington and Harrington, *Rediscovery of the Nauvoo Temple,* 7.

23. Historical Review Committee members were Glen Leonard, Steve Baird, Donald L. Enders, Don F. Colvin, Richard Oman, and Quinn Orr. Extensive research and evaluation was also conducted by Robert Dewey; by his secretary Diane Dieterle; by Roger P. Jackson, Steven Goodwin, and Gerald Tim Maxwell of FFKR; by William Richardson, Neil Richardson, Joseph Coates, Kevin Horne, and Tony Barros of Richardson Design; as well as by Uriel Schlair and Gerald McElvain, from Harry Weese & Associates. Others assisting in the process were Elder Ronald J. Prince, construction project manager in Nauvoo, as well as sculptor and design artists LaVar Wallgren and his partner James Dell Morris.

24. Personal observations of the author, who served as a member of the Historical Review Committee.

25. Hill, "Rebuilding of Magnificent Temple," 6.

26. Ibid., 7.

27. Ibid.

28. Ibid.

29. Ibid.

30. Ibid.

APPENDIX
HIRED WORKERS ON THE NAUVOO TEMPLE

The following partial list of hired workers on the Nauvoo Temple was recorded by William Clayton:

I will now give a list of the names of the officers and laborers on and connected with the temple.

In the office are the trustees, viz:

Newel K. Whitney and George Miller. William Clayton, Temple Recorder. James Whitehead, Clerk. John P. McEwen, Assistant Clerk. Joseph C. Kingsbury, Disbursing Agent for Trustees.

The temple committee are:

Alpheus Cutler, Reynolds Cahoon, Elias Higbee (recently died). William Weeks, architect and draughtsman.

The following are the workmen on the walls of the temple.

William W. Player, principal setter. Edward Miller, his assistant.

The names of the constant hands who attended Brother Player's Crane are Tarlton Lewis, Archibald Hill, John Hill, Hans C. Hanson and Charles W. Patten.

Elisha Averett was the principal backer up, or, in other words, he set the stone on the inside walls and also the inside courses of the main wall. He was assisted by his brothers, Elijah and John Averett, and Truman Leonard.

The hands who worked on the second crane, being E. Averett's Crane were John Harvey, Thomas N. Pearson, George N. Potter and William L. Cutler.

Brother Joshua Armstrong set the greater portion of the upper part of the north wall. He commenced when the third crane was put up. He was assisted by Charles R. Dana. The hands who tended the crane were William W. Dryer, William Austin, Thomas Jaap and William L. Cutler.

For the most part of the time there was only one team to draw the stone to the cranes. Brother Ephrium J. Pearson attended the most of the time. After he left Alma N. Shennan took his place. When the second team was put to work Brother William H. Dame was appointed to attend to it. Old Thomas Travis, a faithful brother from England, was the man who mixed the mortar. This was his business from the beginning of the works; he was sometimes assisted by the tithing hands. He was one of the first who commenced to dig the foundation of the temple.

The following is a list of the stone cutters who cut the stone for the Temple, to-wit:

Alvin Winegar, James Standing, Harvey Stanley, Daniel S. Cahoon, Andrew Cahoon, Stephen Hales, Jr., William Jones (he cut the first plinth), John Keown, Rufus Allen, Samuel Hodge, Bun Anderson and George Ritchey. These persons were among the first who commenced cutting stone for the Temple and have continued to the close. Pulaski S. Cahoon, John Dresdale and Aaron Johnson also commenced to cut stone at the beginning, but did not continue long.

The following persons have cut stone much of the time but not from the beginning to-wit:

William Huntington, Sen., Samuel Williams, John Anderson, David B. Dille, Augustus Stafford, Jerome Kimpton, Buckley B. Anderson, Edwin Cutler, Franklin B. Cutler, William L. Cutler, Charles Lambert, John Pickles, James Sharp, Joseph G. Hovey, Welcome Chapman (he worked on the 3rd crane after it was erected), Joshua Armstrong, James H. Rollins, Lucius Merchants, John Harper, James D. Miller, John Miller, Peter Campbell, Samuel Heath, Morgan Thomas, Ira K. Hillman, Foster Curtis, Joseph Bates, Henry Parker, Andrew Smith, Benjamin T. Mitchell (he cut the first capital which was cut for this Temple), Isaac Allred, Wiley P. Allred, Wilson Lund, Parmelia A. Jackman, Wm. Jackman, William Adams, Thomas McLellan, Chancy Gaylord, Thomas Johnson, David Burrows and William Cottier, The last is a steady, faithful quiet, good workman.

Brother Charles Lambert cut the capstone, which was set on the south east or Joseph's corner on Saturday last. He cut the stone and bought it, and when finished he gave the stone and the labor free of all charges. He has proved himself a liberal-hearted, faithful, good man from first to last.

During last winter, 1843, towards the latter part of it, the Twelve decided to take down the old wood Font and put up a new one of cut stone. The men selected to cut the stone for the Font are William W. Player, Benjamin T. Mitchell, Charles Lambert, William Cottier, Andrew Cahoon, Daniel S. Cahoon, Jerome Kimpton, Augustus Stafford, Bun Anderson, Alvin Winegar, William Jones and Stephen Halles, Jr.

Brother Albert P. Rockwood has been the overseer or captain of the stone quarry from the commencement. He has been assisted by Charles Drury.

The following is a list of the steady carpenters, hired to work on the Temple: Truman O. Angell, foreman over regular joiners, William Felshaw, foreman over tithing donations, Wandle Mace, foreman over the framers, William T. Cahoon, foreman over the raisers and also time-keeper for carpenter shop.

Miles Romney, foreman over the Star builders. He also carved all the capitals for the tower. Elijah Fordham, principal carver.

John S. Schofield, William Carmichael, Addison Everett, Zinni H. Baxter, Hugh Riding, Hiram Mace, Stephen Longstroth, Nicholas T. Silcock, Samuel Rolfe, Vernon H. Bruce, John Stiles, Gideon H. C. Gibbs and Jabez Durfee (carpenters).

The following are employed to frame the timber and raise it on the building: Levi Jackman, William Anderson, Stephen H. Goddard, Easton Kelsey, Daniel McCole, Clark L. Whitney (now in carpenters' shop) Stephen N. Farnsworth and Frances A. Brown.

Jesse P. Harmon is door-keeper to the carpenter shop. His duty is also to keep the shop in order, turn grindstone, and wait on strangers who come to see the works of the temple.

The names of the sawyers are James Bennett, Joseph Busby and Moses Thurston.

Whitney Markham is teamster for the carpenters and sawyers.

The following persons are the painters already hired to paint the works of the Temple, to-wit: William Pitt, Edward Martin, Alfred Brown and John F. Hutchinson.

Copied from William Clayton's Journal, Journal History, 31 December 1844, 12–15.

ABOUT THE AUTHOR

DON F. COLVIN wrote his master's thesis on the Nauvoo Temple and served on the Historical Review Committee that examined the architectural plans for the reconstructed temple. Before his retirement from the Church Educational System, Brother Colvin was an administrator (coordinator) of seminaries and institutes of religion in northern California and in the Salt Lake City and Ogden, Utah, areas. He served for many years as an instructor at the Ogden Utah Institute of Religion.

A speaker and instructor at BYU Education Week and Know Your Religion, he has published articles in the Church magazines and the *Encyclopedia of Mormonism*. He obtained his bachelor's degree in education from the University of Utah and a master's degree in Church history from Brigham Young University.

Brother Colvin has served in many callings, including bishop, counselor in a stake presidency and several bishoprics, and chaplain in the Utah National Guard. He has served three missions and is currently a sealer in the Ogden Utah Temple and patriarch of the North Ogden Utah East Stake.

A former mayor of North Ogden City, he and his wife, Delsa, are the parents of two sons and have ten grandchildren.